I WILL ALWAYS

How One Letter Changed Two Lives

WRITE BACK

CAITLIN ALIFIRENKA & MARTIN GANDA
WITH LIZ WELCH

LITTLE, BROWN AND COMPANY

New York   Boston

Copyright © 2015 by Caitlin Alifirenka and Martin Ganda
"Caitlin, October 2015" chapter copyright © 2016 by Caitlin Alifirenka and Martin Ganda
Discussion Guide copyright © 2015 by Little, Brown and Company

Little, Brown and Company

Hachette Book Group
1290 Avenue of the Americas, New York, NY 10104
Visit us at lb-teens.com

Little, Brown and Company is a division of Hachette Book Group, Inc.
The Little, Brown name and logo are trademarks of Hachette Book Group, Inc.

The publisher is not responsible for websites (or their content) that are not owned by the publisher.

First Paperback Edition: May 2016
First published in hardcover in April 2015 by Little, Brown and Company

The Library of Congress has cataloged the hardcover edition as follows:

Alifirenka, Caitlin, author.
  I will always write back : how one letter changed two lives / by Caitlin Alifirenka and Martin Ganda ; with Liz Welch. — First edition.
    pages cm
  ISBN 978-0-316-24131-1 (hardcover) — ISBN 978-0-316-24134-2 (ebook) —
ISBN 978-0-316-24132-8 (library edition ebook)   1. Alifirenka, Caitlin—
Correspondence.   2. Ganda, Martin—Correspondence.   3. Pen pals—United
States.   4. Pen pals—Zimbabwe.   5. Teenagers—Zimbabwe—Social
conditions.   6. Teenagers—United States—Social conditions.   7. Friendship.
I. Ganda, Martin.   II. Welch, Liz, 1969–   III. Title.
  LB3614.A45 2015
  305.235096891—dc23

                                                                                    2014030355

Paperback ISBN 978-0-316-24133-5

10 9 8 7

LSC-C

Printed in the United States of America

I WILL ALWAYS

How One Letter Changed Two Lives

WRITE BACK

PART 1

Hallo!

Caitlin

⊸⊶⊷⊶⊷

I'D NEVER HEARD OF ZIMBABWE. But something about
the way the name looked up on the blackboard intrigued me.
It was exotic, and difficult to pronounce. It was also the last
country in a long list that Mrs. Miller had written in chalk.
She asked each student in my seventh-grade English class to
pick one place for a pen pal program our school was starting
that year.

I was sitting toward the back row. Usually, I spent that
period passing notes with Lauren, my best friend, or staring out
the window daydreaming about boys. It was late September,
and the leaves on the trees were beginning to turn from vibrant
green to rusty red and mustard yellow. I was an average student.
If I applied myself, I did well. Honestly, I was not all that interested in school, but there was something almost magnetic about
this crazy-sounding place: Zimbabwe. I raised my hand.

"Caitlin," Mrs. Miller said, surprised. She usually had to
call on me to participate.

"How do you pronounce the last country?" I asked. "The one that starts with a *Z*?"

"Zim-BOB-way," she said, sounding it out like it was three words. "It's in Africa."

"Oh, cool," I said. I had a hunch it was there, but couldn't name any other countries on the continent. I had a good handle on Europe, as my family had gone to Germany the summer before to visit my dad's relatives. On the same trip, we went to Switzerland, Austria, Liechtenstein, and France. Other than several trips to Canada, that was my first trip abroad, and it was a huge deal. I'd never imagined traveling to Africa, or even wondered what life must be like there. I had no idea, and that was all the more exciting—like the beginning of an adventure.

"That's the one I want," I said.

I didn't know it then—how could I have?—but that moment would change my life.

Before then, I was a typical twelve-year-old American girl, far more interested in what I should wear to school than what I might learn there. I assumed most kids, regardless of where they lived, had lives similar to mine. And while I imagined that Zimbabwe was radically different from suburban Pennsylvania, where I grew up, I had no idea how much.

My knowledge of Africa consisted of what I had seen in the *National Geographic* magazines my mother subscribed to for our family. I loved looking at the colorful photos of tribal people who wore face paint, loincloths, and beads. I didn't think my pen pal would dress like that, but I had no idea what kids in Africa wore. Jeans, like me? I had so many questions.

I was born and raised in Hatfield, Pennsylvania, a small middle-class town forty miles outside Philadelphia. Both my parents grew up there as well. They met in elementary school but didn't start dating until college. After they got married, they moved to neighboring Lansdale, which was more afford-able than Hatfield. My brother, Richie, was born there. By the time I came around five years later, they had moved back to Hatfield and bought the home they still live in today.

There was no reason to ever move—Hatfield was a great place to live: quiet streets lined with ranch and colonial-style houses with well-kept yards, a good public school, and an old-timey downtown with a deli called the Trolley Stop. There was a Dairy Queen within walking distance of my house, and I'd often meet Lauren there for Blizzards on the weekends. Otherwise, miles of farmland surrounded Hatfield, even though it was less than an hour away from a major American city. Truthfully, we rarely went to Philadelphia because there was so much to do in Hatfield, whether softball games on the weekends, roller skating at the local rink, or just hanging out with friends at the nearby mall. My summer trip to Europe did give me some sense of a world beyond suburban Pennsyl-vania, though.

When I was in Germany, I was struck by how different my cousin Carola was from me. Like me, Carola was tall and blond, but when I first met her, she was wearing cut-off jean shorts and dark brown knee socks with sandals. I thought she looked ridiculous. She also spoke English with a harsh-sounding accent, like she was always angry. She ate sharp cheese and dark bread for breakfast, and liked chocolate with hazelnuts, and salty black licorice—nothing like the Hershey's Kisses and Starburst sweets I had grown up with. I assumed she was a total dork, until I went to school with her one day. The school year started in early August, and as soon as we walked into the building, everyone said hello to her, including all the cute boys. She was actually really popular! And many of her girlfriends were also wearing knee socks with sandals. It was fashionable! Meanwhile, I knew if I showed up at school wearing that outfit, people would say, "Why are you dressed like a nerd? Halloween isn't until October."

That trip opened my eyes to other ways of living beyond my small town. Everything and everyone in Hatfield felt so familiar—even a little boring. I wanted to learn about somewhere radically different, and having a pen pal in Africa seemed like a great way to do that.

Mrs. Miller went around the room, calling on people. Lauren picked Germany, as did many other kids in our class who had some ancestral connection. A few kids picked France, and others picked Italy and England. By the time everyone had chosen, I realized that I was the only person who had picked a country in Africa. I think it shocked my teacher, who had already busted me twice that year for chewing gum in class and once for passing a note to Lauren. Each time I was caught, I was slightly embarrassed. In seventh grade, I just wanted to blend in. I joined the field hockey team because all my friends were on it, even though I did not like running up and down a big field bent over a stick. I guess my trip to Europe had changed me. For the first time, I saw that being different wasn't a bad thing. It was actually kind of cool.

Our homework assignment that night was to write a letter to our new pen pal. Since we did not know who would be receiving our letters, Mrs. Miller said to simply write *Hello!* instead of *Dear so and so.* I was actually excited about homework, maybe for the first time ever.

That afternoon, I sat on the bus next to Heather, my other best friend, who was a year older and lived two houses away from me. I told her about my pen pal assignment.

"That's so cool," she said. "What are you going to ask?"

It was a good question: I had no idea what to write or where to start. I thought about it as the bus pulled out of the school driveway.

Pennfield Middle School is just down the street from Hatfield Quality Meats, a pig slaughterhouse, which my school bus passed every morning and afternoon. That meant most days, I could see the pigs, some as big as miniature ponies, arriving on the back of huge livestock trucks, their pink and whiskered noses sticking through the metal crates. That image, and the squealing sounds they made as if they knew what would come next, always broke my heart. But the rendering days were even worse: The air filled with the stench of garbage cooked in bacon. The smell would stick to your hair and clothes, like cigarette smoke, as it wafted into our classrooms' open windows on warm days back when our school didn't have air-conditioning.

I certainly would not write about that—it was the one thing I didn't like about my hometown. Hatfield was also known for its dairy farms, which I much preferred. I pressed my forehead against the window as the bus passed by rolling green fields dotted with black-and-white cows grazing. They had much better lives than the pigs, I thought. I wondered what my pen pal saw on her or his way to school. I knew there were elephants and giraffes in Africa. Were they like our cows, grazing on the side of the road? There was so much I wanted to find out.

Twenty minutes later, the bus stopped at the end of my street, a cul-de-sac. I knew every family in each of the twelve houses that lined the road. In the summer, I played flashlight tag and kick ball with other neighborhood kids. In the winter, when it snowed, we'd build snowmen in one another's front yards. My family's house was beige with navy-blue shutters and a matching front door, which we hardly ever used. Instead, I always went in through the side door. There Kava and Romeo, our two giant schnauzers, would always be waiting for me, doing their welcome dance, which entailed wagging their whole bodies and jumping up and down at the same time. They followed me through the laundry room that was also a mudroom for all our coats and boots, and then into the family room, where they returned to their still-warm spots on our couch. As always, I threw my backpack at the bottom of the stairs—one of my mom's rules—before heading into the kitchen to grab a snack.

My mom was always home when I arrived. Before I was

born, she worked as an office manager for a doctor in town. Then, when I was still a baby, she decided to go back to school to become a teacher. She wanted to be home when Richie and I finished school every afternoon, and she wound up getting a job as an elementary school teacher in Central Bucks School District in the neighboring county. Now that I was in middle school, I didn't see her during the day, but I always found her waiting for me in the kitchen when I came home.

That afternoon, she was sitting at the kitchen table, reading the newspaper.

"How was your day?" she asked, peering up at me, her big blue-green eyes gentle but curious.

Most days, I filled her in on my softball game schedule or complained about too much homework or mean teachers. But on this day, I had something interesting to report.

"I got a pen pal today," I said. "From Zimbabwe."

"Where?" she asked.

"In Africa, Mom," I said, and rolled my eyes. I couldn't believe she did not know where Zimbabwe was. She was a teacher, after all.

"Oh, do you mean Rhodesia?" she asked.

My mom went to get a world map from the living room, which she laid across the table.

"Rhodesia," she said, pointing to a teakettle-shaped country in the southern part of Africa above a place called Botswana and next to one called Mozambique. My mom then pointed to the date on the map: 1977. It was twenty years old.

"Countries in Africa change all the time," she said in a

matter-of-fact way. She mentioned *colonialism*, a vaguely familiar word.

"What does that mean again?" I asked.

"It's when powerful countries take over other countries and call them their territories," she explained. "Like America—it used to be a British colony, but we fought for our freedom. The Zimbabweans did the same thing."

I had studied American history the year before, but I was having a hard time making the connection. It was all very confusing, but one thing was clear: I needed to learn a little more about this faraway place before I could even begin writing my letter. I didn't want to seem stupid.

When my dad was not traveling for work, he arrived home every night at six. He worked on energy contracts for the government, which sounds as mysterious as it was. All I knew was that he had top government security clearance, and he could not talk about his work with anyone—including us. My brother, Richie, was seventeen years old and a junior in high school. He usually hung out with his friends after school— but he was always home in time for dinner. That was another one of my mom's rules. We ate dinner together every evening at six thirty, and then afterward, my dad logged on to the family computer, a beige Dell the size of a television set. My parents kept it in the den, as my mother had read about predators posing as kids in chat rooms and wanted to monitor the websites Richie and I used. Back then, we had dial-up Internet, which took forever, and then once we were connected, everyone took turns using the computer.

That evening, I went first. I waited for the snap-crackle-pop *You've Got Mail* sound sequence and then typed "Zimbabwe" into a search engine, which led me to the Encyclopedia Britannica site. My mom had a subscription, which meant I could access information. That's how I discovered that Zimbabwe was "liberated" from the United Kingdom in 1980. I was beginning to see parallels: The Africans wanted to be free from British rule, just as colonial Americans did two hundred years earlier. I read that more than 90 percent of the Zimbabwean people were called Shona, but that there was another tribe called Ndebele, which I think was pronounced en-duh-BELL-lay. Shona was the country's national language, but most people spoke English as a result of being colonized.

Phew, I thought. At least my pen pal would be able to understand me.

I wondered which tribe my pen pal was from, and what it meant to be from one or the other. Could you be both? Was it like being German and Irish, like me? It was getting late, so instead of doing more research, I went upstairs to my room to start writing.

There, I took out a piece of lined school paper and sat on the bottom of my bunk bed, where I usually did my homework.

I began: *Hi, my name is Caitlin, I'm twelve years old. I live in Hatfield, Pennsylvania. I'm in the seventh grade. My brother Richie is in eleventh grade.*

I paused. What else should I write to this person halfway across the world? I scanned my room for inspiration and spotted my collection of sports trophies won over the years, usually for good sportsmanship, as I was never the best player, or even very athletic. I continued: *I play softball and soccer and field hockey.* I did not include that I had started taking stats for my field hockey team because it hurt my back to bend over the stick all the time. I was already five foot three, the second-tallest girl in my class. My posters tacked to the wall caught my attention, so I continued: *I like the Spice Girls and the Back-street Boys. And my favorite color is pink.* This was all true. My mother had stenciled pink hearts on my walls, and the rug in my room was magenta, though no one would ever know, since it was completely covered in clothes.

I continued: *For fun, I like to go shopping at the mall on the weekend. I also like to go roller skating and bowling with my friends. And to eat pizza. What do you like to do for fun? And what is it like in Zimbabwe?*

I knew there was more to ask and tell, but this was a good start. I signed it the way Mrs. Miller had showed us earlier that day: *Sincerely, Caitlin Stoicsitz.*

When I turned in my letter to Mrs. Miller the following day, I felt giddy, like this was the start of something big.

Martin
—ᴍᴍ—

MRS. JARAI ENTERED OUR CLASSROOM, smiling.

"Class, I have pen pal letters from America!" she said in a chipper voice. It was mid-October and toward the end of our school year, so this was a welcome surprise.

Everyone started chattering—we all knew and loved America. It was the land of Coca-Cola and the WWF, World Wrestling Federation. Kids with money would Xerox different wrestling photos from American magazines they found in town, and then sell them to other students. It was very popular to have an eight-by-ten black-and-white copy of Hulk Hogan—he was considered a god in Zimbabwe. My older brother, Nation, managed to get one somehow, and we hung it on our wall at home, using bubble gum as tape. It was a status thing. "Do you have Hulk Hogan? Or Macho Man?" This was my view of America—men with big muscles who wore skullcaps and knee-high boots and made lots of money. The big life! I wanted to know what kids my age were like in this faraway country.

Mrs. Jarai only had ten letters—and there were fifty students in our classroom. I was in Group One, so I was one of the lucky ones. The school year in Zimbabwe starts in January, when every student takes a placement test. The kids with the highest scores are put in Group One. I had been in that group for the last eight years, since first grade—my mother made sure of it. On my very first day of school, when I was six, she kept asking, "Who's the best teacher?" An older woman was pointed out, and my mother approached her and said, "This is my son Martin. Make sure he is in your class."

It worked—I wound up in that class. At the end of first grade, there was a ceremony where the top three students were named: Number three was announced first. Then number two. When my name was called for number one, I heard a joyous cry from behind me. I turned to see my mother jumping up and down, like a rabbit, ululating, which is how we celebrate. I had to hold back a smile as her high-pitched cries—"yul-yul-yul"—pushed me toward the front of the crowd, where I received my certificate. On our way home, my mother said, "Martin, if you want to do well in life, you must always be number one."

I was number one again the following year, but then in grade three, I took second place.

"Why didn't you take number one?" my mother asked the day I got my report card, her face screwed so tight, her eyes were squinted slits.

"The other guy is very clever," I explained, handing it to her.

She swatted it out of my hand with such ferocity, I was startled. I watched the paper as it fluttered to the floor and kept my eyes there as she shouted, "That's no excuse. Next you'll be number five, then number fourteen. You must work harder."

"I will, Mai," I said, still stunned. I picked up the paper and smoothed it out on my thigh before trying to give it to her one more time.

"I don't want to look at it," she said, quiet this time, but still fierce. "Or you."

As I turned to leave, the report crumpled in my hand, she whispered, "School is your only hope."

She took a deep breath and finished her thought. "Otherwise you will end up like me."

I understood. My mother wasn't being unkind; she was being protective. My mother was smart, but she had to drop out of school when she was twelve because her parents could not afford the fees. My parents were also poor, but at least I was still in school. I promised her, and myself, that I would always work as hard as possible.

The next semester, I pushed myself and was number one from that year onward. That meant I always got to sit in the front row of our classroom. Since there were so many kids and not much room, four students shared a desk meant for one. It was crowded, but it made it easier to share textbooks—the teacher had only four, which she brought to class every day. I often stayed after school to take notes to make sure I understood what was being taught. We were very rarely allowed to take the books home. They were too precious.

Everyone in Group One got a letter from America, but then Mrs. Jarai ran out, leaving the last four groups with nothing. I felt especially fortunate that I was in the classroom that morning. Due to the overcrowding in our school, each group was also split into teams: 1A, B, C, and D. That meant every day, two teams would start classes inside and then finish outside beneath a big baobab tree—our teacher would travel with us and sit in a chair as we sat cross-legged in the dirt and listened to her read passages from textbooks or lecture us on a topic. On sunny days, it was actually quite pleasant. But when it rained, we had to move into the hallways, which was not as fun. The other teams started outside and finished in. This was called hot sitting and was common throughout Zimbabwe.

Mrs. Jarai handed me the first letter and asked me to read it out loud. We learned English in school—Zimbabwe used to be a British colony—but I spoke Shona with my family and friends. Mutare, where I lived, was 99 percent Shona. I knew how to speak English but used it only in this class, so the words felt funny in my mouth. I tried to mimic the voices I had heard on the radio and television: high-pitched and nasal-y.

" 'Hello, my name is Caitlin,' " I began. It was such a strange name that everyone laughed. I had never heard of Pennsylvania, and had a difficult time pronouncing it. But then I got to the part where she listed the sports she played and smiled: We had something in common. I played soccer daily with my friends but had never heard of field hockey and was not sure how to say the word.

" 'Field hooky,' " I tried.

"HAH-kee," Mrs. Jarai corrected me before I continued.

" 'I also really like the Spice Girls. Do you know them? Baby Spice is my favorite.' "

Someone sang "If you want to be my lover!" and everyone laughed, including our teacher. The Spice Girls were very popular in Zimbabwe.

" 'What is life like in Zimbabwe? I hope you write me back! Sincerely, Caitlin Stoicsitz.' "

The class burst out in laughter again as I tried to pronounce her last name.

Mrs. Jarai just shook her head, smiled, and said, "I cannot help you with that one!"

Mrs. Jarai told those of us who had gotten letters to craft a response and bring it back the following day. I always loved homework, but this felt more important than any regular school assignment: I had a new friend. In America.

That afternoon, I walked home with a bunch of other kids who lived near me in Chisamba Singles. It was a housing development built in the 1960s as a place for men from the rural areas to stay during the week while they worked in different factories on the outskirts of Mutare, the third-largest city in Zimbabwe. My father had arrived there in 1980, after my older brother, Nation, was born.

My mother grew up in a rural village several hours north of Mutare, near the Chimanimani Mountains. She had two older brothers and one sister. She was very clever and always was first in her class. The problem was that her family was dirt poor. They had no electricity and bathed in the rivers. My mother stayed in school until fifth grade, but then her family could no longer afford to send her. She dropped out, and soon after, they sent her to work for my father's family because they could no longer afford to feed her, either. She was twelve years old. Or rather my mother thought she was around that age, as there is no formal record of her birth. She was born in her family's hut, as were her brothers and sister. This is how some people in rural areas of Zimbabwe are born. And it was also common to send children to work for other families—one fewer mouth to feed. My mother worked in exchange for her food and keep, which still happens today.

My father grew up in a nearby village, and while his family wasn't wealthy, they at least had goats and chickens. They were rich compared to my mother's family. She was around fourteen years old when she got pregnant with Nation. My father was twenty-four. It was not like my parents fell in love—in Zimbabwe, if a woman becomes pregnant, our Shona tradition requires that she get married or else she brings shame on both families. Basically, my father was forced to marry her. I don't think it was a choice for either of them. And I know it was why my mom was also very strict about any interactions with girls. I was not allowed to talk to them, or play with them, or even look at them.

Shortly after Nation was born, my dad left the village for Mutare to find work. He got a job at Mutare Board and Paper Mills, the biggest paper mill in Zimbabwe, which was how he wound up at Chisamba Singles. He shared a room with another man—there were four rooms per housing unit. The men worked hard, saved their money, and then headed home once a month with groceries and money for their families. My father's original goal was to save enough to build a house in his village, but apparently he started to misbehave. My father liked to drink, and he liked women, so the story goes that his every-month visit home became every six months. During one, my mother got pregnant with their second son, who died a few days after he was born. People said terrible things to my father, like "Why keep a wife who bears dead babies?" They even told him to get a new wife.

Culturally, any issue around childbirth was the woman's fault, whether the child was crippled, or he died. Polygamy was not common back then, but it also was not a big deal. My father's brother, Uncle Sam, had to get a second wife because his first wife only gave him one child. But my mom was stubborn: After she lost her second son, she insisted on moving to Mutare, into the one-room shack that my dad shared with another man. They put up a curtain in the center of the room, and my parents lived on one side with Nation, and our roommate, Mr. Dambudzo, lived on the other.

I was born there in 1983, three years after Zimbabwe was liberated, which meant I was one of the "born frees." That was what people called children who were born after liberation from British colonial powers. In Zimbabwe, there's often some kind of direct significance to your name. Nation was named after my father's favorite cow. I was lucky: A medical student from England delivered me, and his name was Martin. If you were born on Friday, you could be called Friday. Or if you were born during a dry period, you could be named Drought. I knew people called Disaster and Weakness.

I have a Shona name as well. It's Tatenda, which means "thank you." Nation's other name is Tawanda, which means "We are many." He actually named our other brother Simba, which means "power" in Shona—his English name is Mack, my grandfather's name. And then Lois, my sister, was named after my aunt. Her Shona name is Hekani, which means "surprise," like, "Whoa! Finally a girl!" And then the youngest, George, was named for my father. George does not have a Shona name. I think my parents were too tired by then to think of one.

My father was not the only person to bring his entire family to Chisamba Singles—soon everyone did this, including his roommate, who had two wives. Each wife would swap every two weeks, commuting back and forth from the rural areas with her children. It was chaotic. Some weeks, between our family and theirs, there were twelve people living and sleeping in a room intended for two.

During the day we shared the same space, but at night we pulled the curtain across the room, which was meant to give us privacy, but you could still see and hear everything, a shadow puppet show. My mother and father slept on a single mattress, our only piece of furniture, which took up a third of our space. During the day my mother stored our pots and

20

pans beneath the bed, but at night she stacked them in the corner so Lois and George could sleep there. Nation, Simba, and I slept on the concrete floor beside them. This was how all the kids lived in Chisamba Singles.

I know now this place is called a slum, but for me, it was home. I imagined Caitlin's life as very different from mine, and I was excited to learn more about it, and her.

The little I knew about America I had learned on television. Several thousand people lived in Chisamba Singles, but there were only a few TV sets in the entire settlement. One was a fifteen-inch black-and-white set owned by a man who worked as a manager at the same paper factory where my father worked. Whenever World Wrestling Federation with Hulk Hogan came on, or *The A-Team* with Mr. T, people would cram into his living room and gather around his house, trying to watch through his window. I sometimes climbed onto Nation's shoulders to get a better look as others peered through the door.

As soon as I got home that afternoon, I showed my mother Caitlin's letter. I did not think my mom would mind that Caitlin was a girl—she was too far away to get in any kind of trouble with. And I was right.

"You can learn many things from her, Martin," my mother said, smiling.

I wanted to write Caitlin back immediately, but I had to do my chores first. First, I had to change out of my school uniform—I had only one. It was a pair of green shorts and a green shirt, which I wore every day and washed twice a week, on Wednesday and then again on the weekend. My siblings and I each got a uniform every Christmas and had to make it last the entire school year. I changed into my regular T-shirt and shorts, which hung from my nail—we each had one—and then I went to gather wood for the fire.

Our family shared a fire pit, which was directly outside our home, with four other families. There, my mother cooked over the fire in a large metal can once used for cooking oil that we now used as a stove. This way, we could move the fire into the house if it was raining.

My father left every morning at six to head to work at the factory, and returned by seven PM. We'd usually hear him singing before we saw him, his husky voice bellowing a liberation song by Thomas Mapfumo, a Zimbabwean legend, or "It's only rock and roll but I like it." My father loved the Rolling Stones, Cream, and Led Zeppelin too.

"Baba!" I'd shout, and start running past women selling tomatoes or mangoes on the side of the road, dipping beneath the clotheslines that crisscrossed between the dozens of identical wooden slab shacks. Nation and Simba would always come running, too.

My father used to surprise us with small gifts, perhaps a piece of paper from the factory, or a pen, or a coin for each of us to spend on a pack of peanuts. And he'd usually bring something for my mother to cook—greens or a bag of chicken feet. But these days, he was mostly empty-handed. My dad used the word "inflation" to explain why we no longer ate bread, which rose in price overnight from two to five dollars.

Back home, we'd gather around the fire to eat, sitting

on stones or overturned cans made into stools. My mother dished out sadza, a cornmeal porridge that is our staple food. Sometimes, we had collard greens, too, which were common and cheap. Chicken was a once-a-year Christmas treat. We'd get beans from time to time, if our father could afford it. But lately, it was mostly just sadza.

After dinner, Nation and I had to wash the dishes before we could start our homework. Electricity was rationed from six PM to six AM, though sometimes it did not come on at all. That night, I wrote my letter by the light of the fire. I knew Caitlin was a girl, and I assumed she was white, which made me even more curious about her. White people lived in Zimbabwe, but I didn't know any personally. I had only ever seen a white person up close once before, when a group of people from the Netherlands came to visit our school.

They were so pale, they practically glowed in the dark. They also smelled very sweet, like flowers. We called that the white smell. I think it was from deodorant. We used soap when we could, but if we ran out, we just bathed with water.

That was all I had to compare to Caitlin. I wondered if she glowed in the dark. And smelled like flowers. Did she know Hulk Hogan? Or was she just a regular kid like me?

I did not want to overwhelm her with all my questions. Instead, I wrote a basic letter, using hers as my guide. I told her what grade I was in, and the names of my siblings. I told her that I loved to play soccer, and that I really hoped we'd continue to write each other. I promised her I would not let her down, and I hoped she would do the same.

October 1997

Caitlin
⊸∞∞⊷

AFTER I SENT MY PEN pal letter off to Zimbabwe, I continued on with my life, which in seventh grade consisted of spending a lot of time obsessing about how I looked: I changed outfits several times every morning before settling on one—wide-legged jeans and platform sneakers were popular back then. And then I spent another thirty minutes on my hair.

This was around the same time that my brother, Richie, started calling me The Queen, or Princess, or Prinny for short. He thought I was spoiled—and I thought he was a jerk, because he was. That fall, I came home one day to find that he had hung several of my stuffed animals from my ceiling fan, each with a noose around its neck. It was like a scene from a horror movie, but also classic Richie. He called himself a survivalist and liked to wear camouflage and collect skulls of animals he found in the woods behind our house or on the side of the road. He had a cat, a beaver, a possum, a snapping turtle, and a pig that he got after my parents had a pig roast in our backyard. He also had a dart gun, and practiced shooting at a target *in his room*. I could hear the suck and thump of the darts being launched and landing on his wall, through mine. He had another bull's-eye in our backyard where he liked to practice archery with his compound bow. I was actually glad that he would graduate high school before I started—I didn't want anyone to know that I was related to him.

I had just untied the last teddy bear when I heard Richie clomping up the stairs. Quickly, I hid behind my closed door. As his footsteps grew louder, I jumped out and shouted "Hiya!" and karate-kicked him in the stomach.

I heard the air leave his mouth with a big "pah" as he doubled over. When he stood back up, he lunged for me.

"You little . . ." he said, just as I slammed my door shut.

Through the now locked door, I shouted, "Stay out of my room!"

That night at dinner, I started telling my mom what Richie had done when he came to the table.

"You already got your revenge," he said, glaring at me. "Wait until I get mine."

"What's this about?" We heard my dad's voice from the den. He had just returned from a business trip and was still wearing his trench coat and sunglasses. We teased him that it was his *Men in Black* look.

"Get any aliens today, Dad?" Richie asked.

"I would tell you," he said as he took off his glasses. "But then I'd have to kill you."

My dad was about to sit down when I asked:

"Seriously Dad, what do you do? Every year, all my new friends and teachers ask, 'What type of work is your father in?' and I never have a good enough answer."

"Tell them I work for the government doing energy contracts," he said.

"I do!" I said, exasperated. "But what does that mean!"

"It means I signed a contract with the government that said I would never talk about my work with anyone, including my family," he said.

He then winked at me, and started helping himself to dinner.

When I was young, I imagined that my dad was a spy, and worked for the CIA. As I grew older, I realized he was around too much for that to be true. While he sometimes flew to California or overseas on business, he was never gone for more than a few days. Otherwise, he was home by six PM for dinner and found time to coach my softball team in sixth grade. Not very James Bond–esque.

Over dinner, we usually talked about what was happening at school. I filled them in on my classes and talked about my softball games, which my dad coached, but all I really cared about was boys. I kept a diary of all my crushes in my bedroom closet. My mom let me write on the walls there. She called it my sacred space.

That October, I made my first closet confession. With a Kelly-green Sharpie, I first wrote *10/18/1997* and *I LUV MATT JOHNSON*. Matt was in my algebra class, and while I generally hated math, I loved that class because I got to sit behind Matt. He played soccer, a cool sport at my school, and had wavy brown hair that almost touched his shoulders.

Other than dreaming of kissing Matt Johnson, I did start to wonder if my pen pal had received my letter. Kids in my English class had started receiving theirs from Europe. By late October, I still had not received mine.

I checked the mailbox every afternoon as soon as I got off the bus and felt disappointed each time there was nothing for me. I got concerned. What if my letter didn't make it all the way to Africa? Or what if my pen pal didn't like my letter?

Then one day, a week before Halloween, I saw it amongst the catalogs and bills and coupon flyers. The envelope was a pale blue gray, small and square, and plastered with colorful stamps that took up one-third of its surface. I ripped it open right there in the driveway.

It read: *Hallo Caitlin! Thank you for your letter! I am very happy to have a friend in America. My name is Martin. I live in Mutare, the third-largest city in Zimbabwe. I am fourteen years old, the second oldest of four brothers. Their names are Nation, Simba, and George. I have one younger sister called Lois. I like soccer very much. And I love school, especially math.*

I stood in the driveway reading as Kava and Romey did their welcome dance around me. I felt the same kind of jittery excitement that I experienced every Christmas morning in anticipation of all those gifts. I had a new friend, his name was Martin, and he lived thousands of miles away. I ran into the house, clutching my letter like a winning lottery ticket.

"I got it!" I shouted as I plopped my book bag down on the kitchen floor and waved the letter in the air. "It finally came!"

My mother was in the kitchen, unpacking groceries. "What does it say?" she asked, leaving the bags on the counter to sit next to me at the kitchen table.

I read it out loud—and looked at her with wide eyes when I got to the names of his brothers.

"The only Simba I know is from *The Lion King*," I said.

"I don't think he's named after a cartoon lion cub, Caitlin," my mom said.

I didn't either, but I wanted to know who he was named after—and Nation, too! I immediately whipped out a piece of college-lined paper from my English folder to write him back: *Dear Martin, thank you so much for your letter! It was so great to get it!*

I paused, stumped. I assumed Martin was black, because I thought everyone in Africa was black. And so I figured that Martin was like the black kids who went to middle school with me, kids who lived in houses and listened to music and ate pizza and did homework, just like me. I didn't have many close black friends, though—not since Marlena. We were best friends in kindergarten—until I got in trouble for messing up her hair. It was always done up with either elaborate braids that zigzagged over her scalp, or teeny poofy ponytails that sprouted all over her head, bound by bright pink and orange elastics with marble-size pom-poms. Intrigued, I pulled one off and watched in amazement as her hair slowly uncoiled. I thought it was the coolest thing, until she cried, "Don't touch my hair!"

Her small face crumpled as I saw tears spring from her eyes. She was upset. And I was confused.

"But you braid my hair all the time!" I protested.

"But my hair is different," she said, before stomping off to tell the teacher.

That afternoon, my mother had to explain to me that I was not allowed to touch people without their permission.

"Marlena braids my hair every day at recess," I replied.

"That's fine, if you don't mind it," my mother said. "But it probably takes much longer for Marlena's mom to style her hair—and so she doesn't want you messing it up."

I had never thought about race until that moment. And even after that, I didn't want to see Marlena or any of the black kids in Hatfield as any different from me, nor did I see Martin that way. I know it may sound naïve, but I thought then, as a twelve-year-old girl, what I think now: Regardless of the color of our skin, we're all the same.

I wondered what Martin looked like—and how I could find out. And then I had an idea: I'd send him my photo and ask him to send me his.

I had just had my photos taken earlier that fall. My mom took me to a professional studio, at the mall, right after I got my hair cut—a shoulder-length bob. I was wearing my brand-new blue-and-white-striped button-down shirt. The photographer had me sit on a high black stool, and do all these poses, like I was modeling. I selected a wallet-size picture and wrote on the back: *Please send me your photo so I can see what you look like, too!*

When I was finished writing the letter, I used my Crayola Stampers to decorate the margins. As I pushed the different tips onto the page, each left its own mark, either a small smiley face, a heart, an exclamation point, or, my favorite, a pair of puckered lips. I then placed my photo and letter in an envelope and used my markers to make small hearts and stars to spell out *AIRMAIL* on both sides of the envelope. I ran downstairs and handed it to my mom, who promised to send it off first thing in the morning.

At school the next day, when Mrs. Miller asked, "Did anyone get a reply?" I jumped from my seat and walked proudly up to the front of the class, holding my letter as if it were a rare artifact. As I approached the blackboard, I could not help but think, Africa is *way* cooler than Europe.

Martin
—ɷ—

MRS. JARAI WAS SMILING AGAIN. As everyone took a seat, I could see she was holding a very festive and colorful letter in her hand.

"We have our first response," Mrs. Jarai announced, handing the letter to me. A row of hearts and stars framed my name and address, each perfectly drawn in different colors— a rainbow of blue, red, yellow, green, and orange. I opened it immediately, careful not to rip the excellent artwork, as my desk mates leaned in for a closer look.

When I unfolded the letter, a small snapshot fell onto my desk.

I could not believe my pen pal would send me something so precious. Photos are very rare and quite expensive in Zimbabwe.

I picked up her photo off my desk and was struck by how sweet Caitlin looked, like an angel. Her hair was so blond, it looked like gold.

By then, other students were gathered around my desk, wanting to have a look.

I handed the photo to Mrs. Jarai so she could hold it up for everyone to see, and quickly scanned her letter. My heart was racing as I read each sentence. Caitlin wrote about her hobbies and wanted to know mine. And then she asked about the climate in Zimbabwe. I was already thinking of how I would respond, when Mrs. Jarai returned the photo to me. That's when I saw that Caitlin had written a note on its back. She wanted my photo in return.

My heart went from sprinting to a standstill. This request was difficult, if not impossible. It worried me through all of my classes that day and all the way home, too. I did not know anyone who owned a camera. The only way to get a photo was to hire a professional photographer to come to your house. That cost a lot of money.

I wondered if this was the same in America. Caitlin's picture looked very professional. I couldn't even tell where it was taken—somewhere inside? The background was sky blue, like her shirt. I was so touched that Caitlin would send me something so special, and I wanted to return the favor—but wasn't sure how. And that was not my only worry.

As I was leaving class, Mrs. Jarai said, "Martin, I'm so happy that your pen pal has written again, but the school does not have the funds to send letters for you anymore. I hope your parents will help you keep up this important correspondence."

I understood—stamps were expensive in Zimbabwe. But

so were bread, tea, and milk, and many other things we used to eat regularly that were now rare treats. Inflation was continuing to rise, which meant my father's paycheck bought less and less food. How could I possibly ask for a photograph to be taken, as well as stamps, when we had not eaten bread in more than a month? Since food had gotten noticeably more expensive, my mother started sending me to pick up my father's paycheck every two weeks before he had a chance to spend it on Chibuku, a popular alcoholic beverage made from sorghum or maize. It came in a carton that you shake before you drink to mix the citrusy sediment that settles on the bottom. My father preferred beer, but Chibuku was cheaper and had the same effect. And he liked to have a good time, especially at the end of a long workweek. So my job was to collect his pay before he had a chance to celebrate. After my mother used it to buy food and pay our rent and utilities, there was no money for breakfast tea, let alone alcohol.

I loved this task. It took my father an hour to walk to work every day, but if I ran fast, I could make it there in twenty minutes. The factory was in an industrial area outside of Mutare, as big as a football field. I always entered through the main office, where the men in suits worked. My dad worked on the factory floor, with all the big machines. He wore overalls and rubber boots that covered half his legs. The very first time I went, years before, my dad walked me through the entire paper-making process, starting with where the trees come in and are ground to pulp before being turned into paper. He worked the machines at the end of the line, where the paper is rolled into giant bundles. To do this, he had to run up and down a ladder attached to a huge machine, and push a variety of buttons that made gigantic cranes move like mechanical dinosaurs to lift the bundles. I was in awe.

On this particular day, I found my dad in the break room with bunch of guys his age who were wearing the same overalls and helmets.

"You must be Martin," one said. "The clever one."

"He always brings your report cards to work," another added with a smile.

This made me happy.

I liked my father's friends, but I was more fascinated by the managers in the front. They wore suits and talked on the phone and typed on machines. On that visit, my dad introduced me to Mr. Stephen Mutandwa, the head of human resources. I was standing in front of a black man just like my father, but this one was wearing a tie and let me play with his computer. I punched a few keys, and some symbols came up. I had to stop myself from saying "How do I get to be you?"

I got my chance later that morning. As I was running home, Mr. Mutandwa pulled up next to me in his rusty pickup truck.

"Do you want a ride, young fellow?" he asked.

I had never been in a car in my life. My heart was racing so fast from my excitement that I could barely breathe. As the car started to move, I grabbed the dashboard with two hands to steady myself. Overwhelmed, I began asking all the questions that had piled up in my head, like: "How did you get this car?"

"And how did you become the human resources manager?"
"Where do you live?" "Where can I get a suit?"

"Martin," he cut me off. "You are clearly a smart boy. You must go to university, like I did. That is the only way to truly succeed."

Neither my mother nor my father had finished secondary school, so university seemed out of the question. I knew I was smart enough to go, but I also knew it was impossibly expensive, way more than secondary school, which my parents could barely afford for me or my siblings. And yet, sitting in the front seat of Mr. Mutandwa's pickup truck and watching the dust clouds kick up behind us, I thought I must find a way to go.

"Where did you study?" I asked.

"The University of Zimbabwe in Harare," he responded.

"I want to go there as well," I said. Mr. Mutandwa smiled.

"You will, Martin," he said. "I know you will."

His confidence in me was contagious. If I studied hard enough and stayed focused, maybe I would get there.

Receiving Caitlin's letter gave me a similar confidence. It made me feel special. When I arrived home that afternoon, I showed it to my mother.

"You will learn so much from her, Martin," she said. Then I removed her photo from my pocket and watched my mother's eyes widen.

"Very pretty murungu," she said, smiling.

"Murungu" is Shona for people with white skin. None lived in Chisamba Singles, or anywhere nearby. Besides the

35

teachers who had visited my school, I had only ever seen them on TV, or during a trip into the city center of Mutare, a thirty-minute bus ride from home. Even so, there were not many murungus. And now I had one as a friend.

I was distracted all afternoon. How could I write Caitlin back without a photo? That would be rude. And then, as I was gathering wood for the fire, I heard my father singing in the distance.

I ran to greet him, holding Caitlin's photo in one hand, her letter in the other.

"Baba, look," I said. "Caitlin wrote back!"

I handed him the photo first, which he admired. Then I showed him the letter. He took that, too, and started waving both in the air.

"My son has a new friend in America!" he started shouting to nearby people, some neighbors, others strangers passing through. Chisamba Singles was like a small city—more than ten thousand people lived there, either in shared houses or small shanties built from scraps of metal and wood nearby. I felt a funny mix of embarrassment and pride as my father paraded through the narrow street, boasting of my faraway friend.

"Look at how beautiful she is!" he said, stopping people to show them her photo. "Martin's new friend looks like a movie star!"

Most people smiled, others ignored him entirely, but I shared his deep enthusiasm. Something about seeing Caitlin's face and sweet smile made me know she was a kind and good person. And to have a face to match her words made our connection seem that much more real. I felt in my heart that this was the start of a true friendship.

That night, before I went to sleep, I pinned Caitlin's photo on the wall beside the poster of Hulk Hogan.

The next morning, I woke to see Caitlin smiling down on me. As happy as I was to have her photo there, I was also deeply concerned. I wanted to send her a photo of me as she requested. But how? Hiring a photographer cost the same as a week's worth of mealie meal, the cornmeal used to make sadza. I wrestled with different ideas for a week or so before I finally shared my dilemma with my mother.

Her eyes lit up.

"Martin, do you remember winning the award at school?" she asked.

Two years prior, I had scored the highest on a national placement test in my school. Everyone in Zimbabwe took this test at the end of primary school. At our graduation ceremony, the headmaster announced that my score was the highest not only in our school but in all of Mutare. There was a collective gasp in the audience, followed by an applause that thundered in my bones.

I was proud, but my father was even more so. He seemed to grow another inch that afternoon, walking around with his chest puffed out, his smile brighter and bigger than usual. He was so pleased that he asked the photographer who had come to the ceremony to take our photo. In it, I'm wearing my school uniform. My father is standing to my right and

Nation is to my left, holding the certificate rolled up like a baton. They are both smiling, but I am looking very serious and staring straight at the camera. I had never had my photo taken before or since. To be honest, I was a little nervous. But when we got the photo back, I understood how special it was. The photo actually captured a very happy moment in my life and froze it forever.

"Send her that," my mother said.

"Really?" I asked.

It was the only photo that we owned.

Instead of answering, she got the box where she kept all my report cards and certificates to get the photo. She also handed me money for stamps.

"Your friend is waiting to hear from you," my mother said.

Elated, I went outside to write Caitlin a letter.

6 December 1997

Dear Caitlin

Hallo! Many thanks for your letter. It was so great. My birthday is on the ninth of March.

What do you know of Zimbabwe? Tell me about USA. Thank you for your nice picture. This is mine. On the picture, you look really beautiful. Keep up your smartness, cleanliness.

Hope you are well and we will not let down each other by not replying letters. Say hallo to everyone! Bye. Hope your impatience on my picture has decreased.
Your caring friend,
Martin.

Since the holidays were coming, I added: *Have a wonderful and peaceful Christmas holiday and a prosperous new year. Let's keep our friendship strong. It will never end.*

And then, just to be certain she would not get cross with me for taking so long to send her a photo, I apologized for taking so long to reply and promised to look for a better picture to send in my next letter.

Caitlin

―――❦―――

MY CRUSH ON MATT GREW until I could not take the pressure that whirred inside me every time I saw him in algebra. Lauren was in that class and sat in the row next to me. One day in late October, I passed her a note that read *MATT IS SO HOT. I AM FREAKING OUT!*

Lauren scribbled something quickly and threw the note back to me before the teacher turned around.

I dare you to touch him. No, I DOUBLE dare you.

She had a good point. What did I have to lose? I built up my courage, and then tapped him on his shoulder midway through class. Lauren almost fell off her seat.

"Um, do you have an extra pencil? My tip just broke off," I lied. I had at least a dozen mechanical pencils in my bag.

He turned around and flashed me a smile that I thought might melt me.

"Here," he whispered, handing me his. He then reached into his back pocket for a spare.

At the end of class, I offered him his pencil back. "It's cool," he said. "Just keep it."

"Thanks," I said, hoping he could not feel the heat radiating from my body.

That night, I was trying to concentrate on homework, but could not stop fantasizing about kissing Matt. Finally, I grabbed a black Sharpie and marched into my closet. There, on the wall, I drew an eye with long lashes, followed by a heart and a stick figure, next to which I wrote *Matt Johnson* and dated it: *10/29/1997.* The very next day, he asked me out. It's like I willed it to happen.

That was October 30, which meant Halloween was our first real date. It was official. We were a couple. I made another note in my closet: *Cait + Matt, October 31, 1997.*

Our school had a costume party, and I went dressed as a punk rocker. My mom bought me pink hair paint and I wore a blue sequined minidress and leather jacket. Matt borrowed his friend's football jersey, and his friend wore Matt's soccer shirt. I thought that was pretty lame. As it turned out, Matt was just really shy. Other than the Halloween party, we didn't really do anything besides talk on the phone a few times—and even then, I did all the talking. We once met at the food court at the mall with a bunch of other friends but he barely spoke to me, and he never once tried to kiss me or hold my hand. I started to wonder if he even liked me. And then I noticed Drew, who played soccer with Matt. Frustrated, I wrote in my closet: *I am still going with Matt, but I like Drew.* By the time I dumped Matt, Drew was dating someone else, and I already had a new crush. Nathaniel. We started dating in late November, and then broke up a week later. I still liked him, but so did my friend Chrissy. It was just getting too complicated. By then I had filled up half my closet wall with boy-crazy confessionals. I needed a break.

Taking a break gave me time to think about other things, like school, and softball. I was on the team, but not very good. My coach suggested practicing at home, so I started doing that with my dad on weekends.

We were throwing the ball in our backyard when my dad asked, "Have you heard from your pen pal?" The question startled me. I had not really been thinking about Martin since I sent him my photo. I was too swept up with boys. And then, just like that, his letter arrived the following week.

I could always tell Martin's letters from the rest of the mail. They looked and felt different—thinner paper, more exotic and colorful stamps. This letter was thicker than the last. I ripped it open and gasped when I saw that he had sent me a photo.

Seeing him standing there dressed in his school uniform changed something in me. Martin was no longer this faceless fantasy—he was real. He looked much younger and smaller than I had imagined—like a little boy in his green shorts and shirt. My very first thought was, He's so cute! Not in a boyfriend way, more like a little brother. He had written on the back of the photo that it was taken two years before, in 1995, which explained why he looked so young. He also looked quite serious, though I could see the sparkle of a smile in his eyes. I assumed he was standing between his father and probably his older brother, Nation, who looked a lot like Martin, only taller. I ran up to my room and immediately placed this photo between one of me, my brother, and parents taken at my grandparents' lake house, where we visited often, and another of me goofing around in my backyard with Lauren. I kept all of my favorite photos beneath the glass on top of my desk, so I could see them always.

And then I read his letter several times over.

I loved the way he wrote: While I understood all the words, they still seemed foreign. Every letter began with *Hallo!*, a greeting I'd never seen written before. I imagined his voice to be singsongy and upbeat. In his letters, he used lots of exclamation points, except instead of a dot at the bottom, he drew tiny bubbles. They reminded me of smiley faces, and I imagined him to be as happy as his handwriting. His language was so formal—he sounded so smart!

I wanted to send him something special in my next letter, so I went to the mall that weekend with Lauren to find the right gift. Claire's was our first stop. It was a jewelry store where you could get a pair of hoop earrings for five dollars. We also went to Spencer's, which sold gag gifts. Back then, key chains were super-popular, especially these rectangular metal plates with funny references like *Heartbreaker, Lucky,* or *Diva*. I had about two dozen, which I had clipped onto a huge key ring that was attached to the outside zipper pocket of my backpack. Lots of kids did this, which meant everyone clanged when they walked through the hallways at school, like a jingle orchestra.

I chose one for Martin that had a glittery swirl pattern on

it without any words. I also bought one for Lauren that said *Best Friend*. She got me the same one. We already had Best Friend necklaces. Mine said *Best* and hers said *Friend*.

Back home, I wrote Martin another letter thanking him for the photo, and sent him the key chain and a picture from my winter dance. In it, I'm wearing a headband that looks like a tiara, and a burgundy dress. I asked him to please send me another photo. I hoped it would be more current.

A month or so later, I received a four-page letter from Martin. No one had ever sent me such long letter! This time, instead of writing *Hallo!*, he addressed me as "the queen," which was so funny! It didn't feel like it did when Richie said it. My mom and dad called me Queen Caitlin as well, but in a much nicer way than my brother did. I had no idea where Martin got the idea, but it made me feel that much closer to him, like he was part of our family.

He wrote:

3 March 1998
Dear Caitlin the "queen"
Well! It's me again. I don't know how to thank you. Thank you very very much for sending the nicest letter in my life. Thank you for the glittering and attractive charm. What a friend Caitlin. Thank you for the nice picture of yours. You look extremely beautiful, like a queen. (Queen Caitlin.)

I thought it was funny he called the key chain a charm, and was so glad he liked it. Then I noticed at the very top of the letter, he wrote a PS, which said: *I am making you very nice African-type earrings. I will send them in my next letter.*

How could he possibly know that I collected earrings? I had more than one hundred pairs—a collection of big hoops and long dangly beads and small studs shaped either like hearts or daisies or baby animals. I kept my most valuable ones in a jewelry box my parents gave me for Christmas the previous year. It was blue velvet and had my initials, *CBS*, in gold letters. I also had a pink plastic Caboodles box that looked like a small suitcase, which I had covered in stickers. That's where I kept all the plastic jewelry I got at Claire's. In all my searching for new earrings, I had never seen a pair from Africa.

Martin went on to list all the holidays he celebrated and I was relieved to learn that many were the same as ours— another thing we had in common. But then he wrote that Zimbabwe was still "developing." I didn't quite understand what he meant. I knew I was developing—I had grown two inches since September and had just gotten my first training bra with my mom. But I wasn't quite sure how a country developed. Martin said that there were few schools and hospitals, and wrote that some students learned under trees due to the shortage of classrooms. But then at the end of that sentence he wrote, "Fun!" It certainly sounded nicer than being stuck in a classroom all day—as long as it was not pig-cooking day. When he wrote, *Patients have to stay about ten per bed. Just imagine. Fun,* I couldn't imagine that, no matter how hard I tried. So I skipped to the next line, which made me smile: *Our friendship will always last forever. Sometime we will meet one another.*

I really hoped this would come true.

On the next page, he described life in his country. Lines like *Many workers in Zimbabwe receive a small pay which can't even feed the families* and *Two families have to share a room in some parts of Zimbabwe* stuck out. We had poverty in the United States, though I had never really seen it up close. I figured Zimbabwe was similar.

I also thought that Martin came from a wealthy family because he was wearing a school uniform in the photo he sent. I assumed he went to a private school, which is expensive in America. There was a Catholic school in neighboring Lansdale where the girls wore dark green skirts and the boys wore slacks. Everyone had to wear a yellow shirt. It was supposed to be an excellent education, but I thought I would die from the boredom of wearing the same thing every day. Still, those kids gave me context for Martin and his life. I imagined he lived in a home like mine. But then he wrote that Sakubva, the town where I was sending his letters, was a *high-density suburb* and *filled with poor people and crime, like LA.* I had never been to LA, but knew that movie stars lived there as well as poor people. Maybe that was what Martin meant.

I didn't dwell on it long because the very next paragraph talked about clothes, my favorite subject. *We also have Nike,*

Reebok, Adidas, and many others, Martin wrote. *My best is Reebok.* All of these brands were popular in school—the boys especially liked to wear oversize shirts with Reebok or Nike logos on them. I wanted to get one for Martin on my next trip to the mall.

On the last page, he drew a man wearing a grass skirt and a crown of feathers and wrote, *Our traditional suit but many people wear real clothes.* He also sketched a hut with a grass roof and wrote, *Some Zimbabwean house.* I had seen photos of grass huts in *National Geographic* magazines, but in the photo Martin sent me, there was a brick building in the background that had to be his school. It looked a lot like mine.

The next line really cracked me up: *Have you heard the one from Spicy Girls, which says friendship never ends?*

I laughed out loud that he called them "Spicy," and hoped that the line would become our motto.

At the end of the letter, he wrote, *Send me a US dollar and I will send you ours in my next letter.* I had actually thought about sending him a dollar, to show him our currency. It was like we were on the same wavelength. There was so much else I wanted to tell him about the United States, and to learn about Zimbabwe.

I took out my multicolor pen to write him back. It was the size of a fat cigar and had little levers in different colors circling its top, like a crown. I clicked the green button to describe our seasons, and then the pale blue one to explain that our president was Bill Clinton and our vice president was Al Gore. I chose a dark blue to write, *I have also sent a dollar bill.*

After I finished writing, I opened my desk drawer where I kept all my babysitting money. I found the crispest dollar bill and folded it into my letter. As I addressed the envelope, I felt another kind of fluttering in my stomach. It was a different feeling from my boy crushes—it felt more like an awakening. The world was gigantic, and I had a friend who lived halfway across it.

Martin
—✴—

I HAD ALWAYS WANTED TO see an American dollar. People often said that money grew on trees in America. Seeing this crisp green bill tucked so neatly in Caitlin's letter made me think this may have been true. It looked so new, so hopeful, like a leaf in springtime. I had just laid it on the bed when Nation came into the house.

"Whoa!" he said. "Where did you get that?"

"Caitlin sent it," I said.

We both bent over it, to get a better look: It was bigger than our Zimbabwean dollar, though I rarely saw those either. My parents used coins primarily.

"How much do you think it is worth?" I asked.

Nation shrugged his shoulders.

We both knew it was worth more than a Zimbabwean dollar, especially with inflation, which was escalating daily.

Suddenly the room was awash with a big swath of sunlight. I turned to see my mother's small silhouette in the doorway.

"Why are you all standing around?" she asked. "Your father will be home soon!"

"Mai," I said, handing her the dollar. "I received another gift from Caitlin."

My mother's eyes grew wide, like a child spotting an elephant.

"Why would she send such a thing?" she asked, though it sounded more like an accusation.

Her question startled me—suddenly I worried that my request for a dollar may have been out of line. Truly, I was just curious. We were sharing information about each other's culture, but I realized by the look on my mom's face that I had asked too much.

"I asked her to send it," I said. "I did not think it was such a big deal."

"Well, it certainly is!" she said, still stern. "Your friend must be very wealthy—and you must keep this safe, Martin."

When I showed my father the bill that evening, his face lit up.

"This is the real thing," he said.

"How much is it worth?" Nation asked.

My father shook his head. "I will take it to work tomorrow to ask my boss," he said. "He will know."

My mother winced.

"You must bring that back," she said. "That's Martin's money."

My father turned to me and winked. "Your mother, always so worried."

That following evening, my father arrived more joyous than I had seen him in many months.

"Your friend gave you a very generous gift," he explained. "This may be worth twenty Zim dollars."

I was stunned. It felt too big of a responsibility for me, so I asked my mother to keep it in a safe place until I knew what to do with it.

The dollar stayed put for two weeks. By then, we had been eating sadza for days on end—no beans or even collard greens. And our mealie meal was running low. I could see the strain on my mother. She would make a pot every morning, and we'd eat it clean. In the evenings, our portions were smaller than usual. Simba complained he was still hungry.

"Mai," I said one day as my stomach groaned from hunger. "Let's use Caitlin's money for groceries."

She shook her head. "That is for your future, Martin," she said.

"Our future is now," I explained.

She reluctantly agreed, and then climbed on top of her bed to get the dollar from the box.

We went to the post office to exchange it. The teller did not even have to check any charts or use a calculator.

"One American dollar is twenty-four Zim dollars," she said.

My mother looked as surprised as I felt. My heart quickened. I nodded to her, and she exchanged the dollar.

We went directly to the market and bought enough groceries for two weeks. That night, we ate beans and collard greens with our sadza. And the following morning, we had bread and tea for the first time in many months. It was April in Zimbabwe, but all this good food felt like Christmas—all thanks to my new friend in America.

The next evening, with a full belly, I wrote Caitlin a letter. I thanked her for the very generous dollar bill and told her I would send her something in return soon. I considered sending her a Zimbabwean dollar but knew that was one day's worth of sadza. So instead, I made the only promise that I knew I could keep: that I would always write back, no matter what.

Caitlin

———◈◈◈———

SEVENTH-GRADE SPRING WAS RIDICULOUSLY busy, and dramatic—Drew asked me out again in December and then we broke up on New Year's Eve. I wanted to start 1998 fresh—and that meant dating Brennan. He and I were together for less than a month when Christa told me that she liked him, too. That was tricky. By then, Christa was my best friend. Lauren and I were in a fight—she gave me back the *Best* part of our friendship necklace. Then Christa and I went to the mall and bought a new necklace, together. Then Christa got so mad at me for dating Brennan that she gave me back the *Friend* part of our necklace. So I was without a best friend, but still dating Brennan. I was torn—I really liked Brennan, but he wasn't worth losing a best friend over. I broke up with him and he started dating Christa! I couldn't believe she said yes! I was so upset that I didn't invite her to my thirteenth birthday, on March 28. It was a Saturday, so I had a party and all my friends came—except Christa. Lauren and I were back to being best friends. I had six different best friends that spring, at different times and for different reasons. It was hard to keep straight. At least there was one constant in my life: Martin.

He kept writing. Most of the other students in my English class had stopped corresponding with their pen pals after two or three letters, but by the end of seventh grade, I had at least six letters from Martin. I kept them all in my desk drawer. In the early ones, he'd ask simple questions, like *What's your favorite music?* and *What does your house look like?* But in the last letter he sent me, he asked how much it cost to go to school. I figured he did not realize I was in public school— and I wondered if he would think differently of me as a result. I hoped not.

In that same letter, he said his dad worked at a paper mill. I wasn't sure what that was, or if we even had them in the United States. I bought all my stationery at Staples. And I did notice that while my stationery was either a pristine white with pale blue lines through it or pink with decorative edges, Martin's was always different. Some letters were written on grainy gray paper; some were written on the back of home-work assignments. Sometimes he wrote in pen; other times in pencil. But his penmanship was constant—a bubbly cursive. He always curled the tip of his *h*'s, and his *z*'s looked like chubby *3*s. His letters always put me in the best mood. They were often funny, too.

I had heard monkeys lived in the trees in Africa and asked him if that was true. He wrote back that there were lots of monkeys living in Mutare, and that he actually got into a fight with one once. *Monkeys are really nasty*, he wrote, which made me so sad, because I had wanted a pet monkey for the longest time. He said there were more baboons than monkeys in his hometown, and everyone considered them a nuisance. *I think our baboons are like your squirrels*, he wrote. In my response, I wrote that many people in the US thought squirrels were annoying, but I actually loved them—that's because I loved all animals.

At the time, I had a pet rabbit called Louis. I got him in sixth grade. He had long, floppy ears that bounced off the ground when he hopped. Louis was so attached to me that one day he followed me out the door to go visit Heather, my best friend and neighbor. It was the sweetest thing! He started following me all over the neighborhood. My mom put a little bell on his collar so we always knew where he was, which was unnecessary because he never left my side. He became our neighborhood mascot. When I played kick ball in the street, he'd run whenever I ran. The only time it was a problem was when we played flashlight tag. Everyone always knew where I was, because Louis's bell would ring. I told Martin about Louis, expecting him to tell me about his pets. Instead, he wrote, *The story of your rabbit is very amusing indeed! In Zimbabwe, we eat rabbits! They are quite delicious!*

I was so horrified, I didn't know how to respond, so I put that letter aside and then got so swept up with life. When I finally sat down to write him back several weeks later, I made a point not to mention Louis.

I ended with: *If you could please send me a new picture of you so I can show my friends how nice you are! You are the best pen pal that I have ever had. Again, I am so sorry for not writing back right away! Thank you for being a great friend. Best of friends.*

Before I sealed up the envelope, I remembered that in all my crazy drama, I forgot Martin's birthday, which was three weeks before mine. I also remembered that I wanted to send him a Reebok T-shirt—his birthday was the perfect reason.

I called Lauren to see if she wanted to go shopping later that afternoon. My mom drove us to a discount store in town called Ross, where I found a white shirt with blue trim that had *REEBOK* across the front in matching navy blue. Perfect, I thought.

As I was paying for it, Lauren asked, "Caitlin, are you like in love with Martin?"

The question caught me off guard, and was hard to answer.

"I love him like a brother," I said finally.

"Ew," she said. "That's like incest."

"You know what I mean!" I said, swatting at her. "He feels like a member of my family."

Back home, I wrapped the shirt and attached a note that read, *This is what all the cool kids in Hatfield wear.*

Martin
—m—

THE POSTMAN DELIVERED MAIL to Chisamba Singles every Saturday. I would wait for him to arrive on his bicycle, hoping there might be something from Caitlin. He would always ring his bell and then call out the names of people who had letters and packages. Whenever I heard his husky voice shout "Martin Ganda," I would sprint as fast as I could, knowing it had to be from Caitlin. I'd then spend the next hour reading and rereading whatever she had written. Her stories let me imagine what it was like to be an American teenager. We were growing up together, ten thousand miles apart, as she once wrote in a letter. I'd always share her news and photos with my family and friends, who by now considered her their friend as well. Her letters lifted everyone's spirits. After I had practically memorized every detail, I would give them to my mother, who kept them in the biscuit tin.

One June morning, the postman handed me a large envelope. It was bigger than a textbook and squishy. I knew it was from Caitlin by the small hearts, smiley faces, and stars that decorated the package. Next to my name, she wrote *BFF* in purple glitter ink. I knew, thanks to her, this meant *Best Friends Forever.*

I fought the urge to open the package right there, in front of everyone else waiting for mail. Back home, I decided to go inside our hut. I wanted privacy. Since we shared a common outdoor area with four families, someone was always hanging around. The joke was, if you wanted privacy, you just had to close your eyes. But during the day, our home was usually empty. With no electricity or windows, it was always dark. It was just a place to get dressed in the morning or to sleep at night. I slipped inside, thankful for the cool quiet.

I saw the letter first, taped to a package on which Caitlin wrote *HAPPY BELATED BIRTHDAY, MARTIN!* also in purple glitter ink. I was very touched. I had heard that rich people in Zimbabwe have parties and get presents on their birthdays, but mine always passed like any other day.

The only gift I ever received was when I turned ten.

That evening, my father asked, "Martin, what's today?"

"March ninth," I replied.

And he said, "You know you're ten today, right?"

"Oh yeah," I said, smiling. "I almost forgot."

He grabbed my hand and led me to the woman who sold soft drinks down the road. He told me to choose my favorite.

"Fanta," I said.

We usually got one every Christmas. My father would buy one for each kid, and we would each sip ours slowly, savoring every drop, hoping to make it last as long as possible. That was how we celebrated. The last Fanta I had was two Christmases ago—at the beginning of the economic troubled time. My father could only afford one that year, so we passed it around, taking small sips, holding the sunshine-sweet liquid in our mouths for as long as possible before giving in to a swallow.

I carefully peeled back the tape on Caitlin's gift and could not believe what was beneath the festive paper: an authentic, genuine Reebok T-shirt! Even the wealthy kids who went to my school and lived in houses and ate three meals a day could not afford such a precious thing. Their shirts were knockoffs from South Africa or Mozambique. This one had a tag that said *Made in America!* Proof it was the real deal.

I changed into it immediately. The material felt so good against my skin. I had never owned anything new in my life. Even our school uniforms, which we had to buy each year, were secondhand, and often thin or torn in spots. This shirt was thick and smelled sweet, like ripe fruit. I wondered if Caitlin had sprayed it with perfume, or if this was just how a new thing smelled. Either way, it made me feel powerful, like Superman putting on his cape.

Before I walked back outside, I pulled the *Made in America* tag out of the collar, so people could see this was not some cheap knockoff from Mozambique. And then, smiling wide with lungs so full of air, my chest puffed out, I walked outside.

"Where did you get that?" Nation asked, amazed.

"From Caitlin," I said, beaming.

He grabbed the hem and rubbed it between his fingers. "Wow!"

"It's the real deal!" I said, and pointed to the tag.

Nation whistled and slapped my back. "Now you look like a professional movie star, Martin!" he said.

I felt like one, too. At least a dozen people commented on my new shirt and many asked to touch it.

I wore it to greet my father that evening, but he barely seemed to notice. Usually, he would parade around bragging to all the neighbors that I got another gift from my American friend. Tonight, he simply said, "I'm happy for you, son."

I knew he was preoccupied; there were talks of layoffs at his work. A week before, he came home to say that the company had offered employees to be paid either in Zim dollars or in cups of mealie meal. Many chose food, but my father had to cover school fees as well as rent and food. I could see the concern all over his face; his eyes were always distant, his mouth downturned. He had been working at the mill more than eighteen years—it was all he knew how to do. But if the rumors disturbed him, he did not say. Then one night he came home drunk. That caused a big fight. My mother started screaming, "How can you spend money on beer when your children go to bed hungry?"

He was too drunk to answer.

I knew he was happy for Caitlin's kindness—he just had bigger things on his mind.

I wore my new shirt to school that Monday beneath my uniform, with the tag sticking up out of my collar. When

I finally took it off to wash it a week later, I stood guard as it dried to make sure no one stole it. My father wore it that weekend, and then some days I'd come home from school to see it on my mother or on Nation. I realized that ever since it arrived, it was always on someone's body.

I wanted Caitlin to know how much I appreciated her generosity, but once again was not sure how to do it. That same month, our Post and Telecommunications Corporation, or PTC, fired more than six hundred people, causing the other workers to go on strike. Zimbabwe was in a full-fledged economic crisis: There were riots in Harare and Bulawayo—the government called in the army after people started smashing windows at grocery stores. Their reasoning was "since we cannot afford to buy bread, then we must just take it." People were arrested or beaten as a result. A few even died, trampled or shot by police. Chisamba Singles was already rough—people always fought there. Sometimes it was a domestic dispute that spilled into the street. Other times, it was one man fighting another over an unpaid debt. These days, it was more often about food. Hunger makes people act crazy. I even witnessed one man knifing another for cutting the line to buy bread.

I originally wanted to make Caitlin earrings, but then I spotted a pair of black-and-white speckled ones at the market and thought they would be the perfect gift. I started working on weekends, carrying luggage for people at the nearby bus depot. Now that money was so tight at home, it was the only way to buy postage. And now that the post office was on strike, I had more time to save up.

The earrings cost twenty Zim dollars. After one day of carrying luggage, I had made four dollars in tips. So I went to the market every weekend for two months to save up for Caitlin's gift. By the end of August I had enough for the earrings and stamps. I wanted real stationery—not the back of used homework, which was all I had to write on. My father used to bring scraps from work, but now that the factory was doing so poorly, that luxury ended. I asked him for help anyway, hoping for a miracle. The very next day, at dinner, he handed me two pieces of notepaper with the name and address of the Mutare Paper Mill. "Official stationery," he said, explaining that his manager gave it to me as a gift.

"He often asks about you, Martin," my father said, smiling. I think my father felt good that he could provide something special for me. That same night, after everyone else went to bed, I wrote Caitlin using the fire embers for light:

September 1998
Beloved queen Caitlin:
    Hi. How are you. I did not reply
quickly because the Zimbabwean PTC
where we buy stamps was on strike.
I am very sorry. But never worry, Martin
is always there for his best, Caitlin.
I will always reply no wonder what
happens, I swear.

Thank you very much for the best present, the lovely beautiful high quality shirt I have ever received. Whenever I walk everyone stops me, touches the best quality, asks me where I got the wonderful shirt and I feel special because of you. Oh you are the greatest. I have really a loving AMERICAN friend.

Guess what? I bought some beautiful earrings at a traditional shop for my best friend Cait. I hope you will like them.

Please keep up your excellent art of markers. I really love it. How do you do it?

I added a three-toed lion's paw, a heart, and a star, trying to mimic her handiwork, and added, *I can do it with my pen. You see!*

While there was so much more I could have said—about the crisis, about how hard it was to save money for the stamps, about how hard life was becoming in my country—I decided to keep it light on purpose. I didn't want to trouble Caitlin with my life worries or scare her off. Plus, I didn't think a girl who could send me a dollar bill or a Reebok shirt could ever understand. So instead, I simply wrote:

As I have told you before I am
not a son of a wealthy dad, your gift
increased my clothes. Before I had been
left with only an old shirt of my dad
but your gift made me very happy.

Lots of love, Martin.

After I signed the letter, I placed the earrings in the middle of the page and then drew the image of two hands clasped in a handshake beneath them and wrote in all caps, *NEVER LOSE HOPE. I will always reply.* I underlined "will" and "reply" with three squiggly lines to make this point clear.

I folded the letter around the earrings, and then placed both in the envelope, which my father had also secured for me.

On that, I wrote: *Thanks again for the most beautiful shirt I have ever had. I love you!*

Caitlin

WHEN I HAD NOT HEARD back from Martin by July, I started to worry. He usually replied within a month. I figured he was busy with school and life. I certainly was. I had just started my first real job, as a camp counselor, which meant leaving my house every morning at seven thirty and not getting home until four thirty in the afternoon. It was fun entertaining six-year-olds all day, but exhausting. After work, I usually went straight home. I'd have dinner with my family and then hang out on our back deck with Heather, or play flashlight tag with other neighborhood kids. It was pretty uneventful, until my dad came home one night in early August, looking upset.

"What is it, Rich?" my mom asked.

"Have you heard the news?" he asked.

Mom clicked on the TV to the BBC, her favorite news channel. The screen filled with images of people running through the streets of some faraway city, blood pouring down their faces. Two big men were carrying a limp body in between them, all three splattered with blood. Small fires flared in the streets as police cars arrived and sirens sounded. *Bombing at American Embassy in Nairobi* flashed across the bottom of the screen just as an announcer said, "This was an orchestrated attack. Truck bombs were parked outside the American embassies in both Nairobi and Dar es Salaam."

They were African capitals of countries not far from Zimbabwe. I knew this because ever since I started corresponding with Martin, I had been studying African geography.

"Why would anyone do that?" I asked, dumbfounded.

My dad shook his head and said, "There are evil people in the world, Caitlin."

"Will they strike again?" I asked. I was thinking about Martin. There were only two countries—Mozambique and Zambia—in between Tanzania and Zimbabwe. I knew Martin lived in Mutare—not in the capital, Harare, but still. The thought of him being affected in any way made my stomach queasy.

"Honey, I have no idea," my dad said. He was rattled.

The following day, we learned that many people died from the attacks. The bombings marked the eighth anniversary of American troops arriving in Saudi Arabia. My dad used the word "terrorists." I'd never heard that before and asked him to explain. "They planted a bomb that killed innocent people to make a political point," he said. "They're cowards."

The bombings were front-page news for days: Two hundred twenty-four people were killed in Kenya, ten dead in Tanzania. I was worried Zimbabwe would be next.

That August, my family went on vacation to the Thousand Islands in Canada. We spent a week on a houseboat and brought Romeo, but left Kava home because Romey was a better swimmer and Mom was worried about how we would walk both of them if we were living on a boat. I was worried about being stuck in such a small place with my parents, especially when I realized we were basically sharing the same room—I had a bunk bed, they had a queen-size one, and the only thing that separated us was a curtain. It was like upscale camping and we actually had a blast. Every morning, Romeo and I would jump off the boat to swim. He would paddle over to a nearby rock or the shore so he could do his business. Then we'd swim back to the boat.

On that trip, we visited a bunch of old castles, including Boldt Castle. It was named for its owner, George Boldt, a very rich man who had it built it for his wife. She died suddenly, weeks before they were meant to move in. The tour guide said that George was so heartbroken that he never visited the castle again, but kept it as a shrine to his wife. I was so touched by his story. The place was magical, like something out of a fairy tale. It had a drawbridge, and gardens shaped like hearts. The castle itself had 120 rooms—including a ballroom and a piano room. The Alster Tower was a separate building, twice the size of my home, that George Boldt had built as a playhouse for his children. It made me sad to think they never got a chance to play there.

During that trip, my mom took a million photos. As we were flipping through the stack the week after we got home, I picked out several to send to Martin. In one, I was wearing my mom's big-brimmed straw sun hat so I would not get sunburned on the top of my head. I was so blond that people thought I was an albino, and had such thin hair that my scalp sunburned easily. That shot was my mom's favorite picture of me—I liked it, too. I wasn't looking right into the camera but instead staring off into the sunset.

That summer, I became obsessed with taking photos. My mom bought me an Advantix camera, which was so small it fit in my pocket, but it could still zoom in for close-ups or out for wide angles. I took five rolls of film on that trip alone and pasted them together to make collages when I got back home, one of which I pasted to my bedroom wall, next to my Spice Girls and Backstreet Boys posters. Richie passed my room as I was doing it, and poked his head in.

"What, suddenly you are an artiste?" he said sarcastically, pronouncing it the French way, "ar-TEEST." He hadn't come on vacation, as he was leaving for his freshman year at California University of Pennsylvania, which was four hours west of Hatfield. He wanted to keep working at Sears to save as much money as possible.

"Whatever," I muttered. I was about to tell him to leave me alone, but I stopped. He was about to leave me totally alone that weekend. Instead, I said, "Shouldn't you be packing?"

"I am," he said. I was thinking of a comeback, like, "Actually, you are bothering me," but he was quicker.

"Send this to your African friend," he said as he tossed a T-shirt into my room.

68

It fluttered, like a stingray beneath water, before settling in a tangle on my pink rug. I picked it up and smiled. It was Nike, another brand Martin had mentioned in his letter. Richie was a jerk, but sometimes he was a nice jerk.

"Thanks," I said as he disappeared down the hall.

I sent that with a few photos I had selected from our vacation and several I took specifically for Martin of our backyard, our driveway, and the dogs. I wanted him to see what my life looked like in America.

Several weeks into eighth grade, I finally heard from Martin. He sent me an envelope that had a slight bulge—I tore it open and saw a pair of earrings. They were tiny hand-carved birds, painted black with small white polka dots. He said they were called guinea fowls, which sounded very exotic. I imagined they were very expensive. He also explained that it took so long to respond because the post office had been on strike. I was so relieved that was the reason.

I was also thrilled that he loved the Reebok shirt. He made a strange comment at the end of the letter, that it *greatly increased his wardrobe*. I had no idea what that meant, and was so swept up by his generous gift that I did not give it much thought.

That fall, big gold hoops were super-popular. All my friends wore them, and I had at least a dozen pairs in various sizes and thicknesses. My new African earrings were unique. Nobody else could possibly have had them. And that made me feel special. Still, I was a little nervous the next morning as I slipped them on.

Heather was the first to notice as we waited for the bus that morning.

"Nice earrings," she said.

"Thanks," I said, trying to sound nonchalant. "Martin sent them to me."

"Your pen pal?" Heather asked.

"Yeah," I responded. "He got them at a traditional shop."

"That's awesome," she said just as the bus pulled up.

At school, all my friends commented on them as well.

"My pen pal sent them," I explained every time. No one could believe that we were still in touch.

"He still writes?" Halle asked at lunch.

"My pen pal was lame," Alison chimed in. "I got like one letter and that was it."

"Mine too," Lauren said. "Or maybe I didn't write back? I can't remember because that was like forever ago."

"He must really like you if he sent you jewelry," Alison said.

"Caitlin insists that they are just friends," Lauren said. "But I think she's really in love with him."

I laughed at first, but really, I was annoyed. Lauren knew we were close in a different way. She actually sounded a little jealous, which pissed me off. I wanted to share my news with someone who would understand how special my relationship with Martin was.

Mrs. Miller was sitting at her desk correcting papers when I knocked on her door.

"Caitlin!" she said. "What a nice surprise!"

"I just wanted to show you what my pen pal sent me," I said.

"You're still in touch?" she said, clearly impressed.

"Yeah," I said. "He's sent me eight or nine letters. Oh, and these."

I slipped off one of my earrings and laid it on her desk.

"He bought them for me at a traditional shop," I explained.

"How remarkable," she said.

I knew that—and wished Lauren would see it as well. But that might be hopeless—we'd been fighting again. She never had time to hang out now that she was on the varsity basketball team. And I was getting to be closer friends with Halle, who Lauren thought was lame.

My favorite thing about Martin was that there was no drama. I could be entirely myself with him, and I felt he was doing the same with me. I looked forward to receiving Martin's letters more than going roller skating on Friday nights or to the mall on the weekends. He was introducing me to a whole other world, one I had never imagined before we started writing to each other. These earrings were a physical connection to him, and to that world.

I was excited to send him my next package with Richie's shirt, so I could do the same.

October 2, 1998
Dear Martin,
Hello! How are you? It was so nice to hear from you. Thank you so much for

the lovely earrings that you sent! I wear them all the time and all my friends love them, too.

I'm very glad you liked the shirt I sent! You will find a shirt in this package, too. My brother suggested that I send it to you. He likes Nike, too! I will also look for a Fila shirt for you. I'm glad that you like the clothes we have in the US.

I also included a postcard I bought him in Canada, and several mechanical pencils I bought at Staples. They were my latest obsession and I thought he'd like them, too.

I paused before finishing my letter. I'd been thinking about Martin in a new way ever since the embassy bombings. I could not wrap my head around why anyone would want to harm innocent people, or understand how hatred could fuel such violence. Frankly, I didn't want to understand it. It made me see how truly special my relationship with Martin was. I continued: *As US citizens, we are always mindful of the effects of terrorism. The two attacks on US embassies in Africa were terrible. The radicals who cause this destruction of lives are so nasty and cruel. We hope it stops! Everyone must strive to get along—have an international friendship, like us!*

I also told him about our vacation, and explained all the photos I was enclosing, including the one Mom took of me in the hat, as well as one with me and Romey, and those of our house and cars: *In the driveway on the right you will see my mom's Jeep. My dad drives a 1997 Nissan Maxima and my brother drives a 1987 Nissan Maxima. Richie took his car to university, so we have more room in our driveway now!*

I ended with: *Thank you again for the lovely earrings. I will always think of you when I wear them.* At the bottom of the page, I added: *BF4E-Best Friend Forever.*

October 1998

Martin

—ᴍ—

I DID NOT KNOW ANYONE—besides the human resources manager at my father's work—who had one car, let alone three. That was not the only astonishing thing: Caitlin's house was as big as a castle, and in one photo, she was wearing jewelry on her teeth. I had never seen anything like that before. It was fascinating.

I brought the stack of photos to school to show my friends. I knew they would not believe me if I said she lived in a castle and had three cars and mouth jewelry. I needed proof.

At break that morning, Joe, Paul, and Raymond sat with me beneath the baobab tree outside our school.

"This is her house," I said, taking out one photo at a time.

"Impossible!" Joe laughed. "It looks like the one our president lives in!"

"It's huge," Paul agreed.

"You could fit five families in there, at least," Raymond chimed in.

Raymond also lived in Chisamba Singles. Paul and Joe lived in a township nearby that was a bit nicer, but nothing like this.

Then I showed them the photo of her parents on the houseboat.

"This is the floating house they stayed on this summer," I said with mock authority. "In Canada, people live on boats."

My friends shook their heads in disbelief.

"How is it possible?" Raymond asked.

I did not know the answer, and so quickly pulled out the next photo from the stack. It was Caitlin, wearing her mouth jewelry.

"This is very popular in America," I explained. "Caitlin is going to send me a set so I can show you all how to wear it."

"Wow," Paul exclaimed. "She looks like a princess."

"You should marry her, Martin," Raymond said. "Then you could be a prince."

We all laughed at that idea—and I held back what I was thinking, that my love for Caitlin was far deeper than that.

The next photo was of Caitlin in bed, with her dog Romey.

"In America, dogs are treated like family members," I said.

This photo actually shocked me. Zimbabwean dogs were scrawny and slept outside. They ate only if there were leftover scraps, which was never the case in my house. My friends were amazed, too.

"What happens if the dog poops?" Raymond asked.

We all burst out laughing. It was a good question—and I had no idea what the answer was.

That afternoon, I gave my mother the stack of photos to store with the rest of Caitlin's letters. As I peered into the box, I saw how many pictures she had sent. There were over a dozen. It bothered me that I had only sent her one picture. Worse, she had asked again for another photo of me. Caitlin had been so generous. I had to reciprocate.

This meant we had to hire a photographer to come to our house, take the photo, develop it, and bring it back later. That was expensive. Still, I asked my father to consider it—he knew how important this was to me, so he promised he would do his best to find the money for a photographer. Before I put all the photos away in what had now become Caitlin's box, I selected the photo of her wearing the big straw hat. I had already started calling her "queen" and in that photo, she really looked like one. I pinned that one to our wall, next to the first one she sent.

To buy some time, I decided to send Caitlin an African bangle I bought at the market, which I imagined was the closest thing we had to the American malls that Caitlin seemed to visit every weekend with her friends. The Sakubva Market was five kilometers from my house and called "Musika We Huku," or "the market where chickens are sold." My mother bought our food and other life necessities there. It was adjacent to the central bus station, where I had started working every weekend carrying luggage for tips in order to make pocket money to keep up my correspondence with Caitlin.

The bus station was chaotic, but I loved wandering

through the market. It was the size of three football fields and filled with vendors selling all kinds of things, like fruit, vegetables, and peanuts. You could also buy beef and live chickens there, as well as roasted mice, a popular snack in Zimbabwe. We used to hunt them in the fields around Chisamba Singles when I was younger. It was hard work to catch a small mouse.

People also sold fake sunglasses called Prada or Gucci. One guy hand-painted T-shirts with popular logos, like Puma and Nike with the swish. One said *Reebock*. I now knew that spelling was incorrect, thanks to Caitlin. Whenever I was wearing my shirt, I avoided going by his stand. I did not want to be bad for business.

I spotted the bracelet one weekend. It was made from wood, and had a small cheetah print pattern burnt into it. It was lovely, and reasonably priced, so I bought it hoping it would keep her happy until I could find a way to get my photo taken.

5 November 1998
Dear Caitlin,

Hello! How are you? It was so nice to hear from you. Thank you very much for the Nike shirt. I love it. Now I have two of the competitive modern fashions— Nike and Reebok. Thank you. My parents also thank you for the present.

The pictures are brilliant. I was glad to know your lovely family, nice big house, and beautiful vehicles. Caitlin, I have to tell you what I feel: You are becoming more and more beautiful and lovely! Keep it up!

I have enclosed an African bangle. You wear it on the wrist. I hope you will like it. In my next letter, I am going to give you something bigger and more beautiful.

At our school we wear uniforms so our parents do not bother buying us as many clothes as you have. You are lucky.

Did you hear the new hit from the Spice Girls? "Viva Forever"? I love it! Do you?

We are in summer and it's very hot. We even sweat at night. Are you also in summer? Caitlin, thank you again for the nice shirt, best pencils, lovely pictures, and the nice postcard. Thank you!

Lots of love,
Martin Ganda
BF4E

A few weeks later, my father arrived home in a jovial mood. "Martin!" His deep baritone funneled through our doorway.

I was inside, studying for my Form Two finals that would take place that December. That January I would begin Form Three, which meant I had two more years before I could go on for my A-levels, the last two years before university. My goal was to stay number one in my class, so I would be eligible for a scholarship at the University of Zimbabwe. That meant doing well in all my subjects: math, Pure Science, history, geography, and English were easy. I didn't worry about accounting—I had a 100 average in that class. Shona and woodworking were the problem. Both were also required classes and my least favorite. That evening, I was working on Shona verb conjugations when my father arrived with news.

"What is it, Baba?" I asked, ducking out from our house into the courtyard.

"A photographer will come this weekend," he said. "It's all arranged."

"But how?" I asked.

"A friend offered to help," he explained.

I felt as if I had swallowed several frogs—they were hopping in my stomach. I was so happy, I started jumping, too. I could finally give Caitlin something she had asked for after everything she had given me.

The day my photo was taken, I wanted to look my best. I asked my father if I could wear his button-down shirt and his only jacket even though both were too big on me. He agreed and then also pulled out a tie. I'd never seen him wear it before—it was beige with a brown swirled pattern. Wearing my father's clothes made me feel powerful and strong. We paid the photographer for two photos because you had to pay for the picture even if it came out badly. So if he chopped off your head, you still had to buy it. We took two, hoping at least one would come out okay. One was blurry, but thankfully, the other was fine.

PART 2

Clues

Caitlin

—⊖⊗⊗⊙—

I WAS SURPRISED TO GET such a formal photo from Martin. All the pictures I had sent him of me with my friends were goofy by comparison. In his, Martin was wearing a suit that looked too big for him, and was staring straight into the camera, looking quite serious. Still, I could see the sparkle in his eye and the hint of a smile on his lips. I immediately put the new photo under the piece of glass on my desk, next to the first one he sent. Looking at them side by side, I realized that we were growing up together, so far apart.

It was strange, because even though we had never met, Martin was the only person I felt I could be totally honest with. I never worried that he would judge or tease. On the contrary, I could tell Martin whatever was happening in my life, knowing he'd always take my side, no matter what. Even over the silliest stuff! Like the time I saw Lauren hanging out with some older kids at the mall. I ran up to her and said "Hey!" and she literally turned her back to me and continued her conversation as if I wasn't there. I can still hear her say, "As I was saying…" while I just stood there growing hot from humiliation. That was in the middle of eighth grade. I described the entire incident to Martin, who responded in his very next letter, *That's so rude!*

Another time, I got into a really big fight with Lauren over a Janet Jackson CD. We were dancing in her basement with a bunch of our girlfriends and somehow the CD got ruined. Lauren blamed me. I was so upset! I then thought, I have to tell Martin, and immediately felt better. He knew all about Lauren. I told him the whole story, ending with *She's so mean!* And Martin responded as if he totally understood, like he didn't know anything different—as if he was just like me. By then, he really was my true best friend.

In hindsight, I'm almost ashamed of how ridiculous my teen dramas were. I had no idea what Martin was going through because he never let on. Instead, he responded to my silly stories and never said much about his own life. Not even when I asked him. But there were clues hidden in these upbeat, cheerful notes. Like the one he wrote me in November of that year. In addition to asking me if I had heard the new Spice Girls hit "Viva Forever" he also wrote: *At our school we wear uniforms so our parents do not bother buying us as many clothes as you have. You are lucky.*

I think he was actually trying to protect me from knowing how incredibly hard his life was.

Martin
—〰—

TOWARD THE END OF 1998, things really began to disintegrate for my family. I was just about to finish Form Two, the equivalent of eighth grade in America. Nation and I began working after school as well as weekends in order to help feed our family. My father's paycheck was never enough. It was rough. Worse, I could see how it affected my father. He was no longer singing when he came home, if he came home at all. Some nights, he'd creep in late, well after we had all gone to sleep. I'd wake up, not from any noise but from the sweet, rancid smell of Chibuku.

"How can you drink when there is no food for your children?" my mother would hiss at him the next morning. My father moaned through his hangover, but still got dressed and went to work. It was almost pointless by then. His paycheck barely covered our rent. My mother had begun working in neighbors' gardens and doing pickup work as a maid in town in exchange for mealie meal.

At the end of the semester, I had to take an important exam, which cost one Zimbabwean dollar. My friend Nyasha came to pick me up the morning of the test. He had just moved to Chisamba Singles a few months before and we became fast friends. He was smart and funny. We liked to study together.

The morning of the test, I asked my dad for the dollar. He turned to my mom and said, "Give Martin the money."

She was irate. "Are you crazy?" she shouted. "I don't have any money!"

Nyasha was waiting right outside. He could hear everything. I was crushed. Then I heard Raymond and Paul arrive as well.

"Martin, we're going to be late," Raymond shouted.

I stepped outside as my parents continued arguing inside.

My mind was reeling. If I didn't take this test, I couldn't move to the next grade.

"I can't go," I said. "I don't have the fee."

"You have to go," Paul said. "You're the best in class."

I shrugged my shoulders, and felt a warm sensation rise from my belly and get stuck in my throat. I did not want to cry in front of my friends.

"I have an extra dollar," Nyasha said. "My father gave it to me for good luck."

He reached into his pocket and handed me the coin.

"Are you sure?" I asked.

"I'm totally sure," he said. "Just don't score higher than me!"

I did not bother telling my parents I had found the money. I just left. My friends came from poor families, too, but they all had their dollars. Their parents knew it was important.

The scores came back a few weeks later and I once again received the highest grade in our school. I couldn't wait to tell Caitlin my news—but how? Postage to America now cost fourteen Zim dollars—two weekends' worth of tips. And my father could not afford one dollar for a test.

Around this same time, my parents learned that my younger brother Simba had started to beat up other kids to give him money or to bring extra food for him to school. He was only seven years old, but that's how he dealt with his hunger: He was a bully. One day, all of the parents came to school for a meeting. Many asked, "Who is this Simba Ganda?" That was because their kids would go home and complain about him. One girl begged her mom for two cookies every day. Her mother wanted to know why and eventually she told the truth: She needed one for her and one for Simba.

My parents were so upset—it was shameful not to be able to feed your kids. Plus, they did not expect Simba to go that far. We were getting sadza for breakfast, but it wasn't enough. And now the whole school knew, which was humiliating for my parents. Simba got a beating at home, which was rare. And then the teachers told my parents they had to feed him more, so my mom started giving him extra sadza every morning from the night before. But the problem was, other kids would have a piece of chicken or a muffin or peas—really sexy stuff. And Simba had sadza. So while he was no longer hungry, he still wasn't happy.

I didn't mind the hunger as long as I could stay in school. In the past, if my father didn't have enough money to cover the fees, he'd borrow from neighbors or people at work and pay them back. He often used our boom box as collateral. We kept it on the same shelf with Caitlin's letters and used it to listen to music on holidays and weekends. I learned my father used it to get the money for the photographer when the man he borrowed it from came to collect his debt the day before Christmas. Since my father could not repay him, he took our stereo. That was a very sad day at our house. That boom box was a lifeline to a world beyond Chisamba Singles. It was also my connection to Caitlin. When we played the radio, I'd hear songs that Caitlin wrote about in her letters. I felt like we were listening to them together. As the country became more troubled, my father stopped listening to music, and singing. He was slowly just giving up.

It was early January 1999 when I heard my parents fighting again right outside the house. It was in the middle of the night and I was lying on the floor, beneath the thin blanket I shared with my brothers, pretending to sleep. Nation was on one side, Simba on the other, and though no one said a word, I knew they were both awake as well. I could feel the tension in their bodies, their hearts beating a bit more quickly than usual, but not as fast as mine. Baby George and Lois were fast asleep beneath my parents' bed—I was glad that they were too young to understand what was happening.

My father shouted, "I don't have the money!" And my mom responded, just as angrily, "Find it!"

School fees were due at the start of every semester—my Form Three began the following day. They argued until my dad stormed off into the night. I heard my mom enter the room. She stepped over us, her three eldest sons, and sat on her bed, which squeaked as she lay down. And then, in the darkness, I heard what sounded like a gasp. I had never heard my mom cry before—the sound punctured my chest. I squeezed my eyes shut and stayed very still, trying to keep back my own tears. It was impossible. They started to leak from the corner of my eyes and I prayed silently that my brothers would not notice. If they did, they never said a word.

The following morning, my father was still gone. I got up, built the fire, and ate the leftover sadza my mother had saved from the night before. And then I went to school, as if it were any other day. I walked into my classroom and took my seat at the desk in the front row with the others in my group. I didn't chat with my friends, like I did most days. I quietly prayed that my teacher would overlook the fact my parents had not paid the fees. Instead, the headmaster arrived at the start of class and called out all the names of those students who had to leave. When he called my name, I felt a sharp stab in my throat.

I wasn't embarrassed—many names were called that morning. It was Z$550 per student, roughly twenty American dollars, a fortune for many. Still, most of those kids didn't care about school—for me, it was painful to leave.

As I gathered my things, my mind was racing: I had to get back to school as quickly as possible. I did not want to fall too far behind, as being the first in the class was my only way to go to university. Then another thought struck me: What would I tell Caitlin? And when would I be able to write her again?

Caitlin

A MONTH PASSED WITH NO letter from Martin. I assumed he was busy with school. Or maybe there was another postal strike? Then another month passed and I started to get worried. What if he was getting bored of me? Or had found another pen pal? Still, I kept writing, and checking the mailbox daily for a response. If there was no mail, I'd rush into the house, thinking, Maybe Mom grabbed it. She started shaking her head as soon as I entered, anticipating my broken-record request. Every day that passed without contact started to hurt my feelings. Had I offended him?

And then, one day in late March, my mom looked very serious.

"Oh honey," she said. "I just hope Martin is okay."

"Why wouldn't he be?" I asked, my throat tightening.

She told me she had been watching the news, and that things in Zimbabwe were unstable. She mentioned that the economy was failing and food costs were skyrocketing. People were starving as a result.

"Do you think Martin is...?" I stopped myself—too many terrible thoughts were filling my head.

"He's fine," I said out loud, as if to assure myself. "He has to be."

My mom sat on the couch in the den and patted the cushion.

"Let's watch this together," she said.

It was a BBC News special report on Zimbabwe that my mom had taped. Suddenly, terrifying images flashed before my eyes. There were riots in the streets: Soldiers were clubbing people. Gunfire sparked and crackled, sirens blared. Small fires blazed as terrified people ran, leaving wounded or dead people behind them. It was chaos. The announcer mentioned international sanctions against Zimbabwe in response to the government's aid to Congo rebels. It was all over my head. Then the most terrible thought struck me: What if Martin is dead? I fought back tears until I couldn't take it anymore. I ran up the stairs to my room and flung myself on my bed.

As I sobbed into my pillow, soaking it with tears and snot, I realized how ridiculous I was being. My friend was in serious trouble—he needed my help. There was no time to act like a desperate teenager. I was totally fine, but I had to make sure Martin was, too. And that meant finding him. I pulled myself together and went back downstairs to log onto AOL. I typed

"Zimbabwe" into a search. Several articles popped up about severe inflation and how people were struggling to afford basic necessities like food. As I continued to read, I got more and more upset: There were riots in the street because people were literally starving. Poverty existed in the United States, but even most of the poorest people had access to food. Why had Martin never mentioned any of this?

That night, I went into the den, where my parents were watching TV.

"What's wrong, Caitlin?" my dad asked. "You look upset."

"We need to help Martin," I said.

"Caitlin, we know he means a lot to you," my mother started to say, but I cut her off.

"Can people actually die from hunger?" I asked. My sadness had turned into pure panic.

"What are you talking about?" my father asked.

My mom told my dad about the BBC News report, and how we were concerned that Martin might be affected by the riots.

I suddenly wondered if Martin never shared any of this news to protect me. He knew I would want to do something to help. But I was so far away—what could I do?

The next day, I didn't go to school. I told my mom I felt sick, and that was true. Those BBC images kept me awake all night. I had a stomachache and felt nauseated as a result. What if he had been shot? Or was hurt in the riots? What if either was the reason he had not written—or worse?

That morning, I wrote yet another letter that said, *I'm really worried about you. Please write me back if you get this. I hope you got my last letter. I hope you are receiving my letters. And I hope you are not mad with me.*

I didn't mention the BBC News report, or that I had been researching Zimbabwe, or any of that. I wrote, *I'm praying for you.* I was so distraught that I wanted to buy a plane ticket and go find him. But I didn't share this with my parents— I knew they wouldn't let me go, or even understand why I would want to.

Martin
—ᴍ—

I WAS NOT THE ONLY student expelled from class that morning in January, but I felt the eyes of the students who stayed as I left, like wasp stings on my back. Nation was waiting for me outside.

"Martin, it's not so bad," he said, throwing his arm around my neck. "More time to practice football."

It was a bright, sunny day, but I felt cold in my bones and a big emptiness in my stomach. Nation sensed this.

"You will be back soon, brother," he said.

We walked home with a group of kids who had also been kicked out. Nation was laughing with them and dribbling the ball, which one of his friends had made out of plastic bags and string. No one else seemed too upset, but my mind was going a million miles a minute trying to figure out how I could get back to school as quickly as possible. Form Three was an important year—we had to start preparing for our O-level exams, which we took at the end of Form Four. They were your ticket to university—without those exams, you could not go anywhere or do anything. I was so worried about all those missing lessons and tests. How would I catch up?

Nation was not planning to go to university. He was a really good soccer player and wanted to try to make a career of it. I knew school was my only chance of getting a better life. I felt like I was moving backward. I knew my father wanted me to go back to school, but as inflation skyrocketed, we had less money to go around. How could I help my family, plus save up for school? It all felt so overwhelming.

And then there was Caitlin, who sent a letter every few weeks. I had no way to respond. She also kept asking for more photos. I realized she didn't understand how impossible this was for me. It was my fault for not explaining it to her, but I didn't want her to know of my struggles. They seemed too low for her. I liked that she thought I was a kid just like her.

I also liked living vicariously through her letters. These days it seemed ridiculous, as the life she described was becoming more and more of a fantasy—trips to the mall, family vacations, and Friday night football games. She had all these exciting things to report. What could I write? Still, her letters kept me connected to this idea that things might improve. That there was a better life awaiting me.

As we neared Chisamba Singles that morning, the empty feeling in my stomach grew. It wasn't hunger for food, but for a better life. I had no idea how to get there. So when Peter, one of the other boys who had been kicked out as well, asked if I wanted to go to the market that same afternoon to work,

I agreed. It was bad enough working weekends, but to be here on a school day felt wrong. I was competing with hundreds of people, each trying to make a buck. This type of pickup work automatically put you in the lowest class. I had no choice. If I couldn't depend on my father, I'd have to make money myself.

As Peter and I neared the market, I could smell the roasted peanuts and hear the rumble of the buses and shouts from people selling water, mangoes, and sadza as we crested a small hill. From the top, I could see the sprawl of people selling oranges, avocados, packets of nuts on brightly colored pieces of material or small cardboard tables made from overturned boxes. Others sold live chickens, so there were crates piled as tall as a grown man filled with rustling feathers and frantic clucks. The market was encircled with idling buses and long lines of people waiting to go to Harare or Bulawayo, or to other countries like Mozambique, Botswana, or South Africa. Local routes also ran every hour to Mutare's city center, thirty minutes away. Those buses were always jam-packed with people.

I knew from my weekend experience that the easiest way to make fast money was to carry luggage for passengers: If somebody had a heavy bag, you offered to take it to the bus. It was hard work—you had to climb on top of the bus using the open windows as footholds, and then pull the bag up with you to place on the roof rack. I was excited when a man offered me two bucks to carry his bags. After I lugged them through the market and heaved them up on the bus, he said, "Actually, I only have a dollar." That happened a few times that day: You could either take the bags back to where you first started carrying them, or take the dollar. I figured that it was an extra dollar I didn't have before. But I was still angry about it.

After two more jobs like this, I was exhausted. There was no shelter, and the sun was blistering hot. The worst part of the job was jostling with other kids who were desperate like me. Together we formed a competitive gang. After my third run, I was also famished. I wanted to buy something to eat, but that would take all the money I had just earned. So I kept working all day and felt let down when I came home with only four Zim dollars.

I gave the money to my mom, who shook her head. Every little bit helped, but we both knew I'd never go back to school at this rate. Still, I was determined. Every day that week, I went to the market with Peter to wash cars and carry luggage. By Friday I had earned twenty Zim dollars. Five hundred thirty to go.

My father asked about my day, and could not look me in the eye when I reported my earnings. So I was surprised when he sat next to me at breakfast midway through my second week working and said, "Martin, go to school today. Tell them I'll pay them next week."

I felt a throb in my temples and my throat. The thought of going back to school was exhilarating—but I also knew they wouldn't take me without the full fee. Nevertheless, I felt a rush of excitement when I put on my uniform that morning and thought maybe, just maybe, they'd make an exception.

My chest grew tight as I rehearsed my father's words on

my way to school. Patrick spotted me and shouted, "Martin! You're back!" I waved and kept walking. I decided to go directly to my teacher, who was preparing for class when I knocked on the door.

"Welcome back, Martin Ganda," he said, rising to greet me with a wide smile.

I kept my eyes on the concrete floor as I relayed my father's promise.

"Let's see what I can do," he responded.

I looked up, unable to contain my own enthusiasm.

"Fantastic!" I said. "I will do my best! I promise!"

"Martin," my teacher interrupted. "I already know what a dedicated student you are—I will try, but I cannot make any promises."

The bell rang and kids started arriving in the classroom. I placed my hands together in a prayer position and bowed at him, our way of saying thanks in Shona. And then I took my seat, front row center.

I spent that first class trying to concentrate on the lessons, wondering whom I should ask for the best notes to catch up for all the lectures I had missed. But then, toward the end of that period, I saw the school's financial manager standing at the doorway. The teacher invited him in. I held my breath.

The manager asked which students had returned to class. I was the only one that day, and so my teacher asked him to step outside for a moment. I said a silent prayer.

The teacher returned with tight lips and a grim expression,

followed by the financial manager, who came up to my desk and asked, "Did you pay your fees?"

"No, sir," I started. "My father said—"

Before I could finish, he said, "Martin, I must see the paid receipts before you can enroll in class again. These are the school rules."

The entire class remained quiet as I gathered my things to leave. No one was surprised my father could not pay. This was the story of too many people in Zimbabwe. Why did I think I was I any different?

As I left the room, I caught my teacher's eyes and bowed my head again. He nodded back and I knew he was disappointed, though not nearly as disappointed as I.

I returned to an empty home. My mother had gone to fetch water. That morning a slow trickle of rusty red liquid came out of the communal faucet   it smelled of mud and left a residue on your skin rather than cleaned it. No one could bathe in it, let alone cook with or drink it. This happened frequently in Chisamba Singles. The nearest river was a kilometer away, but if the bed was dry, or the water polluted, my mother might walk three—or ten kilometers to a place she heard from neighbors had a working well. It was still early in the day, so I changed from my uniform into my T-shirt and shorts and headed back to the market.

There, a man asked me to help him pour tea, a new task. I did that for a few days, and while it was a nice change from carrying luggage, I made even less money. So I was intrigued when Peter asked me to help him sell cold drinks.

It was a particularly hot day and he had frozen these small packets of juice. He offered to split any profits we made after he was reimbursed for the cost of the drinks. I was excited, especially since by the day's end I had sold two boxes' worth and had only a few juices left. The sun was casting an orange glow over the market as I headed toward a bus leaving for Harare. There were three and four people to each two-person seat. I boarded holding the box over my head, shouting, "Cold drinks! Cold drinks!"

As I squeezed my way toward the back, I saw William, a friend from school, sitting with his brother, laughing. William was in Group One with me. He was clever, and cared about school as much as I did. But he lived in a house, and both of his parents worked. He never had to worry about school fees or textbooks or money for exams. He had more than one uniform, and several pairs of shoes. I suddenly felt hot not from the crush of people, but from shame. I began walking backward, quickly. I didn't want him to see me doing this work, or knowing that I had gone that low.

Even he knew that Zimbabwe was in terrible shape, but the people who lived in Chisamba Singles witnessed it every day. Food shortages had become a real problem. Fights broke out daily, haggling over prices, or bartering gone bad. This was becoming common. As was domestic violence—I had always heard men beat their wives, since we lived in such close quarters, but now I would see it out in the streets as well. Nothing was being hidden anymore. AIDS, too, had become rampant. The man we split our room with had blisters all over his face as if someone had splashed him with acid. Another neighbor died from it that year. She got so skinny and weak that her family had to carry her outside on sunny days for fresh air. She looked like a skeleton draped with papery skin and scared me so much that I was relieved to hear she had died.

I was only fifteen, but I knew Chisamba Singles was considered one of the worst slums not only in Mutare but also in all of Zimbabwe. We were famous for our poverty. If I had bumped into someone from Chisamba Singles on that bus, he would have understood why I was selling those drinks. William would, too, but not in the same way.

I gave Peter the remaining packets and walked home feeling more down than ever, even though I had made eight dollars that day, a record. I still had such a long way to go. I felt doomed.

That weekend, I got another letter from Caitlin. She had sent three in a row and was disappointed that I had not responded. I understood her frustration. Then I got to the part where she asked if I was mad at her. Mad? At her? This was impossible. I could never be mad at her. That she thought this made me so upset. I had to write her immediately.

I had saved thirty-two Zim dollars and needed sixteen for stamps, which would set me way back from returning to school. But this was important. I still had to find something to write on. My dad was lucky to still have a job. Retrenchment had begun at the factory—they were firing older employees and hiring younger ones, for less pay. I went back to the market the next day and kept my eyes open for something to write on. When I saw a young boy fling the wrapper from an ice-cream bar onto the ground, I grabbed it without anyone noticing. It was still clean, except for a chocolate smear, which I wiped off on my shorts. I ran home to write Caitlin. Since the paper was quite small, I compressed my handwriting to get as many words on the page as I could—this was a big moment in our relationship. I decided to tell Caitlin the truth about why I had not been in better touch. And I prayed that she would understand. And that she would still want to be my friend.

The following day, I took my note to the post office along with extra money my mom gave me that morning to buy an envelope. I knew Caitlin's address by heart, and wrote it in the center of the envelope, trying to leave enough space for all the stamps it needed to make it to my best friend's house.

Caitlin

I CONTINUED TO CHECK THE mail every single day for weeks. And then one day, I saw an envelope so completely covered with stamps it barely had space for my name and address. Martin was alive! I ripped it open, thrilled. But when I unfolded the actual letter, I gasped. My friend was writing to me on trash.

As I read his small cramped words explaining why he had disappeared, I felt a crazy mix of relieved and confused. He wrote that he had been kicked out of school because he didn't have enough money to pay the fees. This made no sense—couldn't he switch to a public one? It was illegal in the United States to just not go to school—wasn't it the same in Zimbabwe? I read the next line: *I've been carrying luggage and pouring tea just to make money so my family can eat.* The pressure that had been building in my chest left no room to breathe. He was a kid! He should be in school! Not working to feed his family. Still, I was so relieved to get his letter that

I ran into the house shouting, "Mom, Martin is alive! He's alive!"

"Thank God," she said, rushing to my side. "Is he okay?"

I tried to answer, but the tears that started in the driveway were now washing over my words.

"What is it?" she asked, concerned.

"He's not going to school," I managed to say before another wave of tears took over. I sunk my head into my mother's soft shoulder. "Mom, he's pouring tea and carrying luggage to help feed his family."

"Now, now," she said rubbing my back. "Martin is a smart boy. He will find a way to get back in school, Caitlin."

I tensed up. She had no idea what he was experiencing. I could barely grasp it. And as much as I wanted to believe her, I knew he could not do it on his own. I wanted to help, but how?

I did not tell my mom any of these thoughts racing through my head. I did not want a lecture about how I needed to concentrate on my own life first. Or about how Zimbabwe was not the United States. I knew that. I had been reading everything I could find online about the country—story after story of poverty, starvation, and disease. It seemed so illogical, so wrong. I had been so worried about Martin for the last two months that I had stopped thinking about much else. My grades started slipping as a result. I had the luxury of not being interested in school, while Martin was actually unable to go. It seemed so unfair.

"I have to study," I lied. I just wanted to be alone.

Upstairs, in my room, I pulled all of his letters out of my desk drawer, looking for clues that might help make sense of everything. All these lines I had glossed over before jumped out: *high-density suburbs, ten people per bed, greatly increased my wardrobe.* There were so many clues that he was struggling, but I never paid enough attention to figure them out until now. I felt like an idiot.

Immediately I pulled out a piece of stationery. The words gushed out of me:

Dear Martin,
    Thank goodness you are okay! I was so worried!! I thought something terrible happened to you. For some reason, I thought you may have drowned! I know that is crazy because Mutare is nowhere near the ocean or even a lake, but still, I had nightmares about it. I have been reading so much about what is happening in Zimbabwe and so I am especially glad you are not hurt. But I am so sorry that you are not in school. I don't understand it. And I cannot begin to imagine what that is like. Here in the United States, we have to go to school. It is the law. Everybody goes, regardless of how much

money you have. Of course, there are kids who drop out, or don't care. But I have never heard of someone who wants to go not being able to.

I had so many questions for Martin, like *How can you get to go back to school? What are your parents doing for money? How are you paying to live? And why are you working to buy food for your family?* But I didn't want to overwhelm him. What if he did not have any answers? It would just make him feel worse.

Instead, I wanted to write something that might give him hope. And I wanted to do something to help—really help. That sparked a thought: I'd just earned twenty dollars from babysitting, which I was planning to spend on silver hoop earrings. Martin needed the money way more than I needed another pair of stupid earrings. Twenty dollars couldn't possibly get him back into school—but maybe it could buy food for his family? Or at least stamps and stationery so he didn't have to spend his money to correspond with me? I stuffed the bill into the envelope and wrote: *I am enclosing some money and hope it helps somehow. Your best friend FOREVER, Caitlin.*

The next morning, I handed my letter to my mom at breakfast and asked her to mail it that same day. I didn't tell her or my dad that I was sending Martin money. I didn't want them to tell me not to.

May 1999

Martin
—∽—

AFTER I SENT THE LETTER TO CAITLIN, I went to the market every day that week to make as much money as possible. It was the only way I could go back to school. Even if I missed a whole year, I'd catch up. That thought kept me going.

The mailman arrived on his bicycle one Saturday as usual. When he shouted "Martin Ganda!" I ran as fast as I could.

I wanted to read Caitlin's note in private and walked to the outskirts of Chisamba Singles. I was so worried about how she would respond to my news. Would she think differently of me? That I was not worthy of her friendship? I hoped not. But I was feeling so bad about my life at that point that I wouldn't have blamed her if she decided to stop our correspondence. I could barely afford to write her letters—and beyond that, I had nothing else to offer.

I slid my finger beneath the envelope seal, admiring the high-quality paper she always used. It felt heavy and soft at the same time. When I pulled her letter out, I saw that she had stuck something inside.

I thought it was another dollar bill, and my lungs inflated. Then I saw it wasn't one dollar, but a twenty-dollar bill! I felt as if I might lift off the ground, like a hot-air balloon. I examined it closely—President Jackson looked so regal. And those words "In God We Trust" that hovered over the White House made me giddy. When my mother and I had taken the dollar to the post office to exchange it, we had walked out with twenty-four Zim dollars. I did quick math. That meant twenty dollars was worth at least four hundred eighty Zim dollars—enough to get me back in school. By now I knew inflation had doubled, which meant the US dollar was even stronger. I had to hold back from shouting in pure joy and relief. Before I ran to find my mother, I read Caitlin's letter to make sure she wasn't upset. I tucked the twenty-dollar bill in my pocket. People were stealing the most basic things in Chisamba Singles these days. Twenty dollars could get me beaten up and robbed, if not killed.

I read Caitlin's friendly letter three times looking for clues that she may be disappointed in me. I could not find one. On the contrary, it was clear that she only wanted to make sure I was okay. She didn't blame or judge me for being poor—instead, she wrote, *I hope this twenty dollars helps.* I knew she was kind, but this generosity was totally unexpected. Caitlin's support felt God-sent.

I raced home and found my mother hanging clothes to dry on the wires strung between our house and our neighbors.

"Mai, I must show you something!" I said. I didn't want to flash the cash out in the open. "Follow me."

Once inside, I handed her the money.

"Where did you get this?" she asked.

"Caitlin," I said.

She studied it closely.

"But how can such a young girl afford this?" she asked. "And why would she send it to you?"

"Mai, Caitlin has a very big heart," I said. That was the only explanation I could come up with.

"Martin, this is enough to get you back in school!" she said.

"I know!" I said, and closed her hand around the bill. "Help me take care of it."

She clasped her free hand around mine, sandwiching my fist between her small but strong fingers. Then she placed her forehead on mine and began to ululate, but softly. She broke free to dance in a small circle, and her joyous cries came out as throaty, high-pitched whispers. Like me, she did not want to attract anyone's attention to our good fortune. But also like me, she couldn't contain herself.

"The post office in Sakubva is closed, but if we go now, we can get to the city bank in time," she said.

It usually took over an hour to walk from Chisamba Singles to the center of Mutare, where several banks were located. We made it in less than forty minutes, as we were practically skipping. Nation was in his last year, Form Four—he wanted to finish up and then focus on a soccer career instead of trying for university. Depending on the rate, the money might help him as well. In the meantime, he was selling used clothes with a friend in the market to make money while not in school. It was better than carrying luggage, but he hoped it was not forever.

We arrived at the bank and joined the queue with men in suits and women in skirts and blouses. Everyone wore shoes. My mother was barefoot and I was wearing cheap flip-flops, my only shoes, which I had repaired with plastic bags fashioned into straps. We stood out among these city sophisticates in their sturdy lace-up shoes or good-looking pumps. But we had reason to be there, too.

When my mother placed twenty US dollars in front of the teller, he looked surprised but didn't say a word as he counted the Zimbabwean bills not once but three times before placing them into an envelope. I was speechless, too: It was seven hundred Zim dollars, as the new rate was thirty-five Zim dollars for one US dollar. My mother placed the slim brick of cash beneath her skirt, tucked tight against her belly, and I followed her out looking all around for any sign of trouble. No one ever would have guessed that the two of us would be carrying so much money. We were safe.

We decided to take the bus home, since it was already mid-afternoon and we had the money to do so. We arrived at the market, where my mother used six Zim dollars to shop for sadza, beans, and greens. When we passed a chicken stand on our way home, she stopped.

"Martin, we have not been able to eat meat on Christmas

for so many years," she said. "Let's celebrate today, in honor of Caitlin."

My mouth began to water as she picked a plump chicken from the stacked crates.

Everyone in our family knew the good news, but we ate silently, smiling. If a neighbor asked, we said the chicken was a gift from our uncle in Harare. We did not want word to spread through Chisamba Singles that our American friend was sending money in the mail. It would make us a target. Many people were complaining of robberies—basic necessities like sadza and cooking oil were being stolen. My mother kept the actual money hidden from my father as well. He wanted a real beer to celebrate the news. Not Chibuku, but a glass bottle of Castle. Instead, he ate sadza and chicken and beans with his family.

That Sunday was one of the longest days ever. I couldn't wait for Monday morning, to march back to school and hand the money directly to the school bursar. When I did, he smiled and said, "Welcome back, Martin."

I had missed several months of school, and exams were coming up, so I stayed after school for weeks to copy notes directly from the teachers' textbooks. And then one afternoon, instead of going home, I headed over to the Mutare Teachers' College not far from my school. I knew there was a library on campus that had electricity, which meant I had light as well as tables to study at. The library closed at seven PM, but I quickly discovered a way to sneak back in after the guard made his last rounds. There was a large unlocked window at the back of the building that I could easily slip through. One night, I waited for the guard to leave—and then I found a rock to use as a step to hoist my body up and through the window's narrow opening. I landed, hands first, on the cool linoleum floor. Surrounded by the quiet of books, I felt at peace for the first time in forever. Rather than let myself get lost in that feeling, I cracked open my mathematics textbook, which was like a jolt of caffeine—seeing the numbers and problems dance before me was like greeting old friends. I was giddy as I dove into my work that night and many more that followed. Within a month, I was back on track.

Caitlin

AFTER HE SENT THE LETTER on the ice-cream wrapper, Martin started to open up to me in a way that made me realize how different our lives were. Until that moment, I did not understand how truly privileged I was. And that was only the beginning. In the next letter, Martin wrote that the money I sent got him back into school, and fed his entire family a dinner he described as a feast. He said, *We ate chicken for the first time in many years. It felt like Christmas.* I was stunned. We always had roast beef or turkey *and* ham for Christmas. In fact, there was such an abundance of food, we'd have leftovers for days. Chicken was a regular weekday night meal. If twenty dollars could do so much, I wondered, what could forty do?

I was working as a camp counselor that summer, and my dad gave me twenty dollars a week for chores I did around the house. They included picking up dog poop in the backyard— and cleaning Louis's cage. I also had to dust the living room baseboards and empty the dishwasher. I had also started babysitting every Wednesday afternoon for the woman who ran the summer day camp. She had three kids. From then on, whenever she asked me to work on weekends, I said yes.

I slipped two twenty-dollar bills in my next letter, and asked him to use some of it on postage. I had never worried about the price of stamps—I just handed my mom the letters I'd written and knew she'd take care of it. I didn't want Martin to worry about the cost of school, let alone buying stamps to write to me. It felt good sending him money to help with these things. He was the first person I had ever known who really needed my help. I wasn't going to let him down. Besides, I got to go to school for free and my parents kept our refrigerator full. I certainly didn't need another piece of costume jewelry, or a candy-flavored lip gloss, or a new CD at the mall.

I couldn't share any of these thoughts with my friends, though. They didn't, or couldn't, understand. I learned this the day after I got the ice-cream wrapper note. I found Lauren and a few other friends hanging in front of our lockers before homeroom and blurted, "Guess what? Martin is alive!"

Lauren did an exaggerated eye roll before saying, "Jesus, Caitlin, enough about you and your African boyfriend!" All the other girls giggled.

"God, Lauren, how many times have I told you: He's *not* my boyfriend," I said. My blood felt like boiling lava coursing throughout my body.

"Yeah, right," Lauren said to more laughter. "It's so

obvious you're in love with him! Why don't you just fly to Zim-wherever he lives to marry him and get it over with?"

"That's gross!" I spat.

But Lauren had already started walking to her next class, gossiping with two other girls who followed her like panting puppy dogs, leaving me smoldering. One girl, Tina, stayed by my side.

"Why are you so offended?" she asked tentatively, trying to be nice.

"That's like telling me to go marry my own brother!" I said.

Tina looked at me like I was crazy, and then ran to catch up with Lauren and the others. Screw them, I thought as I threw my book bag in my locker. Nobody would ever understand my relationship with Martin, except for Martin. So I kept it to myself. It was easy to do. Martin had started sharing what his life was really like with me—which made all my friends' high dramas seem trivial. Strict parents, bad grades, or stupid boyfriends—my friends' complaints seemed so unimportant and meaningless compared to what Martin was experiencing. Mine did, too. I started to look at my own life in a new way. I saw all the things I took for granted—which cereal to eat for breakfast, or whether or not I wanted ice cream or cookies for dessert. These decisions were total luxuries. I got to choose. Even going to school felt different—not so much this thing I had to do, something I was lucky to get to do.

For almost two years now, I'd been so naïve. I had assumed that Martin's life was like mine. I stopped writing to him about going to the mall with my friends or about my dumb friend dramas and instead started pushing him for more details: I'd ask outright, *What do you need? What does your family need?* I also wrote, *I'm so glad you're back into school, but what about your siblings?*

In my early correspondence, I was timid about asking such forthright questions because I didn't want him to think I was stupid for not already knowing. Now I saw that it was my responsibility, as his friend—because his answers would help me make sure that he was going to be okay, no matter what.

PART 3

Generosity

Martin
—ɯ—

THE POSTMAN DIDN'T EVEN HAVE to call my name—I spotted the letter decorated as always with small hearts and stars, Caitlin's trademark.

This time she sent two twenty-dollar bills. I was blown away and still had no idea how she could afford it. But then I thought of the expensive T-shirts she had sent me, as well as the photos of her family's cars, plural. Even her dogs had beds and blankets. In my mind, she was very rich. And so I guessed that money was not the big deal to Caitlin and her family that it was to me and mine. Meanwhile, I did not know anyone who could loan me ten Zim dollars let alone forty American dollars.

The timing was almost spooky, as the retrenchment at my father's work continued. Most of his friends had been replaced. These men were also fathers of families who depended on them, which was why my dad continued waking up every morning and walking the hour to his job as he had done for so many years, even though he was sure he was next to be let go. I admired his resilience then, and still do today.

A lesser man may have been threatened by Caitlin's generosity. Here was a fourteen-year-old girl sending us more money than my father made in several months. My father only had love and respect for Caitlin. Her letters had always been precious to me. Now they were also crucial to my whole family. We were on a ship that was sinking, huddled at the tip before it went under. Caitlin's gift was a lifeboat.

My mother was afraid to keep this much money in our house. It made us a target in these difficult times. That same day, we set up a bank account at the post office. After so many years of relying on my father, my mother seemed happy to have some control. That July, my father's paycheck could not cover our rent for the first time. My mother used Caitlin's money to make up the difference. No one ever said what we all felt: What would we have done if it weren't for Caitlin?

I didn't dwell on that thought—I was too focused on catching up at school. I had nine classes: mathematics, accounts, biology, computer science, and physical science were easy. So were English and history. I continued to struggle with Shona and now English literature, but by the end of the semester, my grades were once again the best in the class. This made my father very proud. He suggested I go stay with his brother in Harare during our winter break that August. My uncle's daughter had married a man who worked at a bank in the capital. They arranged for me to work at the bank as a tea boy.

I had never been to Harare before, so I was extremely

excited. I took the overnight bus from Mutare and wore my Reebok shirt for the trip. I wanted to look cool, not like a country boy. My uncle met me at the Harare bus station dressed in pleated pants, a button-down shirt, and sturdy leather slip-on shoes. I was so impressed. We went to his apartment, which he shared with another family. He had two wives who alternated visits but mostly stayed in the rural areas. His first wife was only able to have one child, which was why he married again. He had another three children with his second wife, one of whom was married to the man I was going to work for.

My uncle pointed to a corner in the living room where I could sleep, and then gave me detailed instructions on how to get to the bank, to meet Alois, my cousin's husband. That was a great adventure. My uncle told me which bus to get on, where to get off, and then what building to enter. Thank goodness—I would have gotten lost otherwise. I'd never seen so many people, or cars, or such tall buildings in my life. Everything seemed faster and louder and brighter in Harare than in Mutare. My blood seemed to pump faster, too, trying to keep up.

Alois was even more put together than my uncle. He wore a suit and tie, like the managers at my father's work, but he was only in his mid-twenties. He greeted me with a firm handshake and a broad smile, and then introduced me to several of his colleagues before taking me to the tea station. My job, he explained, was to make cups of tea for every bank employee at ten AM, one PM, and four PM. If anyone requested a cup in between, I was to do that as well. I liked my new job. The people at the office were very friendly. After a week, I knew everyone's preferences—who liked it very sweet, who wanted more milk.

That first weekend, Alois and his wife, Sekai, invited me to go with them to their favorite cafe. Sekai was very pretty, and funny as well—her name in Shona means "to laugh," and when she did, people wanted to join her. She met Alois during her studies in Harare, and the two got married out of love for each other. I rarely heard of such a thing, but knew I wanted to be like them.

When we entered the cafe, many of the waiters greeted Alois and Sekai by name, which impressed me. I had never been to a restaurant before, so this experience was a mix of intimidating and exhilarating. Most of the patrons were white, and everyone was wearing very expensive-looking clothes. With my Reebok shirt, I fit in.

We ordered our drinks inside and then carried them to the outdoor tables. I ordered the same thing as Sekai, a very fancy coffee topped with whipped cream. It was so delicious that I had to fight an intense desire to gulp it down. Instead, I sipped very slowly. Sitting outside listening to music and surrounded by all these very sophisticated people made me think of Caitlin. I wondered if places like these existed at the American malls she wrote about.

That afternoon, I told Alois and Sekai about Caitlin.

"What a good friend," Alois said.

"Will you meet her one day?" Sekai asked.

"That is my dream," I answered.

"You can, Martin!" Alois said. "You are so clever. Keep your grades up and go on to your A-levels so you can go to university like we did. Then you can do whatever you want."

I drained the last swirl of coffee-flavored foam from my cup and looked around. Sitting at the cafe, no one would have guessed that I was carrying luggage at the Sakubva bus station only months earlier. I can do it, I thought. I can go to university, and I will meet Caitlin one day. The potential of both was thrilling.

I knew hard work would get me there, so I reported to work early every day. When the month was up, I was sad to leave. On my last day in Harare, I bought a special thank-you card for Caitlin that summed up everything I felt about her:

> *We've shared the kind of friendship*
> *that's grown deeper through the years.*
> *We've seen the ups, we've known the downs,*
> *we've shared the smiles and tears.*
> *And through it all, I've learned one thing—*
> *that there could never be*
> *a dearer friend in all the world*
> *than the one you are to me.*

That same afternoon, I also found a place to get my portrait taken. I wore the shirt Caitlin had sent me right before I left for Harare. It was red with blue letters. I wanted to have my picture taken in it as a way to say thank you.

Before I boarded the bus back to Mutare, I wrote a note to Caitlin on the front of the card.

To Caitlin:

Thanks be unto God for making the two of us great friends. Words are not enough for me to express how you and me care for the other though I am not rich.

Below the poem, I added:

Your love and soothing care has changed my life. Our friendship lasts and lasts like a mother's love.

                    Lots of love from
                    your caring friend,
                    Martin.

And then inside the card, I wrote, *You're the only one, Caitlin.* I drew a heart instead of an apostrophe. *All these gifts you have sent me are really great. I thank you very much. I wish I had the money to buy you the greatest gift you've ever received. I used to wear my father's clothes but your love has made me a real teenager in modern expensive clothes. Caitlin, you're the best. I love you!*

I also decided to finally ask her how she decorated her letters. The last one was so ornate that I brought it to school to show my friends. Patrick was certain it was a machine. *Do*

you make these by hand? Or is it a machine or special pen that
helps you?

With that, I signed off.

Since there was no time to find a post office before the bus departed, I packed her card with my things to travel back to Sakubva. I would send it to her from home.

The morning I returned, I sensed something was wrong. My mother barely greeted me, and though it was a Saturday, my father was gone. I asked where everyone was, and she said that Nation and Simba were at the market, working.

"Where is Baba?" I asked. I had been gone only four weeks, so I was not expecting a celebration. But I didn't anticipate such a gloomy reception, either.

My mother took time to find the right words.

"He lost his job last week, Martin," she finally said, shaking her head as if she still could not believe this was so.

I knew this day would come, and yet the news siphoned the oxygen from our already claustrophobic house.

"We used Caitlin's money again for August's rent," she continued, her eyes stuck to the floor. Then she looked up at me and I could see how painful it was for her to share the news. "We need it for September, too."

Now I understood why she was so upset. Without any income, how would we pay our rent in the months to come? We had seen so many neighbors kicked out of their homes for this reason. They'd go to the rural areas to live off the land, but that was not an option for my family. Most families used money from working in the city to build a house in the rural areas to retire to. My father never got to that level, so we had nothing to go back to. If we could not pay rent, we would be homeless.

All these thoughts collided in my head: Money was running out. Father had no job, and no prospects. And that meant there was no money for school. I was starting the last semester of my Form Three in two days.

"It will be okay, Mai," I lied. I had no idea how. I needed air, and room to think.

As I walked down the path to the main road, I brainstormed ways to stay in school—every single solution ended with Caitlin.

On Monday morning, I retrieved Caitlin's last letter and brought it to school with me along with the money I had saved from working in Harare as a down payment. Rather than be called out in class, I went straight to see the headmaster.

Mr. Samupindi spoke at assemblies and handed out awards, but otherwise rarely interacted with students. He was intimidating—a very large man with a gigantic silver Afro. He growled instead of talked, like a wolf. My heart was pounding when I knocked on his office door.

"Who is it?" his gruff voice boomed through the closed door.

"Martin Ganda, sir," I shouted through the door. "I have a request."

"Come in," he bellowed. I opened the door and saw him sitting at his desk, which was covered with piles of paperwork. I had to wave my hand in front of my eyes to clear a patch in the fog of cigarette smoke that filled the room.

Mr. Samupindi took a drag from the nub in between two fingers before stamping it out in one of the several overflowing ashtrays that doubled as paperweights. Ashes scattered as he tamped, and a serpent of condensed smoke escaped into the already thick air.

"What brings you here?" he asked.

"I'm sorry to bother you, sir," I said, approaching his desk. "My father lost his job."

Mr. Samupindi lit another cigarette.

"I don't have all my fees today," I explained, placing Z$52 on his desk. The cost had risen due to inflation and was now $800 per semester versus $550. This was not even 10 percent. "Here's my down payment—and I have an American friend who will cover the rest."

The headmaster didn't flinch, or smile, or react in any way. It was as if I were talking to a statue.

"I promise you, I will have the entire fee in a few weeks," I said, next handing him Caitlin's letter as proof.

"She sent me forty dollars in June, sir," I explained. "This won't be a problem."

The headmaster read through Caitlin's letter before agreeing to a month-long grace period: Things had gotten so bad that even the schools had to be lenient. They needed money.

Emboldened by this good news, I also asked if I could use the one computer that the school possessed to write Caitlin the request that day. This was a very serious request I was about to make. I wanted to type it to reflect that. He agreed.

After my last class, I went back to the main office and told the secretary that Mr. Samupindi had given me permission to use the computer. She was already expecting me.

As I sat down in front of this modern-looking machine, I realized the enormity of what I was about to do: Asking my best friend to pay for my schooling seemed preposterous. With no other options, I started typing slowly, with my two pointer fingers:

8 September 1999

Dear CAITLIN

Hi! I was very happy to receive a letter from you. Thanks very much. How is the "THE KEYSTONE STATE"? I am okay down here in Africa.

We were on a school holiday from AUGUST 5 to SEPTEMBER 6. I enjoyed it a lot. I went to our capital city HARARE, where I was working as a tea boy at a certain company. FUNNY!!!

In Zimbabwe right now we are in SUMMER and it is very hot. Sometimes we go swimming in rivers since we only have one public pool, which is very expensive to use. Caitlin, I love you very much. You have really changed my life through giving me clothes and other nice, expensive gifts. Now I stand as a counted person in my community. My parents have never supported me like that. Thanks very much.

I wrote about Zimbabwean music and asked if she had ever heard of Thomas Mapfumo. Then I added:

I have enclosed my new photo and a greetings friendship card which I bought especially for you when I was working as a tea boy in Harare. I HAVE TYPED THIS LETTER AT SCHOOL ON A COMPUTER.

Just after I finished that line, the secretary tapped me on the shoulder to say she had to lock up the office. I was running out of time and quickly finished with:

Thanks for your love. Say hi to Richie, Romeo, your kind mom and dad.

> *Your Loving Pal,*
> *Martin Ganda*

I retrieved my printed letter and then went outside to consider how best to ask for such a big favor. I couldn't get the machine to say what I needed to, which was: "I need help. Please send money so I can stay in school!" It was a tremendous request, but I couldn't bear going back to the market. I decided to be entirely honest with her about my situation.

I continued writing on the back of the typed note:

Sorry for the late replying. Guess what? I used about three-quarters

*of my pay as a tea boy to buy you
the friendship card!! I adore you!*

*I am back at school now from
the holiday. I have bad news that my
dad is no longer working, so I am doing
all that I can to get money for school
fees, food, for clothes I am okay for
those shirts you gave me. If you could
please help me with school fees if
possible ...*

Mid-sentence it dawned on me. Sure, she had money, but it was her parents who each had a car and bought the castle that Caitlin lived in. Maybe they could help? *... or your kind and loving mom and dad could please help me if possible please,* I wrote to finish the sentence and hopefully take the pressure off my dear friend.

*It costs about Z$800 per term
(4 months), or about US$20. If it is
not possible, don't worry. I will just
do after school jobs to get the money
but it's very tiring. I clean rich people's
cars, carry luggage for people, and get a
few coins which I keep until they reach
Z$800.*

I hope your lovely parents may help
me if it's possible for them. Don't worry
too much if it's not possible. But please
show them my photo! I love your
family! Also please show my photo to
Richie.

After I finished the letter to Caitlin, I decided to be even
bolder, and write directly to her parents. I told them I had one
week to find the fees, figuring that by the time my letter made
it to America, and they responded, it would be even less time
than that. I decided to tell them my situation, and then pray
that they would understand and help me.

Caitlin

━━━━∞∞∞━━━━

THAT SUMMER, I'D GROWN SIX inches. It was like the scene from *Alice in Wonderland* where she drinks the tea and then grows so quickly, she busts out of the house. I was five foot three in June, and five foot nine by August, which meant none of the clothes I wore in the beginning of the summer fit by the end. It also meant I needed an entire new wardrobe for the start of ninth grade. I was thrilled.

I was also happy that I finally got boobs! The summer before, we spent many weekends at my grandparents' lake house in the Poconos. My aunt Kim was usually there—she's married to my mom's younger brother, Jim. Since we lived in our bathing suits on the weekend, I noticed that my aunt Kim's boobs were big but not jiggly. I wanted mine to be like hers, and asked her directly one day, "How did you get those?" Her response was, "Go row the boat for a few hours every day." I followed her instructions religiously—rowing every day until my arms ached. And then the following summer, my boobs popped out! I went from a training bra to a D cup, but could still wear tube tops without a bra.

I loved it—people assumed I was much older than fourteen. I noticed this when I started ninth grade. Guys had always been nice to me, but suddenly, they were *really* nice to me. I loved the attention, but that feeling was soon overcome by pain.

My back started bothering me in eighth grade but really began to hurt earlier that summer. Any time I bent over—to put on my shoes or pick up my bunny—it felt like I was being stabbed at the base of my spine. This made emptying the dishwasher excruciating. It got so bad that by September, I would have to lie down on the floor and breathe through the pain after I was done putting away the glasses and cutlery. My mom thought I was just trying to get out of housework, but then I stopped playing field hockey because bending over the stick became impossible. Red-hot pain radiated down both legs.

My mom finally took me to a doctor, who thought it was scoliosis. Those tests came back negative, thankfully, but the pain never subsided. Next, I was sent for an MRI. That was how we discovered that the corners of my growth plates had broken off. I grew so quickly that my bones broke. Unfortunately, there wasn't much to do about it. I went to physical therapy twice a week for a few months, and did some basic stretching and core exercises, which was a total drag. The only upside was that my mom stopped making me empty the dishwasher and dust the baseboards.

Around the same time that I got the MRI results, I received a particularly thick envelope from Martin. It had been a few months since his last letter, so I was thrilled to see he had sent not one, but three letters. Then I started to read. As I digested what he was saying, I had a flashback to receiving his note on the ice-cream wrapper and started to feel panicky. I was only fourteen, but I understood that if his dad had lost his job and Martin was back working at the market, that meant the money I'd been sending was supporting his entire family—not just school fees, but everything. How could my babysitting money support everyone? Clearly it could not. Meanwhile, my parents still had no idea that I was sending money in the mail to Africa. They knew about the T-shirts and small gifts, but not the money.

In addition to the letter Martin sent me, he enclosed another one addressed to my parents: *Caitlin please, please give this to your parents,* he wrote. *You may read it if you want but please give it to them and tell them it's from me, Martin.*

I immediately opened it.

> Hallo Mr. and Mrs. Stoicsitz.
>
> I know this letter comes as a surprise to you. I am Martin Ganda, the friend of Caitlin, your daughter. Caitlin is my best friend and she has helped me socially and economically and also educationally. I think Caitlin might have

told you that I come from a poor family and this has worsened because my dad, who used to support the family, is no longer working. This has affected me badly. It meant that I was no longer able to get someone to pay for my fees at school. I have tried all means to get money for school fees by doing the following every day after school:

I cleaned cars of people and got a few coins which I saved.

I carried people's luggage to bus stations and got a few coins.

By now I have almost, only Z$48.

I have talked to the principal at our school and he has accepted me to learn for the first week of school only and then I can carry on when I have my fees paid. Please, if possible, I am begging for your help. If it is not possible, do not worry yourselves. But as the parents of my best friend I hope that you might help me. I have written my grades for the past term to Caitlin if you may want to see them.

*The school fees is Z$800 per term
and this is about US$20. I hope you
may help.
    Waiting for a favorable reply.
                Yours faithfully,
                Martin
                African friend of Caitlin*

Reading that letter brought tears to my eyes. He was so proud. He had never asked *me* for help. Asking my parents for help was probably one of the hardest things for him to have to do. He did not want to burden me. He knew that I would get sick worrying about him in such need. But there it was, written on paper, a huge SOS. My parents knew I had a pen pal in Zimbabwe, but they did not know how close we had become. That evening, I decided to tell them everything. It was the only way I could truly help Martin.

It was dinnertime when I came downstairs, steeling myself for the conversation. My dad was already sitting in his spot as my mom placed meat loaf, mashed potatoes, peas, and salad on the table. She asked me to put the dressing out.

I grabbed a Lite Ranch, my dad's favorite, and Thousand Island, mine, and placed both on the lazy Susan at the center of the table. As my mom took her seat, I was still trying to figure out the best way to start this conversation.

"How much money is in my college savings?" I finally blurted out.

140

My dad had already started scooping mashed potatoes onto his plate.

"Enough for you not to have to worry," he said. And then added, "Can you pass the meat loaf?"

I could not think about meat loaf or ranch versus Thousand Island dressing. The amount of food on our table made me queasy.

"I need to know how much," I continued.

"Why?" my mom asked.

"Because I want to send it to Martin," I said. "All of it."

"Your pen pal?" my dad said with a laugh.

"That's exactly who I mean," I replied, furious that he was not taking me seriously.

My mom saw I meant business, and said, "Caitlin, honey, you can't just send all your money to Zimbabwe."

"That money is for you to go to college, sweetheart," my dad added, shifting his tone. "We're saving that for *your* future."

My anger was building, but I kept it at bay to make my case.

"I can go to any college I want," I said. "If I start working really hard, I could even get a scholarship. Martin doesn't have those options." I told them that his dad had lost his job, and that I had been sending my babysitting money, but that it was not enough.

"You've been sending him money?" my mom asked.

"I try to send him ten or twenty dollars in every letter," I said. "I put forty dollars in the last one."

My mother shot an alarmed look at my father, who kept his eyes on me.

"And this is why you have been babysitting instead of going out with your friends on weekend nights?" Mom interjected.

"Mom, Dad, you don't seem to get it," I responded, exasperated. "Martin is my best friend and he is in serious trouble. I need your help. I cannot do it by myself anymore."

Tears were streaming down my face now—this was not going as I had expected.

"I don't know what else to do," I said.

My dad shook his head back and forth. My mom looked down at her plate of untouched food. Everyone stayed quiet.

"Can we see the letters?" my mom finally asked.

"Actually, he sent one to you," I said, and ran to get it.

I placed his plea on the table in front of my dad. My mom was already up from her seat, reading intently over his shoulder.

"He has never done this sort of thing before," I explained. "I know it must be serious."

I watched as my parents read. Everything was dead quiet, except the faint whirring sound of Romey snoring on the couch in the den.

"Sweetheart," my dad said tentatively. "What if it is a scam?"

"Martin would never, ever do anything like that." My voice was faster and louder than usual.

"Honey, your father is just trying to protect you," my mom said.

"I don't need protection!" I shouted. "My friend needs help."

My parents were startled. In my fourteen years, I had never been this adamant about anything.

"Okay! Okay," my dad said. "Let your mom and me discuss what we can do to help."

My mom nodded her head. "We know how important he is to you, Caitlin," she said. "And we're proud of you for being such a good friend."

I threw my arms around both of them. "Thank you! Thank you! You won't regret this."

The next morning, at breakfast, I asked what they had decided. My mom said she was going to do some research, and promised we'd discuss it at dinner.

I left for school feeling a huge sense of relief. My mom and dad knew how to get things done. They would figure it out.

That night, as soon as I heard my dad pull into the driveway I ran outside to greet him.

"Any news?" I asked, following him into the house.

"Do you still really want to do this, Caitlin?" he asked.

"Um, *yeah*, Dad," I said. "And we need to do something now! We can't wait! He only has one week before he is kicked out again."

My dad nodded at my mom, who was listening intently.

"I've already made a few calls," she said. "We're trying to find out the best way to support him."

"Trying?" I said.

"Caitlin, we'll do our best to help him," she replied.

That night, I wrote Martin a letter that said, *I gave my parents your letter. And they promised to help.*

I slipped another twenty dollars into the envelope and wrote that I hoped it would cover costs until my parents could figure things out.

And then every day for the next week, I came home from school and asked, "Any news?"

My mom would share her progress with me: She started by calling the Zimbabwean embassy in Washington, who suggested calling the American embassy in Harare. The receptionist there gave her the name of a woman who might be able to help. My mom left a message for her, but had still not heard back. Impatient, a trait we both share, my mom then called Solange, her friend who lived in Quebec and worked for the Canadian government, to see if she had any ideas. Solange promised to talk to a few friends she had who worked at various embassies.

In the meantime, Mom had also spent hours online, looking up various organizations that might help her understand how much Martin's school fees were—Martin said twenty dollars would cover it, but she wanted to make sure that was actually enough. Even trickier, she wanted to figure the best way to transfer funds.

"Why can't we just send him cash like I was doing?" I asked at an after-school brainstorming session.

"Solange was amazed that your money got to him," my mom said.

"Why?" I asked.

"Mail in impoverished countries is often opened by postal workers," my mom explained. "Are you sure he is getting all of it?"

I didn't know—he sometimes thanked me specifically for money. But other times, he would not mention it, if he wrote back at all. I wondered, for the first time, if he was receiving all my letters. The thought that people would steal things intended for Martin made me a little more cynical about the world. But it also gave me an idea.

"What if I disguise the money?" I asked.

"What, like wearing a mustache and fake glasses?" my mom said, laughing.

"Wait right here," I said. Upstairs in my room, I found a piece of orange cardboard I bought for a school history project and cut a four-by-six-inch rectangle. Then I grabbed a three-by-five-inch photograph of me and Romey that my mom had taken earlier that summer. I took twenty dollars from my babysitting stash, grabbed my glue stick, and ran back downstairs.

"If I hide the money behind the photo, and then affix it to the cardboard, no one will ever know it's there!" I explained proudly.

"Including Martin?" my mom asked, always the devil's advocate.

"I'll write clues in my letter, so he knows to look," I explained.

"Brilliant!" my mother said.

"But wait," she said, grabbing twenty dollars from her wallet. "Save your money. This one is on me."

I folded both bills into the origami hearts we taught the kids how to do at summer camp.

"Thanks, Mom," I said, placing one on top of the other in the center of the orange mat. "But Martin needs as much as we can send him."

I dotted the back corners of the photo with glue before affixing it on top of the cardboard.

"You're a genius," my mom said.

"It runs in the family," I responded.

My mom continued to research safer ways to send money. Her bank could do it, but the Zimbabwean banks charged a 50 percent commission. Mom kept all her notes from every bank teller and embassy representative and African expert she talked to on a yellow legal pad. By the second week, she was on page three.

Around this same time, I was over at Heather's house a lot. Since she lived two houses away, I often popped over after school. She was my only friend who was interested in Martin's well-being. I was telling her and her mom about the great lengths my mom was going to in order to help Martin stay in school when Heather's mom said, "Honey, how do you know he is not lying?"

She wasn't the first to ask this—my mom had heard it from her friends, and I heard it from the family I babysat for, as well as most any adult who learned what we were trying to do. Heather's mom was like my mom. She saw goodness in people first. I hated that anyone would think Martin was a grifter—especially people with big hearts. Martin was the most honest and honorable person I'd ever known. Whenever I said that in his defense, people shook their heads, as if to say "Poor naïve Caitlin." I couldn't stomach that. Instead, I said the same thing to Heather's mom that I overheard my mom say to friends and neighbor: "Well, if he is, shame on him. And if he's not, shame on us for thinking that way."

I understood everyone's concern—Nigerian phishing scams were making newspaper headlines. Criminals pretending to be young Nigerian men or women in trouble would send fake e-mails that said *I've been robbed and need money to get to safety.* Well-meaning people sent money to a mysterious bank account and suddenly their own accounts were drained. My parents were well aware of this—and I think that is why my mom was going to such great lengths to help Martin in the right way. People might also argue that I was an easy mark: I wasn't always the most serious person. But I would just dismiss the naysayers. My attitude was, You don't understand and I don't need to explain myself. That's always how I felt. Thankfully, my parents stood by me 100 percent.

Still, figuring out how to help Martin was taking much longer than I expected. I had promised him we'd sort everything out. What if that was impossible?

November was difficult. We still had no concrete answers from experts and even worse, we had not heard from Martin since his last letter in September. What if he had not received the money I had sent him? What if he was kicked out of school and was back to pouring tea? I could not bear these thoughts. I needed to do something else to help.

Martin had mentioned once that the shirts I sent him had "greatly increased" his wardrobe. I now understood what he was actually saying. Those shirts quadrupled his T-shirt collection, which went from one to four. Meanwhile, I had an entire T-shirt drawer and more clothes than could fit in my closet. That gave me an idea.

"Mom, want to go shopping?" I said once I found her downstairs.

"What do you need, hon?" she asked.

"Actually, not for me," I explained. "For Martin—actually, for his entire family."

She looked at me quizzically.

"It's almost Christmas, and I thought, we've sent him small gifts. Wouldn't it be nice to send his parents and siblings clothing as well?"

"Terrific idea!" she said. "Let's go!"

This moment made me realize how lucky I was. My father worked to pay all the household bills, but my mom worked so she could do things like this. She was as excited as I was.

We drove to Ross, where I had bought Martin the Reebok shirt. We didn't discuss a budget—only that we'd get something for everyone.

Walking through the fluorescent-lit aisles lined with rack after rack of T-shirts, shorts, dresses, and more, I realized I had no idea what size anyone was. I knew Martin was the second eldest of five, but he rarely wrote about his siblings. The most recent photo he sent me was taken from the shoulders up, so I had no idea how big or small he might be. Just then, a slender salesman, shorter than me, approached and asked if we needed help.

"What size are you?" I asked.

He looked at me in a funny way.

"I want to buy clothes for a Zimbabwean friend," I explained. "And my guess is, he is your size."

"Excuse me?" he replied.

"Actually, we're shopping for an entire family in Africa," my mother interjected. "And yes, we'd love your help."

If Martin and Nation were the eldest boys, the other three siblings were younger than me. We went to the kids' section first and selected three pairs of shorts in different sizes. Then we found a skirt with an elastic waist for Martin's mom, since we had no idea if she was big or small. That gave us leeway. All the cargo shorts had drawstring waists for the same reason—we had no idea what size anyone was. We got T-shirts in small, medium, and large for the men in the family. A small mountain was growing in our cart, and we hadn't even hit the shoe section. Since I had to guesstimate, we selected two pairs of sneakers: one for Martin, and the other for whoever in his family might also need a new pair of shoes.

"Let's get socks as well," my mom suggested. "This way he can wear two pairs if the shoes are too big and grow into them later."

We hit the toiletry section next, which was having a super sale: I picked out several bottles of shampoos, an aftershave, and cologne. Tommy Hilfiger and Polo Ralph Lauren were

149

especially popular among the boys at school. I thought Martin might like them, too.

The total was $208, a lot of money, but my mom and I were amazed at how much it bought. We left the store with a shopping bag in each hand, four total. From there, we drove to Staples to get school supplies. I wanted to buy Martin pens and pencils, as well as notebooks and a school bag. There, I spotted Crayola Stampers, the markers I used to decorate Martin's letters. He had recently asked me about them, so I grabbed a pack.

Our last stop was the nearby Shop 'n Save grocery store to get a box big enough to pack everything in. There, I had an idea.

"What if we buy candy to use instead of packing peanuts?" I said.

I loved candy then—and still do. My favorites were Airheads, which tasted like taffy, and Runts, these small hard candies that come in different fruit flavors. I thought it would be cool to send Martin all kinds of American candy that might be difficult to get in Zimbabwe. I still could not believe that my German cousin had never heard of Skittles or Starburst and wanted Martin to try all my favorites.

We filled seven plastic bags meant for produce with Hershey's Kisses, Starbursts, jawbreakers, Bazooka bubble gum, Tootsie Rolls, butterscotch, and the hard candies with the soft centers that look and taste like strawberries.

Back home, we were packing everything into the big box when I had yet another idea: I had three Walkmans. Martin loved music and had recently written about his favorite Zimbabwean musician, Thomas Mapfumo. I went to get one of my Walkmans to include in the package, and then grabbed a Ricky Martin cassette as well, so he would have something to listen to.

After the packing was done, I wrote a letter that explained the contents of the box. I said that I hoped I got his shoe size right –and to send me the right one if not. And then I included a candy dictionary, identifying each kind in detail. Last, and most importantly, I didn't know if he had a telephone himself but figured he could find one. So I asked if he would please let me know when he received the package—I just wanted to make sure it got there okay. I also needed to know that he was okay.

I placed the letter on top of all the clothing and toiletries and school supplies and then emptied all seven bags of candy on top, watching with delight as the rainbow assortment scattered and filled all the nooks and crannies of the package, like three-dimensional confetti.

Mom held the box flaps down as I taped up the box. That night, she called Solange to ask her advice about the best way to send something so big to Zimbabwe. Solange explained that the political situation in Zimbabwe was so volatile it made sending anything there of value a real crap shoot. There was no way to ensure it would get to Martin once it hit the Zimbabwean postal service. There were reports, Solange said, of packages being opened and items sold on the black market. She thought the safest way to send the package was to go through the American or Canadian embassy, and promised she would look into it for us.

In the meantime, I wrote Martin another letter to say that a special package was on its way to him, and that it might take a while to get there. Once again, I included twenty dollars wrapped in aluminum foil, as Solange said that helped hide the fact I was sending cash. Once again, I ended with, *Please write me back and let me know you have received it. Your friend forever, Caitlin.*

November 1999

Martin
—◊◊◊—

I PROMISED MR. SAMUPINDI I would have the money quickly,
but knew it took two weeks for mail to get to the US and
another two weeks to return to Zimbabwe. I still had nothing
by October. Mr. Samupindi was disappointed, but gave me
another week's reprieve. And then, like magic, a letter arrived.

This one, however, had been ripped and taped back
up in a crude way. Someone had written in capital letters
INSPECTED FOR CONTRABAND across Caitlin's beautiful penmanship. It felt like a violation.

I immediately opened the letter and was so relieved to hear
that her parents were willing to help. At the last line, she
wrote, *I hope this twenty dollars will keep you in school until we
find the best way to pay for it securely.*

I looked back in the envelope. Nothing. The money was
gone.

All my hopeful feelings disappeared, water down a drain.
As upset as I was, I also knew that the person who stole the

money must have needed it as much as I did. Things in Zimbabwe were out of control: more companies closing, more people moving back to the rural areas, more food shortages, and more riots. It was also around this time when the government instigated its land reform act. People were starving—and since the government had no bread or mealie meal to give them, they offered land. A mandate was put forth that white farmers who had lived in Zimbabwe for many generations had to give their farmland back to native black Africans. There were stories of men showing up with machetes to claim what they felt was rightfully theirs. People were being killed in the process. It was chaos. Then there were other stories of Zimbabwe aiding a warlord in the Congo that led to more sanctions against our country. The international community was giving up on Zimbabwe—I hoped Caitlin would not give up on me.

When I received another letter in November, I knew she had not. By then, I was back working in the market, as Mr. Samupindi said to keep me in school would not be fair to the dozens of other kids he had expelled for nonpayment. I understood.

This letter was shorter than usual. She enclosed a photo of her and Romey, and wrote in her note, *Behind every great dog is a way to stay in school!* I was confused and had to read that line five or six times before its meaning dawned on me. I peeled the photo off the card, and saw two hearts overlapped.

The next day, I went directly to Mr. Samupindi's office and laid my tuition on his desk.

"Your American friend came through," Mr. Samupindi said, pleased.

"I knew she would, sir," I said. "Now may I return to class?"

"What are you waiting for? Go!" he bellowed. I could hear him laughing as I ran down the hallway to my first-period class.

December 1999

Caitlin

THANKSGIVING IS USUALLY MY FAVORITE holiday, but the one that year was miserable. I appreciated all the work my mom was doing, but we still had not heard from Martin, or figured out how to send the funds securely. I felt like a hamster running in place on a spinning wheel. Solange finally got back to us with advice about sending the care package—the political situation in Zimbabwe was so dicey that the embassies were not willing to act as our go-between. She suggested sending it through the regular mail, and putting "used school supplies" on the customs forms so no one would bother opening it. That was disappointing. We had wasted so much time.

I didn't share any more news or worries with my friends, not even Heather. No one seemed to understand. But that didn't stop everyone coming to me with their problems. It was one after another that fall—Lauren was crushed that her boyfriend broke up with her, Lesley was upset that her parents were so strict, Jen was devastated that Tim liked

Christa and not her, and Brittany was having stomach ulcers because she was failing algebra. When Laura, who had been complaining about how Lauren was ignoring her, got mad at me for not sitting with her at the cafeteria one day, I just lost it. She cornered me that afternoon right before I got on the bus, fighting back tears, wondering how I could be so cruel. "Especially since you know what I am dealing with!"

I said, "I didn't even see you!" which was better than how I really felt. I wanted to scream, "Actually, I would have avoided you if I had noticed because I cannot deal with you or any of your totally made-up problems anymore!"

I was so boiling mad when I got home that afternoon that I threw my book bag on the floor and flopped onto the couch. I felt like a pressure cooker that was about to explode—waiting to hear how we could help Martin with his very real problems, while getting barraged daily by all my friends' petty dramas, was more than I could handle.

"What's wrong?" my mom said when she saw me splayed out in the den.

I told her about Lesley—and Brittany and Laura and Lauren. I was detailing all of their dumb dramas when the tears came in torrents. "Who cares about stupid boys? Or dumb algebra?"

"Caitlin," she said, rubbing my back as I vented. "You're a really good listener. And sometimes people just need to dump."

"All these people are dumping on me and the only person I care about has basically disappeared," I wailed. "I can't take it!"

A new wave of tears came. What if something terrible happened to Martin? He could be badly hurt or in danger, and how would I ever know?

"We're doing everything we can to make sure he's fine," she said. "These other folks and their issues—put it this way: Unless you think someone is going to harm herself or someone else, then they really are just dumping on you. And you need to dump them as friends."

As soon as she said that, I saw how I was making everybody else's problems my own. From that moment on, I changed my attitude. People could still tell me stuff, but I wouldn't take it on. Instead, I'd say, "That's too bad." Or, "I'm sorry you feel that way." The only person I was willing to expend any emotional energy on was Martin.

And then one day a friend of Solange's who worked for the Canadian embassy in South Africa sent my mother helpful news, a first.

November 22, 1999
Anne,

Thanks for the interesting message. Yes, the schools charge, even though they are government run. Usually charges are around Z$1400 per year (three terms) but they will vary from school to school. As to sending money, that is not so easy. Sending cash in that quantity (a lot in Zimbabwe) is very risky. You would have to send US dollars and he would change it there. Alternatively, does

the school have a bank account you could wire
the money into? That way you would be absolutely
sure that the money goes to the intended place.
Ask Martin for his school's address and contact
them directly. They will be happy to assist you
with paying the fees.

If you need further details, please do not
hesitate in contacting me!

Regards, Chris

This should have been good news, but we still had no word from Martin. Christmas was coming and I had no idea if he had received any of the money I was sending or the large package I hoped would be there in time for the holiday. The waiting was taking a toll on me. All I could do was write him again. This time, I snuck five dollars in our family Christmas card and hoped it would make it to him.

I woke up Christmas morning to carols playing on the radio and the scent of bacon and eggs wafting through the house. On my way downstairs, I peeked into the living room, where our tree looked propped up by the piles of presents that had magically appeared overnight. It would take half a day to open them all. That year, I got a 24-karat-gold necklace that said *Caitlin* in script and a Tommy Hilfiger denim jacket I had been coveting. Richie got a computer, and he almost fell off the couch.

"You'll need it for college," Mom said.

We went to my grandparents' house for dinner and feasted

on ham, turkey, and more side dishes than could fit on their table.

"Eat up," my dad teased.

I was scheduled to have my wisdom teeth removed on December 27, which meant I would be drinking a liquid diet for a few days afterward. I was dreading the surgery, but my orthodontist said if I did not do it now, then the last two years of braces would be a waste.

I was still recovering in bed when I wrote Martin yet again. Even if my letters were getting intercepted, my strategy was to keep trying. One had to get through.

12/30/99
Dear Martin:
 A belated Merry Christmas and my wishes to you for a happy New Year! My holiday break has been both fun and not-so-much fun. Let me explain.

I told him about our Christmas, and how my parents took me the mall to go shopping the next day. I wrote, *I picked out things I wanted. I know, I am very, very fortunate.* I felt compelled to include that, as, thanks to him, I realized how true it was.

Then I told him about my wisdom teeth, summing up the procedure with, *What a mess!* The anesthesia made me nauseated, and my mouth throbbed for days. I knew better to complain to him, though.

I really wanted to know if he had received the care package. And I needed to let him know that my mom learned that sending tuition directly to his school was the most secure way to support him. I added:

> My parents would like:
> 1. the name of your headmaster or principal
> 2. the complete mailing address of your school
> So there you have it! My family and I would really like to help you continue your education and also help your family since your father is currently unemployed. So please respond as soon as possible so we can get the tuition money to your school.
>
> My best wishes to you and your family for a healthy and happy New Year. And, if you did get that large box I sent, I hope you and your family enjoyed the stuff.
>
> Please write soon!
>
> Your friend, Caitlin

I showed my mom the letter before we sent it off, to make sure I got all the money instructions right. I did, but she wanted to add something: On the bottom right-hand corner, she wrote, *Martin, here is another twenty dollars to pay your tuition until we hear from you. Anne, Cait's mom.*

Martin
—ᜋᜒ—

THANKS TO CAITLIN, WE ATE chicken for Christmas that year, a miracle considering what our friends and neighbors were experiencing. In Zimbabwe, if you have food, you share it, so our neighbors ate chicken with us. Once again, we said it was a gift from the uncle I had visited in Harare. Everyone knew I had spent the past August there. It was an easy ruse. Now that Caitlin was concealing cash in her letters, we had to be extra careful.

In every letter, Caitlin asked me to respond. I hesitated. Things were so difficult, and as much as I appreciated her family's efforts to get me back in school, I was starting to lose hope. It also dawned on me that I had never been 100 percent honest with Caitlin about my life. I kept so many things hidden from her because I was ashamed. I didn't want our relationship to be in any way impacted by my family's poverty. With every new card or photo or dollar bill she sent, I saw that she truly loved me for who I was, not for where I came from.

I decided to write her a letter that told the truth about my life. The whole truth.

January 13, 2000
Dear Caitlin,
    Hello! I am very glad about the way your loving family and you are helping our poor family. Words cannot express how deep your love is for me and my family's life. Caitlin, your mom, dad, and Richie, you are really larger than life as Backstreet said. May the Lord bless your unconditional love. If I had money I would buy something expensive for you. When I sit and think about what you have done, I start to cry because no one has ever helped me like that. My poor parents are really happy of you.

I told about our life in Chisamba Singles in full detail:

    Because of poverty and too many poor people, the one-room houses are shared by two families....There is no constant supply of electricity and therefore we use wood as a source of fuel to cook and sometimes homemade paraffin

lamps. The life we live here is tough but
it has been reduced because of your love
and help.

I reiterated that without her, we would be homeless: *If we don't pay rent on time, we are chased out and another family enters.* There was so much else to say—including thanking her for the Christmas money. I also wanted to respond to her concerns about sending money:

I too was worried about people
stealing the money you sent here but
I have been inquiring about how to get
money safely and was told that THE
WESTERN MONEY TRANSFER would
help by making the money travel safely
and quickly. How about that?

Caitlin and her mom were so focused on my schooling fees, which were critical. But with so much time passing, I also had another concern: the registration for O-level exams was fast approaching, so I decided to be bold once again.

This is my last year at school, as
I am doing the ordinary level (SCE). If
I pass, I will proceed to advanced level
education. I must pay for these tests,

which cost roughly $585. If you could help me please. The headmaster of our school is Mr. George Samupindi. I am very sorry for troubling or annoying you with "large" figures. The deadline for the payments has not been announced yet but I think it is mid-February.

You can contact our headmaster, Mr. George Samupindi, at the same mailing address where you sent the very first letter:

Sakubva High School
PO Box 3059
Mutare
Zimbabwe

I am very sorry for making the letter so long! I hope your sore mouth has healed and you are back at school.

I was also curious what Caitlin's plans were after high school. We had not talked much about that, and I was interested if she felt the same way I did about university. *What are your plans for college—what do you hope to do there?* I asked.

There was no room left on the page, so I signed off: *See you my "sister" Caitlin. Your "brother" Martin.*

January 2000

Caitlin

⸺⊗⊗⊗⸺

I WAS BACK IN SCHOOL when I finally heard from Martin in late January. All the stress and worry that had built up inside me dissipated. I could breathe again.

I gave my mom the letter, with Martin's headmaster's name and address.

"Terrific," Mom said. "I'll start making calls tonight."

We both knew that Zimbabwe was seven hours ahead of Pennsylvania, which meant three AM our time was ten AM theirs.

I had a hard time falling asleep knowing we were getting closer to being able to help Martin. I finally drifted off and then awoke to a voice downstairs.

"Sa-KUB-va."

My mom was speaking loudly into the phone, pronouncing Martin's hometown as if it were several words. I looked at my clock: It was 4:11 AM. I fell back asleep.

Two hours later, I woke to a voice again.

I jumped out of bed and ran downstairs.

"Okay, thank you!" she shouted into the phone before hanging up.

"This has not been easy, Caitlin," she said with a sad smile. There was a notepad on the kitchen counter with a string of long numbers on it, each starting with *011-263* and then several combinations of numbers, each scratched out.

"I started with the American embassy in Harare, and they suggested I try calling the British council," she said. "This was at three AM. I wanted a head start. A lovely lady with a British accent said she would see if she could help me, and gave me the number to someone in Mutare who might know this school."

My head was spinning.

"Who were you just talking to?" I asked.

"I am not even sure!" my mother said. "The connection was so bad, I could barely hear a word."

My heart sank a bit. "What next?" I asked.

"Caitlin, don't you worry," Mom said. "I'm going to find that school."

I saw how hard she was working to make this happen. But I began to worry. What if she couldn't?

The following day, I could barely concentrate in my classes. I kept thinking about my mom, and Martin, and wondering if she got through. I also worried that the money we'd been sending had been intercepted. I couldn't stand the thought of him back at that market.

That afternoon at lunch, Lauren asked, "Caitlin, what's up with you lately?"

"What do you mean?" I asked, confused.

"You seem distracted," she continued. "Honestly, you're so not fun to hang out with. And I'm not the only person who is saying that."

I realized this was a test: I could either scream—"Funny you should mention it, because my *true* best friend may be homeless and starving in Africa for all I know, so I'm sorry if I seem a little distracted! Oh, yeah, and my growth plates snapped off in September, which felt like someone taking a knife and putting it in red-hot coals before plunging it into my back, and then my wisdom teeth were yanked from my jaw last month, but again, I am so, so sorry that I'm not all that fun!" Instead, I took a deep breath and said, "I'm sorry you feel that way. I just have a lot going on."

Just then, the bell rang for class. I'd never been happier to hear that shrill clang.

"I'd better run," I said. "Thanks for being so honest with me, Lauren."

I left her standing there dumbfounded. She wanted to pick a fight, but I had more important things to focus on.

That afternoon, I ran off the bus and found my mom still on the phone. I wondered if she had ever left that spot.

She saw me and frowned. After she hung up, she put her hands in the air.

"This is harder than I ever imagined!" she said. "People don't have phones in Zimbabwe like we do in the States. I'll keep trying, but let's write Mr. Samupindi to be safe."

We drafted the letter together.

January 24, 2000

Dear Mr. Samupindi:

We are writing on behalf of our daughter's pen pal, Martin Ganda. It is our understanding that Martin's father is no longer employed. This unfortunate situation is making it extremely difficult for Martin to continue his education. We would like to remedy that situation, and sponsor Martin's educational process.

The difficulty we are facing is how to quickly and safely transfer US funds to Martin. Currently we are exploring options. Martin corresponds that the Western Money Transfer (equivalent to our Western Union) will work. Also a personal check against our account will work. But US banking officials claim that Martin will not receive the full benefit of our written check amounts, as the bank removes some fees, thus reducing the amount our dear friend will receive.

Please advise us as to the cost of keeping Martin in school. This will provide us with an accurate amount so we will not be "guessing" how much is needed. We should like to keep Martin out of the process and only inform him that his tuition is paid and up to date. This is in lieu of sending funds to him. It will also keep Martin

safe from anyone who suddenly realizes that this
young man is receiving US funds and an easy
target for thieves.

In this letter we are enclosing a $20 check paid
with US funds, which should provide ample money
for Martin to continue his education without
interruption. But, from this $20, will you please
purchase enough postage to reply to the above
address?

Also, since Martin is interested in transferring
to the Advanced Level education, we understand
he will be writing a public examination. He would
like to write nine subjects. Please give us the cost
of this as quickly as possible so we do not miss the
deadline for test taking.

Thank you in advance for your assistance in
this important matter. Any suggestions, ideas,
or insights on how best to handle this matter
efficiently will be appreciated.

> *Sincerely,*
> *Anne Neville Stoicsitz*

"Perfect!" I said.

"I'll send Martin a copy so he knows we are going to take care of this. Then he can concentrate on school," she said.

She then took out another piece of paper to write a note to Martin.

January 24, 2000

Dear Martin:

Thank you for sending Caitlin the lovely letters.
She is sharing them with us, as she knows we are
able to help you more than she is. Her gift to you
is friendship!

Enclosed is a copy of a letter we have sent
to your headmaster. Hopefully the mail will
move quickly and he will be able to respond!
Rest assured we did enclose a check for $20
to help continue your education. He will tell
us what we need to do so funds are put directly
into your tuition fund. We are anxious for
a reply.

Mom left space at the bottom of her letter to Martin so I could add my own note: *Martin, I hope we have helped you with all your needs.*

I drew a smiley face. And then I remembered I wanted to share more good news! *My family and I will be hosting a German exchange student from April to May. We're all very excited. Good luck in school! And tell your family I said hello. Keep your heads up and keep smiling!*

Right before we sealed the envelope, my mom took out her checkbook and added one final note: *Enclosed is a check for your family's use. If you are close to the deadline for your examinations, perhaps you could use the check for that?*

Martin
—ᴟᴟ—

A WEEK INTO THE NEW YEAR, the postman told me that there was a large package waiting for me back at the main post office.

"Bring a friend to collect it," he said. "A strong one."

This must be the mysterious package Caitlin had written about. I went to find Nation, who was playing soccer with his friends.

"Brother, I need your help," I called from the sidelines as he dribbled the ball down the dusty pitch, weaving in and out of his friends like a gazelle.

"Come back after I've won this game," he shouted, and then *pow!*, he took a shot at the goal. The ball flew between the two twigs doubling as markers. Nation pumped his fist in the air as his teammates ran to give him high fives.

"I need you *now*," I said urgently.

He looked annoyed.

"It's important!" I said.

He called a time-out, and jogged over to me. I my reason in his ear.

"I'm off!" he shouted, and then we sprinted to post office, two kilometers away.

There, I gave my name to the postmaster, who pointed at a box almost as tall as my sister, Lois, and too wide to wrap my arms around. I thought there must be a mistake, until I saw Caitlin's handwriting on the side, spelling out my name and address in large capital letters.

Nation and I each took a side of the box and sidestepped out of the building.

As much as we both wanted to rip the tape off and look inside, we knew it was best to do this in the privacy of our own home.

"New TV?" someone shouted as we passed by.

Nation glared and the guy left us alone. My brother was tough. People knew better than to mess with him.

Back home, my parents and siblings gathered inside to open the box together. My father used his knife to carefully slice through the sturdy brown tape and then unfolded the top. Simba cried, "Whoa!" Inside, scattered everywhere, were little sweets that looked like jewels.

"What is it?" my sister, Lois, asked, peering into the box. She was six, and had never eaten a sweet before. I had tried bubble gum once or twice, when school friends shared theirs with me. But these real sweets were a new experience for everyone in my family.

I picked up the letter and read Caitlin's greetings aloud. She explained that these were called candies in America.

I handed one called Starburst to Lois. "You try first," I said.

She unwrapped the pink paper and placed the small square into her mouth tentatively.

"It tastes like sweet fruit," she said, smiling.

George Jr. wanted to try one, too. I chose an orange square for him, and then gave my mother a red one. My father took a small colorful ball called jawbreaker, which Caitlin described as impossible to bite into. This inspired Nation to have one, too. We all watched as they both tried to chomp down on these large candies, but no luck.

"A sweet rock!" my father said. He then took it out of his mouth and tried smashing it with the handle of his knife. No luck. We were amazed. He popped it back in his mouth.

I tried a Tootsie Roll. It was the most delicious thing I'd ever eaten in my entire life.

Beneath the layer of candies were neatly folded clothes. I started pulling items out, and was suddenly overcome with that same perfumed scent that my Reebok and Nike shirt both had. This was what "new" smelled like, I thought. So many new things! T-shirts, shorts, and then soaps and deodorants that smelled even more gorgeous, like a whole garden of flowers.

When I saw the Walkman, I had to sit down. I had seen people wearing these small machines in Harare. Alois explained that it was a way to listen to music on your own.

That was a funny concept—shouldn't music be shared with everyone? I recounted this story as I placed the headphones on my ears. Nation had found the cassette Caitlin sent, buried in the box. It was Ricky Martin. I knew his music. "La Vida Loca" was blaring from every boom box and radio in Mutare practically. I popped the tape in and hit PLAY.

The music swelled in my ears and startled me. My family, riveted, erupted in nervous laughs.

Then I heard a deep voice start singing, "She's into superstitions, black cats, and voodoo dolls."

I found the volume dial and turned it up. It was too loud for my ears. I took the headphones off and handed them to my father, who held them in the center of our room as we all huddled around.

By the time it reached the chorus, "Upside, inside out!" my whole family was dancing.

"Living la vida loca!" my father started to sing. His voice filled the house and reminded me of the better days, when he would wake up and go to sleep singing. We had not had music in our home since the radio was taken from us two Christmases earlier. The clothes and toiletries were great gifts, but this Walkman was the biggest hit by far. And we were only halfway through the box.

Simba pulled out the markers, and I knew immediately these were the tools Caitlin used to make her exquisite designs! There was a box of crayons for Lois, a coloring book for George, and a book bag for me! We were nearing the bottom when I spotted the sneakers, stacked side by side. I pulled out the first pair and my mother gasped. My father was the only person in our home who had proper shoes, which he needed for the factory. The rest of us wore flip-flops called pata patas because that was the sound they made when you walked in them. They were the cheapest thing to buy at the market, and made of rubber. Mine had been repaired several times since my father bought them for me two years earlier. My mother, however, did not even have a pair of pata patas. So when I handed her a pair of white sneakers with silver stripes down their side, she bowed her head very quickly.

"You try first, Mai," I said.

She put her head in her hands, covering her face, and her smile.

"Put them on!" Simba urged as I pulled the other pair from the box. These had a blue stripe, and a note from Caitlin: *I hope they fit you, Martin! If not, please send me your size.*

I waited. This was my mother's very first time trying on shoes. She slipped her foot into one, then the other.

"I will show you how to tie them," Nation said as he bent over her feet.

She stood up and jumped up and down, once, then twice. Then she walked around the room, bouncing a bit with each step.

"How do they feel?" I asked.

"Too good for words, my son," she said.

I tried mine on, so thrilled to finally have a pair of real shoes! But my foot was too big. I pulled and tugged and pushed, but there was no way I could get my heel to go in.

This meant they would not fit my father or Nation, who had bigger feet than me. Or Simba, who wore my size shoe. They were too big for Lois and George, of course. I handed them to my mother, to see if they fit her. She placed them next to her new sneakers and saw they were a bit bigger, but certainly would work.

"Mother, now you have two to choose from," I said, smiling.

She bowed at me and said, "Une moyo wakanaka."

In Shona, this means, "You have a good heart." It's one of several expressions for giving thanks.

I said, "Mother, Caitlin is the one with the good heart!"

And she said, "So do you, my son. It is why Caitlin is your dear friend."

That night, so many joyful feelings were swirling inside my chest. These gifts and what they meant to me and my family were too good for words, but I tried anyway.

January 18, 2000
Dear the loving Stoicsitz family
   Hello everybody.
   Hie Cait, your loving mom, and
caring dad. I finally got that huge
expensive parcel! Oh! I am very happy.
My family members are over-excited
and are feeling really great with the huge
box with the high-standard clothes,

perfumes, shampoos, shaving creams....
Books. Oh! I thank you please. My
parents are not very literate in English
but they told me to say a big thank you.
We really appreciate your love.

I tried to list everything she had sent, which took up two whole pages. I included the shirts, and the cassette player, and candies.

Thank you for those durable shoes
you gave us! Though they were not my
size, they are the best I have ever seen.
My mom is the only one whose shoe
size they were so we gave her all the
two pairs. Faithfully, these are her
first durable, expensive nice pairs of
shoes, I thank you for this. She no
longer walks barefooted and she is
now counted in society.

I thanked Caitlin for the pens, crayons, and school supplies, as well as the scented perfumes and soaps. We never had such things before! At the end of two long paragraphs, I summed it up: *Our life is changing now through you.*

At the end of Caitlin's note, she asked me to call her on the telephone to let her know the package arrived. Once again,

I was in a bind. Like cameras, telephones were only for rich people. I knew there was a telephone at the post office where I could arrange to receive a call. I wrote:

> *We do not have a telephone because it is very expensive to buy and use and maintain. But you can contact me through the POST OFFICE in Sakubva. You call them and tell them you want to speak with me so that they can contact me and I will be there in time to receive the international call from you. I hope this is the only way we can speak together on the phone. What do you think?*

I also caught her up on my school schedule. I had learned that the O-level fees were due by March 15, and that I needed Z$540. Just writing that fee took my breath away. They had already given us so much money—more than that amount—but asking for this on top of everything felt like too much. Still, it was my only option. I wanted to make sure she knew how much their financial support was appreciated by us.

> *The money you sent came at a time when we were drowned in poverty and hunger. This is why I always say you*

> are a loving family. The money really
> helped us! Thanks be unto you the
> loving and caring friends.

I was overcome with emotion as I wrote this sentence. What would we have done without their help? Then I heard my father out in our courtyard singing, "Living la vida loca!" And saw Lois coloring with George on our bed. And then I saw my mother bounce by me in her new shoes. All these tremendous feelings crashed over me, a warm wave:

> Thank you for your effort, love, and
> time. Thank you for the shoes you gave
> us. My mom, I repeat, is now counted
> as human in the society.

I was now more than ever determined to repay this kindness. I said in closing:

> I promise you this: One day I will be
> one of the African students at one of
> your universities. I would like to be a
> doctor or a chartered accountant so I
> can help my poor family, visit our loving
> friends (the Stoicsitzes) in Hatfield, have
> fun, send great gifts of appreciation
> to you, and if possible find a job in

180

Hatfield or any American state near you.
Isn't this a good wish! I pray this will
happen.

Cait, your dad and mom and Richie,
I say

> Warmest regards from
> Martin Ganda and Ganda
> family

PS, I have recently stopped cleaning
cars and carrying luggage and have left
this for my brother Nation so I can
concentrate on school. I have two
more years before I go to university.
How many do you have, Caitlin? Thanks
thanks.

After I finished writing, I took out my new box of Stampers. I chose lips, hearts, stars, and smiley faces to decorate each page, and then encircled Caitlin's name at the top, like a halo.

Caitlin

⸺◈⸺

AS HAPPY AS I WAS to get news that Martin had received the package, several sentences in his letter upset me. To this day, they still make me cry. He wrote: *My mother wants to thank you for the shoes.* And *Now she will be counted in the society.* That just floored me. I thought, How can someone be over-looked or ignored just because she doesn't have shoes? It made me realize how much injustice was happening in the world—and probably in Hatfield, too.

I started obsessing about how ridiculous it was that people were treated badly because of how much money they did or did not have. I was halfway through ninth grade and could see how all these cliques formed in school around money. The popular girls were all from families like mine that could afford to buy them the trendiest clothes, shoes, and makeup. They went on vacations to cool places—like Florida or the Bahamas—and to see concerts, or to Six Flags amusement park with their families. Then there were also kids who had money and used it to gain access to these cliques, like Marie. Her family was really wealthy, but she was very shy and a little nerdy—the opposite of her mother, who went to high school with my mom and was on the prom queen's court. I think it bothered her that Marie was not more popular. So she bought six tickets to see 'N Sync and then told Marie to invite all the popular girls, including me. None of the other girls liked her—they'd say mean things about her behind her back. But they all accepted the tickets, which made me feel nauseated. I told Marie I couldn't go because I had to babysit, which was true. I was relieved. I didn't want any part of that.

A few weeks after I received Martin's letter, my mom took me to a luncheon at Gwynedd Mercy University. She had decided to go back to school to get her bachelor's degree in education when I was still in elementary school, and she was still an active alumnus. They served brick oven pizza at the luncheon but had ordered way too much, so there were two entire pizzas left over at the end. The woman who had organized the event asked my mom if she wanted to take them home.

"We'd love to!" I said, before my mom could even say a word.

My mom looked bewildered.

"We can give it to that guy who lives in Lansdale, mom," I said. "The Vietnam vet."

There was a homeless man who lived in the nearby town. The rumor was that he had fought in the war and came back slightly crazy. Not in a scary way—more in a "he prefers living on the streets" way. I remember the very first time I saw him. I was in fifth grade and riding in the car with my mom. He was searching through the garbage outside of a diner dressed in very dirty jeans, an old stained sweatshirt, and an army jacket.

"What's he doing?" I asked.

"Probably looking for food," my mother answered. "Not everyone is as fortunate as we are, Caitlin."

I had seen him a dozen times since then and he was always wearing that same jacket.

We looked in all his usual spots—the Shop 'n Save parking lot, the train station, the town park. I finally spotted him in the bushes behind the Burger King drive-through. Mom stopped the car, and I got out with the pizza boxes.

"I thought you might like this," I said, handing over the boxes. "It's really good pizza."

He took the boxes without looking at me or saying a word.

I got back in the car with all these thoughts buzzing in my head, from How can a person be homeless in our country? to What happened to him in Vietnam that would make him choose that lifestyle? I didn't have answers, but I made a pact with myself that I would never be mean ever again to anyone because he or she had dirty hair or smelled bad or was poor or didn't have shoes.

I'd begin with Amanda. She sat in front of me in Mr. Sinkinson's English class, so I could see that her scalp was covered with whitehead zits. Worse, she'd pop them during class, and then run her fingers down clumps of her already greasy hair. I tried to ignore it at first, but it was hard. To be honest, it made me want to puke. She only had two or three outfits, and didn't wash them very often—on hot days, she smelled like salami. I never mentioned any of this to anyone, until one day a huge dandruff flake landed on my notebook. That afternoon, I ranted to a few friends about how gross she was. Later that week, I passed Amanda in the hall with one of those friends, who said, in a really sarcastic voice, "Um, have you ever thought about washing your hair?"

Amanda sunk her head into her shoulders and sputtered, "I do wash it," before scurrying away.

Driving home with my mom, I started connecting the dots. Amanda had seven siblings, three outfits, and always ate the lunch plan, which was soggy canned vegetables and mysterious meat. I had a debit card that allowed me to buy anything I wanted from the cafeteria—pizza, bagels, sandwiches, or a salad. I had no idea what Amanda's parents did, but I understood then that it was not her fault that she had zits on her head. If that was my problem, my mom would take me to doctor after doctor to make them go away. I vowed never to be mean to Amanda, or anyone else like her, ever again. If anything, I would stick up for her.

Martin
—〰—

MY MOTHER DIDN'T WALK IN her new sneakers. She floated. When people asked about them, she'd jump up and down to demonstrate how durable they were. She kept all our new gifts neatly stored in the same large box they arrived in, placed in the corner of our room, and would invite friends in to see them. This was new—she never had guests in our home, but my mom was very proud to have all of these things, and she wanted to show them off. We were, too, though the new clothes were complicated. We spent the first few days trying everything on seven or eight times in a row, swapping with one another, having fun. But then we realized that we couldn't wear any of them to school, as we had to wear our old uniforms. We did not want to wear them when we got back home, to do our chores or play around, as we were afraid to get them dirty. Everyone wanted to save them for special occasions, and there were not many of those happening in our lives. So they mainly stayed in the box. My father, however, woke up every morning and put on his brand-new shirt and shorts to go look for work. It made him appear—and feel— less desperate.

I particularly appreciated the package of ten toothbrushes. Inside, there was a booklet that discussed "dental hygiene." It said you should change your toothbrush every six months— I was shocked. I had had mine for seven years. The bristles were all beaten down. I was so happy to exchange it for a new one.

Caitlin

WHEN MY GERMAN TEACHER, FRAU KANZ, had asked if anyone was interested in hosting a German exchange student in the spring, I had raised my hand.

I loved visiting Carola in Germany, and thought it would be fun to reciprocate. Frau Kanz told me to discuss the possibility with my parents, but I already knew they would say yes.

Later that week, Frau Kanz handed me a folder.

"Everything you need to know about Stephie is here," she said.

I looked at her photo first—she had short, dark brown hair and almond-shaped brown eyes. She was wearing a jean jacket with jeans, and I smiled. She reminded me of Carola! I'd never wear denim on denim! But I'd never wear socks with sandals, either! I was excited to show Stephie how American girls dressed. I was excited to be her American ambassador.

Back home, I read Stephie's bio to my parents. For fun,

she wrote that she liked to "go to disco," which cracked me up. There were no discos in Hatfield, and I had outgrown the Friday night roller-rink scene. I'd take her to school parties, and to the Cineplex near the mall. I'd also take her midnight bowling—which was what my friends and I did for fun.

My mom spent a week transforming Richie's room for Stephie, since he would not be home from college until June. Once she removed the Star Wars wallpaper, she had to spackle all the dart-gun holes he had shot into the wall over the years. That took an entire day. Then she painted the room taupe and navy. I was jealous—Richie already had the bigger room, and now he had the nicer room, too!

Still, it was for Stephie, I had to remind myself. She deserved it—not Richie.

Only, she didn't. I figured that out pretty quickly. When I first saw her, I thought she seemed fine. I was a little alarmed by how much stuff she brought: two huge suitcases stuffed with more clothes than even I had. We got home and I showed her the room Mom had worked so hard on. Stephie looked as if she had bitten a lemon. She did not say a word, so we left her to unpack on her own.

When it was dinnertime, I went upstairs to find her sitting in her room, her bags still packed, playing one of the video games she brought with her.

"Aren't you going to unpack?" I asked.

"Don't you have a maid that will do it?" she said, annoyed.

"A maid?" I responded.

"Back home, I have a nanny and a maid," she said.

"A nanny?" I said, my voice high-pitched because I thought she must have been joking. "Very funny," I said. Stephie didn't laugh.

"Okay, well, we don't have a maid or a nanny here," I said, slowly realizing that maybe this girl was not as cool as I had hoped she would be. "But I do have a mom who made a really delicious dinner to welcome you to our home."

I turned around to walk back downstairs, but Stephie stayed put.

I walked back to her room, now pissed. "Aren't you coming downstairs?" I asked.

"I'm not hungry," she said, and then asked me to close her door.

At dinner, I was fuming. My mom and dad ate quietly.

"Who does she think she is?" I asked, stabbing at the lasagna my mom had made especially for her. I was too mad to be hungry.

"Cut her some slack, Caitlin," my dad said. "She's in a new country and probably feels overwhelmed."

"Or even homesick," my mom added. "Let's give her a few days to settle in."

I agreed to give her another chance, but when I went back upstairs to apologize for being testy, her lights were out. Jet lag, I figured. Germany was, after all, six hours ahead of us.

The next morning, I knocked on her door and was glad that she invited me in. "We have the whole day to do whatever we want!" I said. I suggesting going on a bike ride. I wanted to show her the neighborhood, and introduce her to Heather and a few other nearby friends.

"Can we go shopping?" Stephie asked.

"Yes," I said, relieved. "We can go to the mall. That is a very popular thing to do!"

Soon I learned that was all she wanted to do. She wasn't even interested in going to school with me, which was the whole point of the exchange program! When she asked my mother to make her breakfast in bed that first week, my mom finally lost it.

"Stephie, I appreciate that you have a maid in Germany who makes you whatever you want whenever you want," I overheard my mom say one day. I was in my room, and Mom was standing in the doorway to Richie's out in the hallway. "But in America, and specifically in my house, that's not what we do. So if you want to eat, you are more than welcome to join us downstairs."

Yes, I thought to myself. You tell her, Mom!

We learned quickly there was no telling Stephie anything. When she came downstairs for breakfast, she would barely pick at her food, and then she dragged herself out the door to get on the bus to go to school with me, complaining the entire time.

"Everything is so booooor-ing here," she said. "Nowhere to have any fun."

By the end of the first week, I realized I had made a terrible mistake by inviting her to live with us.

That Friday, all of my friends planned to go midnight

bowling. Stephie will love this, I thought. There was even a disco ball in the alley, and they played music really loud. But when I told her what we were doing that night, she twisted her face into a knot and said, "Can you get beer there? In Germany, we can buy beer at discos!"

"This isn't Germany!" I said, starting to lose my patience. "And it is illegal to drink beer in the United States until you are twenty-one."

"Then I stay home," she countered.

"Suit yourself," I said. What I really wanted to say is, "Why don't you just go home?" Instead, I had to tolerate her for another entire month. I didn't think I was going to make it.

I gave up on trying to please Stephie, but my parents had already planned a trip to Washington, DC. I dreaded going, but we had a nice time. We even have a photo of the two of us standing in front of the Washington Monument, where we both are smiling, a miracle. Another weekend, we took her to Philadelphia to see *Les Misérables*. Those were the only times she seemed impressed. Meanwhile, I quickly appropriated the musical's title: *The Miserable*. Starring Stephie.

My anger at Stephie was a good distraction from the fact we still had not heard from Mr. Samupindi. My mom was worried that Martin didn't get the money for his exams and that he might not even be in school. It was like we were sending notes and checks into a big black hole. She kept checking her bank to see if her check had been cashed: nothing. I could tell she was getting frustrated, which broke my heart. I knew all this time and effort was worth it, that Martin was worth

it. But Mom was losing hope. She sent him a postcard in late
April, which she showed me before she posted.

April 25, 2000
Dear Martin,
  We have not heard from you. Our letters of
January 24, 2000, to you and your headmaster
contained important documents. Due to political
unrest in Zimbabwe, we are very concerned about
you and your family. Please try to contact us
with your whereabouts. We are unable to help if
we don't know where you are or what you need.
Please contact us.

  Love, Rich, Anne,
  and Caitlin

I flashed back to the months before I received the letter on
garbage. What if he was back working at the market, with no
way of contacting us? Hearing Stephie complain about doing
her own laundry and dishes —two rules in my house—made
me want to throttle her. I didn't even go to the airport with
her to say good-bye. But I did do a victory dance as soon as
the door shut behind her.

By late May my mom finally said enough is enough. "Caitlin, I am just going to send a hundred dollars to Martin via
Western Union and pray that it gets to him. What else can
we do?"

She made all the arrangements, and then wrote Martin a postcard instructing him to go to his Western Union branch to collect the funds on June 5. When she did not hear from him that day, she was sick to her stomach. The next day, she wrote again:

June 6, 2000
Dear Martin,

By now we hope you have received the postcard indicating you are to go to the post office bank to collect your Western Union money. We wired the money to you on Monday June 5, 2000, as the postcard said. According to Western Union, US$100 is being converted at a rate of Z$37.07 as of today. But it may be converted to a greater or lesser amount on the day you arrive to collect the funds. In any event, at today's rate, you will receive Z$3707.56. We tried to figure out how much money you and your family need for school and rent. We believe this amount will maintain your family for a few months.

We both crossed our fingers and said a prayer that the money would make it to him.

My junior high school graduation was only days away, but I was too concerned about Martin to get that excited. That changed two days after we sent that postcard.

"I did it!" my mom announced that afternoon. "I found him."

She jumped up from her chair to wiggle her hips and wave her arms like a crazed cheerleader.

"Martin?" I asked.

"No," my mother said. "Mr. Samupindi! I finally got through to the Sakubva post office and told the postmaster that I needed to speak to the headmaster at Martin's school."

"And?" I was on the verge of breaking into my own dance.

"And they promised to send word to him," she continued. "So I'm going to call the post office at two AM and hopefully Mr. Samupindi will pick up."

My head started spinning at that moment and did not stop until I heard my mom's alarm clock go off hours later, at 1:55 AM.

I quickly got up to follow her downstairs.

"Hello, I am calling for Mr. George Samupindi," she said after punching a long list of numbers into the phone. Her voice was calm and formal.

In the silence that followed, she winked at me.

"Yes, hello, Mr. Samupindi, thank you for taking my call," she continued. "My name is Anne and I am calling from the US about Martin Ganda."

I placed a chair next to her just as my mom's face fell into a frown.

"Why?" she said.

By then I was close enough to hear Mr. Samupindi's voice booming through the receiver. He seemed to be shouting, as if he thought that was necessary to speak to someone so far away. I was glad as I could hear every word: In a clipped British accent he said, "Martin is one of our brightest students."

I caught my mom's eyes and smiled wide. I knew it!

But then he said, "If he does not finish his O-levels and go on for his A-levels, he will rot and die in Zimbabwe."

I covered my mouth but not soon enough to catch my gasp.

"What do you mean?" my mother asked, staying calm.

"Between poverty and AIDS, a poor boy like Martin doesn't stand a chance," he continued. "What makes his case particularly sad is that he is easily the brightest student we have ever seen in these parts—smarter than many of his teachers."

My mom's eyes started filling with tears. "Mr. Samupindi, how can we help Martin stay in school?" she asked.

She jotted a number down on her notepad, and asked, "What about his siblings?"

I sat back, so proud.

She wrote *US$80* on her notepad and circled it twice, smiling so hard her eyes turned into happy slits.

"How can I get this money to you?" she asked. "I'll send you a check today. Please keep Martin Ganda and his siblings in school. I will be one hundred percent responsible for their tuition."

I heard Mr. Samupindi say "Happily" before he hung up.

Tears were rolling down my mother's cheeks.

"You did it!" I said as I squeezed her hard.

"This," she whispered into my ear, "was a team effort."

When I pulled back, my mom was sobbing and laughing at once.

"Mom!" I said. "This is no time for tears! We need to call Martin immediately!"

He had mentioned in a prior letter that we could call the post office in Sakubva for emergencies, which this was. News this good couldn't wait for another letter.

Martin

—◇—

I WAS CLEANING THE MORNING dishes when a boy my age came running down the path shouting, "Martin, America is calling. For you."

I started sprinting toward the post office and could hear both Nation and Simba running behind me.

Once there, I pushed through the heavy glass door and past the long queue of people waiting to send or collect packages. The phone operator was in the corner, holding the receiver in both hands.

"You must be Martin Ganda," he said.

I took a deep breath before I placed the phone to my ear.

"Hallo?" I said.

"Martin?" a high-pitched and twangy voice responded.

"Caitlin," I shouted. "Is this really you?"

"It's me!" she answered. "I have good news!"

Goose bumps blanketed my body.

"My mom spoke to your headmaster," she said. "You don't have to worry about school fees anymore!"

By then, Nation and Simba were on either side of me straining to hear the conversation.

"Caitlin, this is the best news ever," I said, fighting back the emotions swelling up in my chest and throat. I thought I might choke on them.

"How will I ever repay you?" I asked.

"Knowing that you and your family are okay is the only payment we need," Caitlin said.

I don't remember much else of the conversation. I do remember hanging up the phone and knowing, deep in my bones, that my life would never be the same.

I ran straight to Mr. Samupindi to tell him I had heard the good news.

"Martin, these people care about you," he said. "You must not take that lightly."

"Yes, sir," I said.

"If you study hard, you can go to any university," he continued. "These people will help you. You must make the most of this opportunity."

"Yes, I know," I said. "And I will."

The O-levels were only a few months away. If I aced them, then I really could do anything. This was my chance.

I started sneaking into the teachers' college library again that August and September to prepare. In between, I got another note from Western Union that more funds had arrived. My mother and I went to collect them on August 31. The note said:

TO: MARTIN GANDA
FROM: ANNE NEVILLE
AMOUNT: US$100

Caitlin was not the only angel in my life.

This money was in addition to the first wire we received in June and the check she had already sent Mr. Samupindi for my schooling as well as Simba's, and Lois's, too, as she had just started school.

When I handed my mother the Western Union receipt, I saw something in her face that was new to me. The deep lines carved into her face between her brows and around her eyes softened. This money gave her relief.

12 September 2000
Dear Cait and family,
    Hallo! First I would like to apologize for a late reply. I first wanted to make sure that the large sum of money you sent had arrived. Thank you very much. May the Lord bless you. You are the greatest. I have enclosed the receipt/ invoice. We used some of the money to pay some bills, and food, and saved the rest.

Right now we are on a holiday. I will begin our General Certificate of Education public examination on 13 October 2000. I am working hard and hope to pass. I thank you for your efforts you are taking in order to help me and my family.

Life in the community as you know is deplorable but your efforts are reducing the problems. Thank you for that. Sometimes it's difficult to believe how we live because in the US there is nothing like that. The families sharing a room, unemployment, poverty. I wish you could one day visit us and see how many Zimbabweans in Chisamba Singles are living. For food, Mom and Dad sometimes go help clean the churches and the houses of the rich, though this is very infrequent. Here they are given a few coins from which they buy food (very little) and keep a few dollars for rent. This is a very difficult task, as the money we are paid cannot even buy a loaf of bread costing Z$20. Imagine how much money we need for bread only! The government is doing nothing to help us.

They say if you cannot afford to live in town or city, then go die in the rural areas and give chance to those who can afford to live in the city.

Thank you again for your love.
My family feel great about your unconditional love.

From that moment on, I spent all my spare time cramming for the O-level exams. Elias started joining me at the library as well. He, too, wanted to go to university. We took mock tests and grilled each other on the more difficult questions. We studied problems that we thought might show up and asked our teachers to borrow textbooks that we studied all night and returned the following morning. This meant spending two to three nights every week studying until three AM and then falling asleep beneath the desks in that quiet space lined with books. The sun streaming through the big windows acted as our alarm clock, waking us each morning in time to get home for breakfast before heading back to school.

The day of the exam, I felt well prepared. And a little bit excited, too.

Caitlin

I COULDN'T WAIT TO START tenth grade. I was finally going to North Penn High. All of the kids from my middle school plus kids from two other middle schools meant there would be one thousand students in my grade alone. I'd been to the campus before, when Richie went there, but showing up for my first day of class felt different. I was no longer the little sister, but an actual student. And I was taking a lot of classes—English, World Culture, geometry, biology, German, Mechanical Drawing, health, Study Skills, and Aquatics, which was basically an excuse to swim in the school's Olympic-size pool. The campus was so huge, it took thirty minutes to walk from one end to the other. I liked all of my classes except geometry—I still hated math. This year, there was not one cute boy in my class to sway me. My favorite class, though, was World Culture. Ever since I had met Martin, I became interested in how people lived in other countries— their customs and traditions.

We had to choose a region to focus on, and I picked Southern Africa. For an early assignment, I researched the climate. That was how I learned about monsoons, where it rained hard for days. Martin had described this in his letters as their "rainy season." I did more research and learned that neighboring Mozambique flooded almost annually. Did Sakubva flood as well? I wondered. If so, what did Martin and his family do? Did they collect the water to drink so they did not have to rely on the county taps? I had so many questions—and another idea for a care package.

I started making a list: tarps, buckets, rain boots, ponchos. Water purification tablets.

I didn't want to ask my parents to spend any more on Martin's family. They were already covering the basics. I wanted to do this on my own—and that meant getting a real job.

Ray's Pizzeria was down the road from my high school. The owner was married to the lady who ran the summer camp program where I had worked the last two summers. I knew they needed a waitress, so I applied. In addition to making nine dollars an hour, I got tips: On busy days, it could be as much as three hundred dollars.

Making this much money gave me even more independence, something I was craving now that I had started high school. I sent some cash to Martin and saved most of it to buy him things on my growing list. I didn't need to spend it on clothes—my mom bought me whatever I needed. Though I did make sure I always had money in my wallet, just in case. Fun money.

Now that I was fifteen, I started meeting friends at the

mall on Friday and Saturday evenings instead of the afternoons. It was a good place to find out where the closest party was, whether a keg party in Lansdale or a dance party in North Wales. Our high school served five different towns, which meant there were at least three or four parties to choose from every weekend.

Lisa and I met on the tennis team and became fast friends. She was a year older than me, which meant she could drive. I told my mom I was spending the night at Lisa's one Friday, which was the plan. But then we went to the mall looking for fun, and met Johnny and Jim. They were older than us, and wore leather jackets and their baseball hats so low, I couldn't see their eyes. When Johnny asked me how old I was, I said seventeen.

"Want to go to South Street?" he asked.

It was only eight PM. South Street was in Philly, which was forty-five minutes away. I'd never been there at night. Lisa looked at me and shrugged.

"Sure," I said.

We followed them outside to Johnny's Cutlass Supreme. It was as wide as my mom's Jeep, but much lower to the ground. I got in the backseat and slammed the heavy door shut. It didn't latch. I tried again, pulling even harder. This time it stayed in place, but was still ajar.

"Fasten your seat belts, ladies," Johnny said before he peeled out of the parking lot, leaving tire marks behind on the pavement.

I tried—but they didn't work, either. I pushed my body

close to Lisa's in the center of the backseat and grabbed her hand. I could tell she was the same mix of excited with a sprinkle of scared. Still, I swatted away the small thought that this might be a mistake and decided to just go with this exhilarating feeling, like I was nearing the top of a roller coaster.

Our first stop was a liquor store, where Jim popped out to buy beer for the boys and fruity wine spritzers for us. I cracked one open and clinked my bottle to Lisa's before we guzzled the neon-pink watermelon-flavored liquid down. It was cold, but my stomach and face felt warm by the time it was empty.

I opened another, and then looked out the window as the trees whirred by in the dark night. This was turning into the most fun night ever.

When we arrived at South Street, Johnny shoved two more beers into his leather jacket pockets before hopping out of the car.

He opened my door and said, "Ladies..."

Lisa and I stumbled out of the car. I felt this fun mix of woozy and warm. Heavy metal music streamed out of one bar window clashing with the reggae sounds that escaped another. Neon lights blinked and glistened in the dark night as people spilled onto the streets, tipsy. I followed Johnny past several bars wondering how we would get past any of the burly bouncers that flanked each doorway. We'd been wandering for ten minutes when a cop tapped Johnny on the shoulder.

"You know you can't have an open container on the street," he said. Johnny shrugged his shoulders and tossed his open beer into the trash. "This one, Officer, hasn't been opened yet," he said, holding the other Coors can in his hand, in a mock salute.

"Make sure it stays that way, Johnny," the officer said, and walked on.

"Why does he know your name?" I asked as Lisa and I followed Johnny and Jim back to the car. Instead of answering, Johnny revved the engine and drove to another place called Club Malibu ten minutes away. There, the bouncer unclipped the velvet rope as soon as we walked up and gave Johnny a fist bump as we walked in.

Inside, the music pulsated through the floors and the soles of my shoes. My whole body was vibrating. Johnny shouted, "You girls want a cocktail?" We both nodded.

As the guys went to get drinks, I soaked it all in: Everyone was drinking, dancing, laughing, and having a great time. I was just about to ask Lisa if she wanted to dance when I felt my back pocket vibrate. I pulled out my phone and saw "Mom" flash across my screen. I hit IGNORE. The boys returned with drinks when I felt my phone buzz again.

"I'll be right back!" I shouted, and then looked for an exit. I knew I couldn't ignore her all night, so I decided to do a preemptive strike.

"Finally!" she answered the phone in one ring.

"Sorry, Mom!" I said. "Lisa and I are at a party. I didn't hear the phone ring."

"Oh really," Mom said. "Where?"

"Warrington," I said. It was about thirty minutes away from Hatfield, so it wasn't a huge lie.

"Well, I need you to come home now," she said.

"Why?" I asked.

"Because I'm your mother, and I said so," she said.

"I can't," I said, thinking fast. "There's no one to drive me."

"How did you get there in the first place?" Mom asked.

"Johnny," I said.

"Who's Johnny?" she replied.

"A new friend," I said. My wine cooler buzz was quickly being overtaken by pure panic.

"Well, tell your new friend Johnny he has thirty minutes to get you home," she replied. "Or give me the address and I'll come get you."

I hung up and ran back inside.

"We have to go," I said to Johnny.

He looked at me like I was crazy.

"Now," I said.

I told him I was actually only fifteen, and that my mom wanted me home in thirty minutes, or else she was going to come looking for me. I was kind of amazed that he agreed to drive us home. As he was going ninety miles an hour down the turnpike, I started to worry. Was he really going to take us home? What if he slipped something into our cocktails? Why did he wear his baseball cap so low? I could never pick him out of a lineup. And why did that policeman know him by name?

Horrible thoughts raced through my head as we sped down the turnpike. When I saw familiar town signs flash by, I started to relax. When Johnny took the exit for Hatfield, I finally exhaled. I gave him directions to my house and he pulled into the driveway. We made it back in thirty-eight minutes. Close enough.

I swung open the door, but Johnny popped out of the driver's seat just as quickly.

"Don't I even get a kiss?" he said.

I did not want to kiss him, but I also didn't want to be rude. And I certainly did not want my mom to come out in her terry-cloth robe to start questioning him. I closed my eyes and leaned in for a quick peck. His breath smelled like dirty feet.

"Thanks for a great time!" I said, pulling back quickly.

Lisa, meanwhile, clearly did not want to kiss Jim, either: She was already speed-walking toward the house. I ran to catch up with her, waving at the guys before we slipped into the house, knowing we would never see them again. My parents were waiting for us in the den.

"How was the party?" my mom asked in a deadpan voice. She knew something was up.

"Really fun," I said.

"Glad you made it home safely, sweetheart," my dad said as we bolted up the stairs.

"Lisa," my mom called after us, "Does your mom know you are here?"

"Yes!" I shouted down. "Good night! Love you!"

Once in my room, we both collapsed on my lower bunk bed. Lisa called her mom to say she was spending the night, and then borrowed some PJs.

That night, as I drifted off to sleep, I couldn't help but think how lucky I was.

November 2000

Martin
—ɷ—

THE O-LEVEL EXAMS STARTED IN mid-October. Each test lasted three hours, and I signed up for nine. They were scheduled every few days and I felt like a marathon runner. I was careful to rest up in between, and stay focused. The last one took place at the end of November. I had to do well. Not just for me and my family, but also for Caitlin and hers. I wouldn't have been able to even take the exams without their support. I wanted to prove to them that I was worthy. My future depended on them in more ways than I could fathom. I wanted to do something to repay them this enormous kindness and decided to send them more photos—not just of me but of my whole family.

We used some money that Caitlin's mom had sent to hire Mr. Masamba, the same photographer who had taken the other two shots of me. We weren't yet dressed for the occasion when he arrived with his camera, as everyone wanted to wear something that Caitlin had sent. While my parents changed inside our house, I stood outside with Simba and Lois, waiting to do the same.

"Say cheese!" Mr. Masamba said. I thought he was joking, until I heard the click.

My father had paid for four photos. Mr. Masamba knew we were sending these photos to America and promised to make sure they were extra professional. Still, I asked him to wait before he took any more—Simba was wearing the track pants Caitlin had sent, but with his own worn-out vest and nothing else underneath. I wanted him in a proper polo shirt. And Lois was wearing an old shirt that had been passed on from me to Simba to her. It was so thin in places, you could see her skin. We saved Caitlin's clothes for special occasions, like this.

"Hurry, go change," I told them after that first shot was taken.

They went inside, and I followed. Soon, we were all outfitted in our American clothes: My father and I wore white matching polo shirts. Nation chose a bright yellow parka, and my mother put on a bright red skirt and a navy-blue rugby shirt. She dressed George in the smallest T-shirt sent, and Lois in another white polo shirt that fit more like a dress. Mr. Masamba asked us all to gather together on the bed so we could fit in one frame.

I sat between my mother and father, and Nation stood off to the left. George sat in my mother's lap, and Lois and Simba leaned up against my legs.

"Say hallo!" Mr. Masamba said as he snapped a photo. I smiled wide and hoped everyone else remembered to as well.

I suggested the third shot be of me and Nation, since they often asked about him.

"Baba, Mai," I said. "Let's have the last one be your portrait."

My father eagerly hopped on the bed, and my mother sat next to him. George climbed in the spot between them just as Mr. Masamba started counting, "One, two, three..." My father smiled broadly while Mother remained very still and serious. George started to cry—and I hoped that wasn't captured on film.

Mr. Masamba returned with the photos a few days later. As I flipped through each, I thought, No more hiding. Caitlin would now really see in these shots how we truly lived. I could soften our poverty with my words, and dress it up in her clothes, but these images told the truth. I prayed that she could handle it.

November 2000
Dear Caitlin.
Hallo. How is everybody over there? How is school? We are all fine here in Zimbabwe.
We finally managed to get ourselves photographed. The photos were taken

in our one-room house. I hope you
are going to like the photos. This is my
whole family including my big brother
Nation, whom you were fond of!

I am still writing my O-level exams
and am going to finish on the 21st of
November. From there I will be on a
school holiday till early February 2001.
And then I will proceed to advanced
level education. If I pass, I will go to
university maybe in the US!

I would like to thank you very
much for the ample support you have
and you are supplying to me and my
family.

God bless you.

        Yours,
        Martin Ganda.

I looked at the photos again and felt compelled to explain
them, so I added a PS:

Do not get confused by our house.
The photos were taken when we were
sitting on the bed where my mom
and dad sleep. This can confuse you
while comparing it with how you live

in the US. Below the bed are some
of the utensils we use. At night, we
remove these and squeeze ourselves
under the bed and sleep. I know this
can make you doubt, but now you
understand how we live. I love that,
your understanding.

Caitlin

⊸⊷⊷⊸

THE PHOTOS WEREN'T WHAT I EXPECTED. Yes, Martin was the same smiling person I had grown to love like my own brother. In these images, he looked like a more grown-up version of that little boy in kneesocks whose photo remained beneath my glass desktop, but I was expecting sunny, bright blue skies, and tall, bleached-out grass. I imagined his mom and dad wearing colorful traditional clothes—made of hand-dyed fabrics. The dark and grainy photos Martin sent me were the opposite of those Technicolor images. In one, Martin was leaning against a building that looked like a wooden shack—not the thatched-roof hut in my mind. My first thought was, That can't be his home. Our backyard tool shed looked bigger and sturdier. I flipped through the pictures several times, though, and realized, that *is* his home. The ground around it was packed dirt scattered with jagged gray pebbles. There was a tree off in the distance, the only green spot in an otherwise bleak field of beige and gray.

I studied the shot of Martin sitting between his parents on a bed in a dark, cramped room with all his siblings gathered around. I figured that must be his parents' bedroom. There was another shot of Martin and Nation on the same bed, and then another of just his parents with the youngest boy, George, again on that bed. I read the letter to see if it referenced the photos. That was how I learned that this was not their bedroom. It was their *entire* house. Martin wrote that he and his siblings had to move pots and pans in order to make space beneath his parents' bed to sleep.

I went through all the photos again, looking for more clues about Martin's life—none of the kids were wearing shoes, including Martin.

Does Martin even own a pair of shoes? I wondered, flipping again through the stack, looking for proof that I was wrong. Nothing.

I looked up from my bottom bunk, stunned. My biggest complaint for the past year had been "Why did Richie get the bigger room?" I could never imagine having to sleep beneath my parents' bed. As for shoes, my closet door could barely close from all the pairs I had piled up in there, most of which I never wore. It seemed wrong that I had so much, and Martin and his family had so little. I felt it was my responsibility to share my good fortune with my best friend.

I showed the photos to my parents that evening. They, too, were shocked by how hard his life looked.

My mom kept shaking her head, saying, "Wow," over and over.

"It's time for another care package," I said.

My dad agreed. "How can we help?"

I went to get the list I'd been compiling.

"They're in the rainy season now," I explained. "They experience something called monsoons."

"Like heavy tropical rains?" my mom asked.

"Exactly," I responded. "But look at their house—you can practically see the gaps in the walls."

"What are you proposing?" my dad asked.

"Tarps," I said.

"They sell them at the army-navy store," my mom added.

"I also want to get them collapsible water buckets," I added. "His mom can use them to collect rainfall."

"Smart," my dad said.

"We'll go shopping tomorrow," my mom said. "Meanwhile, let's all clean out our closets."

I used to give all my hand-me-down clothes to my two cousins who were several years younger than me, but my uncle Jim and aunt Kim could afford to buy them new clothes. Martin's family could not. I selected several pairs of shoes from my own: sneakers, flip-flops, and a pair of sandals. I realized they would only fit a few family members, and so I wrote a note to Martin asking him to send me everyone's shoe size, so no one was left out.

The following day, we went to the army-navy store, run by a guy wearing camouflage pants, work boots, and a Harley-Davidson T-shirt.

"Hi, Jeff," my mom said as we entered the store, Richie's favorite shop.

I explained what we were looking for and Jeff selected several large tarps, two collapsible buckets, and rain ponchos in sizes small, medium, and large.

"Do you have water purification tablets?" I asked as we piled things on the counter to buy.

"Right on!" Jeff said, grabbing four bottles of iodine tablets called Potable Aqua.

"They'll kill whatever is gnarly in the water," he said. "Guaranteed."

Next, we went to Ross to get rain boots for everyone—we still did not know everyone's size, but these were easier to guesstimate than actual shoes. My mom also grabbed an umbrella. Back home, we added batteries for Martin's Walkman, lotions, pens, notebooks, and envelopes to the box, which Mom set up in the dining room.

By mid-December, it was full. We included our family Christmas card, though I knew it wouldn't get there in time. It didn't matter. I just hoped it got there.

I woke to familiar sounds and smells on Christmas morning, but when I got to the kitchen, my dad said, "Santa left your present outside this year."

I was still in my PJs when I went outside to find a dark green 1996 Acura Integra with brand-new shiny silver rims in the driveway. The license plate said *C8LIN*.

"She's all yours!" my dad said, handing me the keys on a red ribbon.

I started screaming, which prompted Mom to tease, "Don't wake the neighbors!"

I had a hunch I was getting a car: My dad promised me I'd have something to practice driving by my sixteenth birthday that March. I didn't think my Christmas could get any better, but then back in the house and beneath the tree, there were still mounds of presents to open. That year, I got clothes, jewelry, socks, pajamas, and a dwarf white bunny. I decided to call her Lois, after Martin's adorable little sister.

It took a few weeks for me to finally write Martin back about the photos he had sent. I didn't mention them in my care package letter. Honestly, I was still figuring out the best way to even talk about them. I knew Martin was poor, but I had never seen that kind of poverty. I certainly didn't judge him for it. Instead, I was in awe. He remained so hopeful, so hardworking, so kind. My love and admiration for him grew even deeper.

January 7, 2001
Dear Martin:

How are you doing? I am fine and so is my family.

For me school is going really well. I have lots of homework and enjoy the whole process. How is school going for you? Have you heard about your O-level exams yet? How was your Christmas?

I hesitated telling him about all the presents I had received. But then I realized that he had been totally honest with me. I needed to be honest with him as well. I knew our friendship could handle it. I wrote about the small stuff first, and then:

The biggest surprise for me was a CAR!!!!
Now everyone in my house has a car.

I also told him about Lois.

I got a dwarf white bunny and I have
named her Lois. I selected that name
because she is sweet, cute, and little,
like your sister! I hope you and your
sister don't mind! She is now about
ten weeks old and she joins Louis, my
male medium lop bunny. I keep them in
the house because we have about twelve
inches of snow and it's too cold for them.
Anyway, I can pet them all the time and
carry them around.

I still had not mentioned the photos. I wasn't sure what exactly to say about them, so I decided to speak from my heart.

Thank you so much for the photos!
It was wonderful to see you and your
beautiful family. It is sad that in this
world you must still live in poverty.
I understand this is, unfortunately,
commonplace in many nations. We
do have poverty in the US, but our
government is frequently able to
rescue the needy, but not always.

I wished there was more I could say on the issue, but truthfully, Martin was the reason I was finally opening my eyes to the fact poverty existed—not just in Africa, but everywhere, including Pennsylvania. He was opening my eyes to so many things that had always surrounded me, but that I never noticed until he came into my life. He was the reason I tried to join the African American Awareness Club earlier that year. Lauren came with me. Our friend Tina had just started dating Brian and it bothered me that everyone referred to him as a "black guy." I always corrected them with, "Why not just Brian? Why does his skin color matter?" By then, Lauren had finally stopped teasing me about dating Martin. We both were interested in learning more about African and African American culture, so we were excited to join the group.

When we showed up at the first meeting, there were already seven or eight kids there. They were all black, and older than us. Not one said hello, or welcomed us. Instead, they just turned and stared. One girl glared. She didn't say one word, but her look said, "What the hell are you doing here?"

I immediately felt out of place. Lauren and I quickly found seats and listened to the organizer—a senior who wore wire-rimmed glasses and a button-down shirt—talk about his goals for the club. "We have to empower young African Americans to rise up," he said. "We are not a minority anymore. And we need to show white people that we matter."

I was so confused. Of course he mattered. Everyone matters. But he certainly did not feel that way. He seemed so angry. And he never once even looked at me or Lauren. It was like we were invisible. The meeting adjourned, and no one asked me or Lauren why we were there. If anyone had, I would have said, "My best friend is African." But it was clear that no one was interested in me, or what I had to say. I don't think they were interested in Africa, either. They just kept talking about empowerment. After we left, I said to Lauren, "That was awkward." She agreed, and added, "So much for joining that club."

I didn't include that in my letter, though I did tell Martin that I had joined the Break Dance Club. That also lasted one session, as when Lauren and I showed up, once again we were the only white girls. Everyone else was Asian.

I also told him about the mix tape I was making for him. I'd been making lots of mix tapes for my friends that year, so it was fun to make one for Martin, especially since he might not know all the music American kids were listening to.

I had this radio cassette player with a microphone attachment, so I could tape-record my own voice as well as music. One weekend, I spent two hours making a recorded letter, introducing all my favorite songs along the way.

"And now, here's Pink singing 'Most Girls...'" I'd say in a goofy fake radio voice, and then hit PLAY and, "Most girls want a man with the bling bling" filled the space right behind my voice. I also included "Who Let the Dogs Out," which had become a huge hit that summer, and Eminem's "The Real Slim Shady," my latest obsession. His photos, torn from magazines, were quickly replacing the Backstreet Boys on my bedroom wall.

I ended the letter asking Martin about his father's employment status, and catching him up on the latest drama in our home: namely that Richie had moved back in:

Richie felt as though he was making poor decisions at California University and needed to be home to have my parents guide him back to make the right choices.

That was code for Richie preferred partying to going to his classes and so my parents refused to pay for another semester until he straightened out.

I included some candid shots from Christmas, including a photo of my new car, and one of me with Lois.

I have enclosed a few photos for you. I hope you like them! I feel pictures help us

"know" each other better. This is important
when you come to the US to study!!!!
Have a wonderful summer (winter in
Hatfield) and give your family lots of
hugs and kisses from me.
Love Caitlin.

PS Here's some of my Christmas money
for you, too.

I didn't tell my parents that I sent Martin cash this time,
but I knew by now they would not mind one bit.

PART 4

A Future

Martin
—⚏—

CHRISTMAS PASSED WITHOUT MENTION. We couldn't even listen to music on Caitlin's Walkman, as we wore out the batteries. While we still had money in our savings account, we knew better than to use it for batteries or even special vegetables or chicken feet. My mom wanted to guard every penny to make sure we had enough to cover our rent and school fees. She continued to look for work, as a maid or helping in someone's garden, in exchange for food. My father kept looking for new employment as well, along with hundreds if not thousands of other men from Sakubva. It was bleak.

By then, our American friends were literally keeping us alive. We were beyond thankful. So when another box arrived on January 10, everyone was surprised. Caitlin's family had already given us so much. This package was totally unexpected and as large as the first one. I was most excited about the large pieces of waterproof canvas that Caitlin sent to put on our roof. The rains had been so heavy and unrelenting that year that water seeped through the floor and between several spaces in the walls. George caught a nasty cold—and had a cough so deep, I worried his lungs would collapse. His little body would convulse each time he hacked, which was so often, it kept everyone up at night. My mother blamed the dampness and tried to fill the holes with sticks and straw. That did not work. So when a neighbor suggested trying paper, my mother wound up using all we had: Caitlin's letters.

She didn't tell me until after the fact. One evening in early January she pointed to the three spots where she used several letters to stuff between the slits. They were already mashed into a pulp.

"I chose the shortest ones," she explained, sensing my disappointment.

"It's fine, Mai," I lied. I understood why she did it, but seeing Caitlin's words used as wall putty hurt my lungs.

So when I saw that Caitlin had sent tarps, and read why, I was elated. That same day, Nation and I spread one large plastic sheet over our roof and secured it with the strong elastic cords Caitlin had packed as well. We lay another tarp on the floor of our hut, and enjoyed our first dry night's sleep in more than two weeks. The rain boots were also a big hit. There was a pair for everyone, including George, and ponchos, too. I had seen people wearing these waterproof capes in town before and thought they looked foolish, to be honest. Skin is waterproof. Soon I understood how nice it was to walk around in the rain without getting your clothes soaked. This was a revelation.

As were the water purification tablets. So many people fell ill each year during the rainy season, as Chisamba Singles didn't have a proper sewage system. The water overwhelmed the streams and ditches, which led to contamination and deadly cholera outbreaks. The newspapers ran weekly reports on the rising toll—thousands of people were becoming sick from unsafe drinking water. The buckets Caitlin sent meant we could collect rainwater, and the tablets ensured that it was safe to drink. That alone saved my mother hours every day and saved all of us from the threat of contaminated water.

In that same package, I received my first pair of dungarees and my first pair of shoes: real Nikes. I could hardly believe my eyes. I tried to stay calm. The last ones Caitlin had sent were too small. If these didn't fit, I would give them to someone else. I was giving myself this internal pep talk as I removed them from the box and unlaced them. When I slipped my foot in, and then tied the first one closed, my face broke into a wide grin. They were a little big, but worked. Wearing them and my new denim pants, I felt closer to Caitlin than ever. Like a real American.

I wanted to send her something in return, but what? There was no news to report. Things in Zimbabwe were as dismal as ever and getting worse with the cholera outbreaks and increasing poverty. So I decided to wait for my O-level results to post. Hopefully, they'd offer a bit of good news and another way to thank Caitlin for all she had done for me.

The morning that the scores were due, I headed to school early. There, I saw my friend Patrick.

"Congratulations!" he said.

That was odd, I thought. Results were not usually posted for everyone to see. Your teacher gave your grades individually. I passed another student on my way to the classroom, who said, "Way to go, Martin!" Another shouted, "Number one!"

There was a line of students ahead of me when I arrived to collect my results. When my teacher saw me, he stood up and said, "Martin! We're so proud of you!"

I felt the hair stand up all over my body.

"Thank you, sir," I said. "I'd like to know why!"

"Because you got nine As," he said. "Out of nine tests."

I was speechless.

"Your scores were not only the highest at our school, but in the entire region," he said. "You should be so proud."

Everyone in the class was applauding and some even started to ululate. I fought the tears that had flooded the backs of my eyes and made my mouth taste slightly salty.

"You should become a doctor!" someone said. "Or a lawyer!" another chimed in.

"Martin, this means you can be whatever you want to be," my teacher said as he handed me the envelope with my scores. "Mr. Samupindi would like to see you before you leave."

I could smell the smoke through the headmaster's door when I knocked.

"Enter!" Mr. Samupindi said.

He stamped out his cigarette when he saw me and let out a deep belly laugh.

"Martin, you just set a record for our school," he said.

I was shaking from happiness.

"You must go on for A-levels, of course," he continued. "And I think you should consider doing them at Marist Brothers in Nyanga."

"What's that?" I asked.

Mr. Samupindi told me it was a boarding school that was more like a college campus—students sleep, eat, and study there.

I immediately thought of the kids I sometimes saw boarding a bus at Sakubva station when I worked at the market. They stood out in their matching navy-blue blazers with a golden crest on the front pocket. Some even wore cricket hats. I asked Nation why they were dressed like that, and he said they were students at a prestigious school—that must be Marist.

"You'll meet students from all around the country," he said. "And you won't have to worry about any issues at home. Your job is simply to study and do well."

This sounded like a dream.

"But how?" I asked. "It must be expensive."

"Yes, and worth it," he explained. "Students there become doctors and politicians. There must be scholarships for bright students like you. Or perhaps your American benefactors could assist you."

My mind was swirling. Fifteen minutes earlier, I was planning on doing my A-levels in Sakubva, with all my other friends. Now I was being encouraged to apply to a private school in some faraway place where I would have to wear a suit to class. It was chaotic, in a good way.

"Sir, A-levels start February nineteenth, less than two weeks away," I said.

"Those test results are your ticket, Martin," he said, slapping me on the back.

I left his office with all these exciting thoughts bouncing in my head like those small silver balls in a pinball machine. This school was my jackpot.

I saw Elias, who had heard my good news.

"You did it!" he said, slapping my back.

"How were your results?" I asked.

He got six As and three Bs and was number two in our school. I started to really understand how significant my results were.

"What have you heard of Marist Brothers?" I asked.

Elias whistled, and then said, "It's the best school in all of Zimbabwe!"

A few other friends had gathered around. "Oh, Marist is the place!" one said. "You can become whatever you want if you go there," another added.

My head was still swimming with these thoughts when I arrived back home. I showed my mother my grades.

"I'm so proud of you, son," she said, her eyes growing glassy.

When my father learned the news, he started to sing "You are the champion of the world!" at the top of his lungs. This brought Nation running, who lifted me off the ground when he heard the news, and started running down the path, holding me by the waist, shouting, "Martin is going to be a doctor!"

Everyone was so happy—but none was as happy as I. My future was looking bright for the first time—and I had Caitlin to thank.

February 2001
Dear Caitlin and family

Hallo! How are you doing over there? Thanks greatly for the great and big parcel with beautiful expensive easy to use items. Thank you very very very much. I have received the nice fitting dungarees and shirts of real quality! I don't know how to thank you for the Potable Aqua. It is of utmost usefulness here in Mutare, where some of the piped water could be unsafe for drinking especially in summer now when we are experiencing heavy downpour....

I want to thank you for your efforts to improve our lives. I received the parcel on 10 January 2001 so sorry for a bit of delay. I wanted to include the results of the O-level exams that you paid for. I had distinctions in all nine classes/subjects, i.e., an A in every subject. I have photocopied my results for you to see. If possible I am kindly asking you to help me with my levy and fees since they are now more expensive and I need to buy some textbooks to supplement those at school. If impossible, please do not strain yourself. I'm doing advanced maths, advanced physics, and advanced chemistry. I hope to go to an overseas medical university in the US, since my ambition is to become a doctor.

I forgot to write that I have the best grades in the whole of Mutare. So I just want to give God the best of glory and you, too, for maximum support both emotional and financial.

I was very happy to hear that you (Cait) received a large gift, a nice car. I really congratulate you and another bunny. I'm not worried that you named her Lois but I think this will strengthen our friendship and families. I am happy that you liked the photos we sent.

I want to thank you for the
Christmas money you gave me. That
was great of you. That money has
helped our declining cash reserve.
Thanks very much.
We all send you great greetings and
wish you the best in all you are doing
over there.

Your loving and faithful,
Martin

I sent the letter off, and then continued to ask people about
this amazing private school. No one knew anyone who went
there, or how to apply, so I decided to find out for myself. I
found a bus that left Sakubva every morning for Nyanga. It
took three hours, I was told, which meant I could make the
trip there and back in one day.

On the bus, I watched the industrial outskirts of Mutare
give way to grasslands where an occasional scraggly tree
punctuated the sunburned bush. Nyanga is northwest of
Mutare, in Manicaland, home to Mount Nyangani, Zimbabwe's tallest mountain, and Nyanga National Park. Every so
often, I'd see a skinny cow or several patchy goats nibbling
roadside. Less frequently, we passed a cluster of traditional
mud and grass-roofed huts. It felt like I was headed to the
middle of nowhere.

I finally arrived in Nyanga and was shocked at how small

and slow everything seemed compared to Sakubva. The town has roughly two thousand residents, a post office, a bank, and a few small shops. Several women were selling mangoes and peanuts at the bus stop, a roadside dirt patch. One lady was selling sadza, and though I was hungry, I decided to wait to buy something for the trip back later that evening.

I asked an elderly man for directions to Marist Brothers.

He pointed down a different dirt road, that led away from the town's small center.

"I meant the school," I said.

"Yes," he said. "Marist Brothers School is that way."

I looked down the road, which disappeared into a forest.

"How far?" I asked.

"About thirty-five kilometers," he said.

"Is there another bus that will take me there?" I asked.

"It left two hours ago," he said. "Try again tomorrow."

I was planning on taking the five PM bus back home, so I started jogging down the new dirt road, hoping to hitch a ride. An hour later, I heard a rumble behind me. I turned to see a pickup truck in the distance, kicking up dust in its wake. I planted myself in the middle of the road and started to wave my arms. This was my chance.

The truck slowed down and a man my father's age peered out the window.

"Marist Brothers?" he said.

I took it as a good sign that he thought I was a student already. I nodded.

"Hop in," he said. "I'm making a delivery."

The back of his truck was filled with onions, potatoes, carrots, and kovo—food for the dining hall, he explained. My mouth started watering.

I was so relieved to be moving quickly again.

Twenty minutes later, we emerged from the forest and a lush green lawn unfurled before my eyes. We parked in front of a freshly painted building where dozens of guys in navy-blue blazers, white shirts, and gray flannel pants were milling about. A few wore the cricket hats. I had made it.

I hopped out of the truck, proud to be wearing a Caitlin shirt and my Nikes. I wasn't wearing a suit, but I fit in.

I quickly found the headmaster's office and asked the secretary for a meeting.

"Mr. Muzawazi will be back late tonight," she said. "You can see him tomorrow morning."

"I'm due to head back to Mutare this evening," I explained.

She suggested I speak with the deputy headmaster, Mr. Nyamandwe, right down the hall. I told him I wanted to do my A-levels at Marist Brothers.

"You and every other bright boy in Zimbabwe," he said, barely looking up from the papers on his desk. "School starts next week, and we're full. It's impossible."

"There must be a way," I countered.

We went back and forth. When he saw that I wouldn't take no for an answer, he said, "Well then, I suggest you see the headmaster tomorrow. He's the only one who can find room for you."

"I wasn't planning to spend the night," I replied.

"Go introduce yourself to some of the students," he said. "Someone will surely find you a bed."

"Thank you, sir," I said. "I promise you will see me studying here this year."

"I don't see how," he said, shaking his head.

Outside, I scanned the courtyard. All the students looked the same in their pristine uniforms, but then I noticed one kid was wearing cheap sandals sold at the Sakubva market we called Rafters. All the others were wearing leather shoes or sneakers. As I made my way closer to this one guy, I overheard his accent and knew he was from the rural areas. He spoke as if he were singing, more lyrically than the tight and clipped way of city people. When someone called him Rabbit, my hunch was confirmed: He was from the countryside, even worse than Chisamba Singles. He probably didn't even have electricity where he came from. He would understand my dilemma.

I introduced myself, and then told Rabbit my story. His eyes lit up. "You must see the headmaster tomorrow," he said. "He will listen."

Rabbit told me that he also came from a very poor family but was the top student at his school.

"I'm here on full scholarship," Rabbit said. "The headmaster set the whole thing up."

This made me hopeful.

Rabbit gave me a campus tour. Each classroom had individual desks, and the library was bigger than the one I had snuck into all those months, lined with books floor to ceiling.

"Twenty-four-hour access," Rabbit explained when he saw my eyes pop out from my head.

The dorms were large rectangular rooms with six beds lining either side, a locker in between each. Rabbit took me to his.

"This is where you sleep?" I asked.

"You can get used to a mattress, Martin," he said with a wink.

"I would like to," I replied, laughing.

"Last year, I was eating one meal a day in Marange, sleeping on dirt," he said. "Next year I will go to medical school in Harare."

That afternoon, Rabbit introduced me to many students. He was very popular—all the guys respected him. Every time, he said, "Meet my new friend Martin! He's coming to school here!"

I started to believe him.

The dinner bell rang at five PM. My stomach rumbled in response. I hadn't eaten since seven AM. I followed Rabbit and two friends to the huge dining hall, which had twelve long tables, one per dorm. Rabbit found an extra plate for me, and grabbed two forks and knives. This made me nervous. I had never used silverware before—we ate with our hands at home. I kept my cool as we found our seats with ten other guys. I could tell by their haircuts and shoes that they came from wealthy families. They appeared blasé about this place, like they expected life to be this way. Rabbit, however, remained amazed and amused. He knew poverty—and privilege.

A platter of steaming sadza came out first, followed by several heaping bowls of beans. My mouth was watering, but I waited for Rabbit to make the first move. He kept talking with friends. Then the rice and kovo arrived. I'd never seen so much food on one table. One kid asked, "Any meat tonight?" The server replied, "Not tonight, but definitely tomorrow." The kid who asked looked disappointed. I was speechless.

Rabbit helped himself to everything and told me to do the same. I waited for Rabbit to start eating, to watch how to hold a fork. Mine felt clumsy in my hand. Rabbit must have sensed my discomfort, because he said, "You can eat with your hands. No one will judge you." I looked around and saw every single kid was using a fork. I tightened my grip and dug into the steaming pile of beans on my plate. Some fell onto my lap, but thankfully no one seemed to notice. I quickly picked them up and popped them into my mouth. The second try was more successful and before long I had finished everything on my plate. Rabbit encouraged me to have more. After my third helping, I was so full, my stomach ached. One guy noticed how much I ate and called me the bean eater. As we walked back to the dorm, two other guys said, "Oh, you're the kid who ate all the food!" Everyone laughed, including me.

I didn't mind. I still couldn't believe that much food was possible. We couldn't finish it all. I asked Rabbit what they did with the leftovers.

"They throw it out," he said. "You and I know how crazy that is. But these guys have no clue."

Most of the students were the sons of judges, politicians,

businessmen, and soccer stars. Their families lived in houses in Harare with maids and had not one but several cars. None of them had ever known hunger.

I continued asking Rabbit all the questions bombarding my brain: I'd found the perfect guide.

That night, Rabbit secured a bed for me in his dorm room. Another bell sounded, which meant it was time for quiet hours. Rabbit informed me that everyone got up at six AM. Breakfast was at seven, followed by an eight o'clock church service on the lower campus.

"The headmaster will be there," Rabbit said. "That's your chance."

I thanked Rabbit for all his great help and said good night. As I lay down and pulled the covers up to my chin, I thought, This can't be happening. I had never slept on a mattress, let alone had my own linens. At home, I shared one thin blanket between two brothers. These sheets felt crisp and cool on my skin, and the blanket was heavy yet soft. It warmed me immediately as I pulled it up, all the way to my chin. I closed my eyes and listened to the faint breathing of my roommates as I drifted into one of the deepest sleeps ever.

A siren startled me awake. I hopped out of bed and followed Rabbit to the showers. I turned on the spigot and laughed out loud when warm water came rushing out. I had only ever bathed with cold water before. Rabbit laughed as well—the only person in the room who understood what was so funny.

Breakfast was eggs, toast, and porridge. Beans were one

thing, but eggs were even a bigger luxury and unheard of where I came from. And yet there I was helping myself to not one but two. I turned to Rabbit before I began to eat and said, "I love this place!"

Mass took place in an old stone church with all the students on both the lower and upper campuses. Following the sermon, a large man with a big bushy beard and matching Afro that floated on top of his head like a crown approached the podium.

Rabbit elbowed me. "That's him," he whispered.

As soon as everyone was dismissed, I went looking for this formidable man. He was outside the church chatting with students. Everyone else was in a suit and tie, so I stood out in my Nike shirt and shoes. When Mr. Muzawazi spotted me, he said, "You must be Martin Ganda. Follow me."

We walked to his office, where several people were already waiting to see him. I took a seat and waited until his secretary called my name.

As I walked into his office, he asked, "I hear you wanted to see me?"

"Yes, sir. I want to do my A-levels here," I started to explain, but he cut me off.

"You're too late! We're already filled up," he said. "Besides, there are many qualified students here who need to get in; we don't even have space for them."

"I've come all the way from Chisamba Singles to speak to you," I countered. "Please give me a chance."

That quieted him.

"I have an uncle that lives near there," he said. "That's a tough place."

I saw that he was impressed and I just kept building up on that—I told him that I had been kicked out of school time and time again for lack of fees, and still managed to graduate number one in my class.

"Okay, let's look at your grades," he said.

As I handed him the envelope, I said, "I got the highest grade in my school—and in all of Mutare, too."

"How did you do this from Sakubva?" he asked.

"Hard work and study, sir," I explained.

"What does your father do?" he asked.

I think he expected me to say "teacher," so when I said that my father lost his factory job after sixteen years of dedicated work, Mr. Muzawazi was even more surprised. I explained that my parents didn't even finish their O-levels, and that they were barely literate. And I added what I knew was the urgent truth: that I was their only hope. As I spoke, I felt a big ball of emotion forming in my chest.

"Sir," I said finally, "this is my only chance. If you don't allow me this opportunity, I'll die a poor man."

"And if you do come here, what next?" he asked, his tone softening.

"I want to go to university," I explained. "I have young siblings. We're sharing one room; there's barely enough space for us to sleep, let alone for me to study."

"Okay," he said. "Get me a deposit by tomorrow at five PM and I will find room for you."

My mind started reeling.

"How much?" I asked.

"One thousand Zimbabwe dollars will secure you a spot," he said. "The rest will be payable by the middle of March."

The deposit alone was four months' rent, impossible to access in twenty-four hours. We didn't even have that in our savings, which was already earmarked for living expenses. I thought of asking Caitlin, but she was too far to get the money so quickly. Then I thought of Alois. He worked in a bank. He may be willing to help—and was my only chance.

"I can do that," I said, reaching out my hand to shake on it.

"Then you will be a student here," he said.

He knew he was asking me to do the impossible, but he also believed in me.

I thanked the headmaster and ran out of his office. It was eleven AM, and I was in the middle of nowhere. There was a lot to accomplish in thirty hours. I quickly caught a ride to Nyanga and hopped a bus back to Mutare. When I arrived home, I told my parents everything and then went to call Alois from the post office. I tried him at home first. No answer. Then I tried his cell. No answer. I tried him at home again, and was thrilled when I heard, "Hallo?"

"Alois, it's Martin," I said—and then breathlessly recounted the entire situation, from getting the highest O-level scores to the headmaster's offer. "I promise to repay you, cousin."

"Let me see what I can do," he said.

"They need it by tomorrow," I explained. "School starts the following day."

246

"What else do you need?" he asked. The headmaster gave me a list of supplies required to attend Marist Brothers, which included the uniform and a specific trunk, all of which I needed by Tuesday.

After I rattled off everything on my list, I heard Alois speak to Sekai.

"You are in luck," his voice boomed through the receiver. "Sekai can come to Mutare tomorrow morning to help gather all these things."

"Fantastic!" I shouted.

Sekai and Alois understood how important this was.

The next morning, Sekai stepped off the bus looking as beautiful and vibrant as I remembered her.

"We have a lot to do, cousin," she said. "Let's go."

Sekai was paying for everything—so I had already crossed off unnecessary items, like the tracksuit, the extra shirt, and the lace-up shoes. I had to get the black metallic trunk, to store my personal belongings. Everyone had one, including Rabbit. Back home, I filled it with a few clothes from Caitlin, notebooks, and a blanket my mother had secured for me.

"I traded this for work," she said. My mom had picked up a part-time job working as a maid for a wealthy family. I didn't know how many hours it would take her to pay off such a lovely thing, but it became my most prized possession, my connection to her. I packed my Walkman, a few cassette tapes, and a dozen or more of Caitlin's photos.

After dinner, I walked Sekai to the station to say good-bye.

"Alois is very proud of you, Martin," she said right before

she boarded the bus. "He'll do his best to get the deposit in time."

I clasped both my hands around hers and bowed my head into our interwoven fingers.

"I don't know how I can repay such kindness," I said. "But I promise you, I will."

Sekai smiled and said, "Focus on your studies, Martin— that's all we want in return."

I barely slept that night. After the first rooster crow, I jumped up. My new uniform was draped over my trunk. Slipping into the long pants and proper shirt and jacket that morning made me realize that my life was truly about to change. I felt ready.

My trunk was too heavy to carry to the bus station, so my family accompanied me to the main road, where I hailed a small tut tut taxi. I hugged my younger brothers and sister good-bye. Before I got in the vehicle, my mother placed both hands on my shoulders and stood on her toes to look in my eyes.

"Work hard," she said. "Don't do crazy stuff there."

My father put his arm around me and said, "You'll do just fine. You have made us so proud."

"I will miss you, brother." Nation was the last to say good-bye.

"And I you," I replied. "All of you."

As the taxi took off, I realized I wouldn't see any of them again for months. I felt sad as I watched my family, still waving, disappear. Then I realized, I'm doing this for myself, and for them. I was starting a new chapter.

In Nyanga, a van collected me and a few other students. I quickly found Rabbit, who had saved a bed for me, next to his.

"I knew you'd be back," he said.

This meant we shared a cabinet, too. His side had several photos pinned to it. One of his family visiting on parents' day, another of his girlfriend back home. I started unpacking and took out the photo of Caitlin wearing her sun hat.

"Wow," Rabbit said. "Who's that?"

I pulled out all the other photos and started telling Rabbit about Caitlin.

"So she's your girlfriend?" Rabbit asked.

"She's my best friend," I countered.

By then, a small crowd had gathered around to look at the pictures of Caitlin, her family, dogs, house, and her new car.

"She looks like a movie star!" Bonaventure said. His bed was on the other side of mine.

"Is that how you got those Nikes?" asked Gregory, another dorm mate.

The questions kept coming rapid fire. Finally, I put up my hands and said, "Okay guys, enough! I have to unpack!"

When I was done, I adhered all of Caitlin's photos to my locker with tape borrowed from Rabbit. From then on, I was no longer known as the bean eater, or the kid from Sakubva, but as the new guy with the gorgeous American girlfriend. I didn't argue. They would never understand our bond. Besides, it raised my cache on campus.

Caitlin

———— ⊗⊗⊗ ————

I WAS HANGING OUT AT the food court in the mall when I spotted Austin. I knew him through Heather—they were dating even though he went to Pennridge, a rival high school. That meant the other three boys he was with probably went there as well. One of them was really cute. My friend Amy saw me staring and said, "I dare you to go talk to him."

Propelled by the thought of kissing the tall, lanky boy with the sandy-brown hair one day soon, I stood up and heard Amy say "No way" as I walked across the court. The boys must have heard, too, because they turned toward me as I approached.

"Hey, Austin," I said. "What's up?"

"Not much," he said. I was waiting for an introduction, but couldn't stand the suspense. I turned to my new crush and said, "Hi, I'm Caitlin. And you're really cute."

His other friends all busted out laughing, including Austin, who said, "Your move, Damon."

Damon's cheeks turned red as he looked away for a moment before turning to me to say, "Okay, well, you're cute, too."

I found a slip of paper and a pen in my bag and wrote down my number.

"Call me," I said, and then walked back to my friends, who each high-fived me when I sat down.

"I cannot believe you just did that!" Amy said.

I couldn't, either, but loved the warm tingly feeling flooding my body.

My friends and I popped into Aeropostale to try on the skinny cargo pants that were all the rage. There, I fell in love with a backless halter top and a leather miniskirt that I dreamed of wearing on my first date with Damon. I hoped he'd call.

As we rode the escalator up to the next level, Amy spotted Damon and Austin below.

"Caitlin, there he is," she said.

"Hey, Damon," I shouted as all my friends laughed. He looked up at me and I blew him a kiss and winked. I'd always been outgoing, but even I was amazed at my forwardness.

That night, I was in my room when my cell phone lit up with a number I didn't recognize.

"Caitlin?" I recognized the gravelly voice and felt that same tingly feeling again. He called.

We talked on the phone for over an hour that night. I told him I was about to turn sixteen, and that my dad had already bought me a car.

"I've actually seen it," he said. "I dropped Austin off at Heather's last week, and I noticed it in the driveway."

"You drove past my house?" I said.

"Your driveway looks like a parking lot," he responded. "And your car stuck out."

I got goose bumps. "Well, now you know where to come pick me up!" I said.

Damon showed up the next day. My mom and dad already knew he was coming over. They were very cool about my having boyfriends, as long as they got to know them.

"Nice to meet you, young man," my dad said, greeting Damon at the front door.

Damon and I went to the mall to meet up with Heather and Austin, both of whom were excited that we could now double-date. I was, too. Damon was different from the guys I dated in middle school. He was more mature, and sensitive. I understood why when I met his dad. He had MS and was in a wheelchair as a result. That meant he needed full-time care to do anything from eat to go to the bathroom. Damon's mom took care of his dad, and basically let her kids fend for themselves. His parents turned the downstairs den into their bedroom, and let Damon and his older brother take over the second floor, which meant they could drink beer and smoke pot in their rooms, as their mom never really checked on them.

The first time Damon offered me pot in his house, I was mortified. My mom had recently found Richie's bong in a brown paper bag in his underwear drawer. She took the bag out to the garage, smashed it with a hammer, and then put the bag of broken shards back in the drawer. I kept waiting for Richie to get yelled at—and so did he. The look of fearful anticipation on his face remained for days. She never said a word, which was somehow worse than being grounded.

I knew better than to bring pot or any paraphernalia into my house, but I thought it was cool that Damon could. I also liked that I could tell him anything. We were in his room hanging out when I first told him about Martin. At first I worried that he, like everyone else, would think Martin was my boyfriend. After I told Damon the whole story starting from the first letter to the phone call with Mr. Samupindi, he smiled and said, "That's so cool."

April 2001

Martin
—〰—

I SETTLED IN TO MY school that Tuesday and waited for confirmation that Alois had sent the funds. Everything was happening so fast, I did not have time to write Caitlin with my news. I wanted to wait for everything to be settled first. The fees were due by five PM. When Wednesday morning arrived, I woke up nervous. At breakfast, the deputy head-master called several students' names, including mine. We were all instructed to report to the bursar's office. This felt too familiar.

I was the first in line at the bursar's office, desperate to know the status.

"The deposit did not arrive," he explained.

"There must be a mistake," I said.

"Regardless, it was due yesterday," he responded.

"I know my cousin will pull through," I said. "May I call to see what the holdup is?"

The bursar gave me a week to sort things out, so I reported

to my first class that morning confident I could. The teacher entered the room and all of the students took out their notebooks and got quiet immediately.

"Mangwanani, class," the teacher said. That was the only Shona spoken for the next forty-five minutes. Classes were taught in English, and all of my teachers were brilliant. I felt like a dried-out sponge being doused with water. I soaked every word up, and wrote each one down verbatim. By the end of the day, my hand was aching. So were my arms, as each class came with its own textbook. When that first teacher handed them out at the start of class, I was in awe as students wrote their names inside the covers.

I held back from raising my hand to ask the question straining at my lips: "We get to keep these?"

That evening, I lugged seven textbooks back to my room and carefully placed them in my locker.

"There are thousands more books at the library," Rabbit said. "And you can use them at any time."

No more sharing, or borrowing, or sneaking around, I thought. This was my heaven.

At the end of my first week, I saw how challenging my new school was. My classmates were smarter and more diligent than any I had encountered before. I decided to go study at the library, like I did in Sakubva. I thought I could get ahead that way, and so I was shocked to find I was not the only one with this idea. Kids didn't brag about sneakers, or music, or money. Instead, they'd say, "I stayed up until four AM studying." The harder you worked, the cooler you were.

I knew I could work hard and keep up with the rest academically, but not if the money didn't arrive. Alois sent me a message on Friday—he needed a few more days. I spent that weekend feeling enormous dread, knowing at any moment I could be kicked out.

Monday morning arrived and all of the A-level students were called to an assembly after breakfast. The headmaster spent fifteen minutes giving everyone a pep talk. "This is your chance to show the world how smart and dedicated you are," his big voice bellowed across the wood-paneled room where we all had gathered.

I was standing in one of the back two rows, with my class. The upperclassmen were in the front two rows. Everyone was dressed for inspection, which came next. The headmaster walked from one student to the next, eyeing each up and down, and whispering notes to the deputy, who followed him with a book. If your shirt was wrinkled, or your hair was a mess, you would get written up.

"Stand up straight," Rabbit had coached me earlier that morning as we all walked toward the assembly. "And don't look him in the eyes. Just look ahead." I did as I was told, and thought I made it when no notes were taken in front of me. But then the headmaster resumed his position at the front of the room and bellowed, "Jonathan Chinweze." Jonathan raised his hand. "Lovemore Mugonda," the headmaster shouted. Another hand shot up. And then he said, "Martin Ganda."

Electricity coursed through my veins as I lifted my arm in the air.

"Come see me in my office," he said, before dismissing the rest of the students.

As I walked down toward the office with Jonathan and Lovemore, my head was spinning. How could I raise this money? I had to stay. I couldn't imagine going back to Sakubva now.

I was the first to go in.

"You said your cousin in Harare was going to pay Friday, but nothing happened," Mr. Muzawazi said. "I have protected you as long as I possibly can. It would not be fair to the other students if I kept allowing this to happen."

"I understand, sir," I said. "Please allow me to make one last call. I will tell my cousin if we don't receive the funds today, then it's over."

"Fair enough," he said.

I went directly to the secretary, who placed the call. When Alois heard my voice, he said, "Perfect timing! I just sent the money this very minute!"

"This is such great news!" I said as all the tension drained from my body. "I was sure I would be taking a bus back to Chisamba Singles this evening."

Alois explained that it was more difficult than ever to sell stocks these days, as the market was on the verge of collapse. "I could help with the deposit, but I won't be able to do anything more," he said. "You'll have to find another way."

I said I would, and then reported the good news to the receptionist. "Please let the headmaster and bursar know to expect the deposit today," I said. I did not mention the rest of the tuition. I first had to figure out how I could get it. That would take some time. And I did not feel I could ask Caitlin for this much money. It was twenty times more than my school in Sakubva, and she was already supporting my family. It was too much. I decided to just throw myself into my work. Perhaps, if I did well, the headmaster would make an exception. All I knew how to do was study. So I focused on that.

By the end of the semester my grades were good and I had never once gotten called out for a messy room or rumpled jacket. I even got the highest grade on an early math test, but I knew that wasn't enough to keep me in school. The semester was coming to an end and I still hadn't figured out a way to raise the rest of my tuition. I kept focused on my work and prayed for a miracle.

The last Monday in March, the headmaster announced that anyone who still owed tuition was going to be sent home the following week. I knew he was talking about me. That familiar feeling of dread consumed me.

That morning, the headmaster called my name with three others. I was sure it was over. I was heading back to Chisamba Singles.

This time, I wasn't first in line. I did not want to learn my fate but savor every last second I had as a Marist Brothers student.

I watched as the three guys before me left his office with their mouths tightly drawn, or trembling. When the headmaster called my name, I felt like I was walking to the guillotine.

I entered his office with my head down.

"Martin, I have good news," he said.

I thought it was cruel of him to make light of something this serious. I glared at him. He was sitting at his desk, his hands behind his head, like he was stretching. I wanted to punch the smile off his face. This was my livelihood, my future. All those months of stress turned into rage, now boiling in my belly. I remained quiet. I had nothing left to say.

"I'm on the board of this company, and they offer scholarships," he explained, handing me a piece of official stationery that said *DELTA CORPORATION*.

I was trembling as I read the note:

Dear Sir:

This is to inform you that Martin Ganda is a recipient of the Delta 2001 Scholarship Award for two years up to A-level exams.

Kindly send the school invoice for the whole year for the above named student. Payment will be made directly to the school.

Thank you for your assistance.

Yours faithfully,
G. T. Mutendadzamera
Corporate Affairs Manager

I looked up at the headmaster, who said with a huge grin, "You may now return to class."

I slowly turned toward the door, still reeling from this news.

"And congratulations on your math score, young man!" he said. "Keep up the good work."

All I could say was, "Thank you, sir. I will."

When I left his office, I started to sprint. There were so many emotions swirling inside of me, I started running down the driveway toward the main road with the scholarship letter rolled up in my right hand. I felt like the runner who starts every Olympic game. This was my torch! And my ticket. When I was far enough away, I started to ululate. My cries floated up in the air, and caught on the tree branches above, where they startled birds into flight. I kept singing, and running, tears now streaming down my face, until my vocal cords started to ache and my lungs felt empty. I slowed to a walk and drank in the country air as if it were a cold glass of water on the hottest summer day. And then I turned around to walk back up to class.

Caitlin

WHEN MARTIN SENT ME HIS O-level scores, I wanted to make copies and hand one to everyone who doubted him, and me.

"Remember the grifter scam artist kid from Zimbabwe you warned me about?" I'd say in my revenge fantasies. "Well, guess what? He just got *nine* As on a national exam. *All* As." Then I'd whip out his report card and say, "See?!"

I never once doubted Martin, and so I wasn't in the least bit surprised that he did so well. And now that my mom finally figured out how to send him money safely, I could focus on being sixteen.

I celebrated my birthday that March with my extended family. My grandparents from both sides came, as did several aunts, uncles, and cousins. My mom added another table to the end of our dining room table, which extended into the adjoining living room to fit everyone. She bought me an ice-cream cake from Dairy Queen and I got lots of presents, but the best gift was being able to finally drive my car. The day after my birthday, my mom took me out of school to go get my learner's permit. Damon met me at the DMV—he had skipped school, but lied to my mom when she asked him why he had the day off.

"Parent-teacher conferences," he said. I knew that wasn't true; we had planned the whole thing the night before so we could spend the day together. My mom fell for it.

We'd only been dating for a month, but I was falling in love with him. He was my first serious boyfriend, and more independent than any of the guys I'd ever dated, probably because his parents gave him so much freedom. Like us, they started dating in high school. Damon's mom was sixteen when she had Damon's older brother. Damon's dad was diagnosed with MS when he was twenty-one, a year after Damon's little sister was born. His mom was so busy taking care of his dad that Damon was the only guy I knew who could cook dinner, wash his own clothes, and make sure his little sister did her homework. He also helped teach me how to drive, which I'd been doing for a month when I received more good news from Martin.

He wrote that he had won a scholarship to a prestigious private school two hundred kilometers north of Mutare, in a town called Nyanga. I pulled out the new atlas of Africa that my mom had bought. I had already circled Mutare and Harare on the Zimbabwe page. I wanted to circle Nyanga, too, but no matter how hard I looked, I couldn't find it. Neither could my mom.

"It must be really rural," my mom said.

Martin also wrote in his letter that he was even more serious about coming to university in the United States. That news made me want to do cartwheels and a backflip. I read that section of his letter out loud to my parents.

"Can you imagine?" I said. "We'd finally get to meet him!"

"I can," my mom responded. "Lots of international kids come to school here. Martin is so bright, I'm sure he could even get a full scholarship."

He sent the list of universities he was interested in applying to, which included Harvard and the University of Pennsylvania. He asked me to contact each to have application material sent to him at his new school.

"That will be good practice, Caitlin," my mom said.

I was halfway through my sophomore year, which meant I needed to start thinking about college myself.

At the time, I was thinking about pursuing a degree in technical education. It was my favorite class. We did mechanical drawings using a computer-based program called CAD. It came so naturally to me that my teacher encouraged me to consider it as a career. That was the first time I even thought about my life after high school. I was in awe of how organized and focused Martin was. In his letter, he said, *My aim of becoming a doctor is to help some primitive Zimbabweans who still resort to traditional medicine and end up dying. My other aim is to increase the number of doctors in Zim because there are few and cannot serve everyone.*

Inspired, I logged onto our computer to send a few

requests on Martin's behalf. I started with Harvard and then let out a deep sigh as I sent the last e-mail.

"Everything okay, hon?" my mom shouted from the other room.

"Everything is more than okay, Mom," I said as I clicked the computer off. Martin was going to come to school in the United States, I thought. I felt it in my bones.

Martin
—∿—

AS MUCH AS I LOVED going to Marist Brothers, I missed my family. Nation would write every so often to keep me posted on things. Thanks to Caitlin and her family, money wasn't an issue. Knowing my family wasn't going hungry or homeless allowed me to study worry free.

Still, I couldn't wait for the semester break, which started in late July. I was so eager to see everyone, and was all the more disappointed to learn that my mother was not well. She got out of bed to greet me, but then had to lie down immediately afterward. Nation had mentioned that she was ill in a letter I received a few weeks earlier at school. I was surprised that she had not recovered. Everyone assumed that it was a bad flu or cold. But the following day, she did not even get up to make breakfast. Nation said she had been sleeping a lot lately. He was concerned. After she spent two consecutive days in bed, I was, too.

Malaria and cholera were rampant in Zimbabwe. Both are

potentially fatal. I wanted to get her to the hospital as quickly as possible. This was no easy task. The closest clinic was only five kilometers away, but due to a fuel shortage, there were no taxis on the road. I was lucky to get a bus back to Mutare, as gasoline prices had skyrocketed, costing Z$110 per liter. Even if we had money to spend on a taxi, we couldn't find one. Instead we borrowed our neighbor's wheelbarrow, which I lined with a blanket for padding. Nation and I gently placed her on top of it, taking extra care not to startle her, as she winced at the slightest jostle. Everything hurt. She was thinner than usual, and delirious with a fever that drenched her with sweat. We covered her with another blanket and took turns pushing.

"We must move quickly," I said as my mother moaned in her sleep. If she had cerebral malaria—and it entered the brain—it meant permanent damage.

The rainy season had turned the roads to mud, which made pushing the wheelbarrow that much more difficult. I was thankful we had Caitlin's boots and rain slickers. While one of us pushed, the other held our new umbrella over our mother.

After two hours of pushing, I was relieved to finally see the hospital in the distance. We neared the entrance and I saw that there was a line of at least fifty people waiting to be seen. We joined the end and I ran ahead to see if there was any chance of bumping my mother to the front. As I walked toward the admitting door, I passed many people who looked worse off than my mother. One woman was limp, almost lifeless, in her husband's arms. An older man was covered in open sores that wept clear liquid like tears. I returned to our spot and told Nation we had to wait like everyone else.

My mom was so weak that she barely knew where we were or how we got there. She looked so small, almost childlike, curled in the cart. Her breath was so shallow that I placed my hand on her throat several times to make sure life was still pulsing through her veins. It was so faint, I worried that she might die, right there, as we waited. If that happened, what would we do? My mother may have been strict, and tough on all of us, but she was the spine of our family. We walked upright because of her. Caitlin was the reason I could go to school; my mother was the reason I wanted to. She had to survive. Life without her was too terrible to imagine.

Hours later, a nurse confirmed it was malaria—thankfully, not cerebral. She needed IV fluids immediately. She was so dehydrated that she was at risk of dying without them. But the hospital couldn't afford to supply any medicine. Instead, the nurse told us what we needed, and then we had to secure it.

"There is a man outside wearing a blue shirt," she said. "He sells IVs."

She told us to look for another guy in a red bomber jacket, who had the pills my mother also needed. Both were selling drugs like people sell fruit or wood carvings at the market: out in the open, negotiating prices, haggling. If you didn't have the money, or something worthy of trading, you were screwed. I had heard that people died all the time because of this. Now I saw how it was possible. Nation and I both knew how lucky we were to have enough money to get my mother what she needed, but we did not mention it. Nor did we speak the more terrifying truth: Without Caitlin's help, my mother would have died that day.

As soon as the nurse gave my mother the IV and pills, she perked up. It was like giving water to a droopy plant. When she sat up in bed for the first time that evening, I fought back tears. She was going to be okay, but needed to spend another two days in the hospital, to gain back strength. Nation and I returned home with the good news. My father let out a deep sigh. It filled our small hut and escaped out the door, taking so much tension with it, as if he'd been holding his breath for weeks.

I returned to the hospital the following day with food for my mother, since there was no meal service there, either. This time, Simba came with me. He needed to see for himself that she was going to be fine. Nation and I returned the following day with our neighbor's wheelbarrow to bring her home.

My mother didn't want to get back in it.

"I'm not an animal to be carted around," she said.

"Of course not, Mother," Nation said. "But it's a long way home."

Finally, we convinced her it was more dignified to ride in the wheelbarrow than on either son's back, the only other option. She complained the entire way home. This made me happy. She was her old self. It meant she was going to be just fine.

With her safely back home, I could finally relax. That included seeing my friends and going to the post office, as I had heard there was another package for me. Caitlin hadn't mentioned anything, so I was intrigued.

This box was filled with pencils, pens, crayons, glue, and erasers. Caitlin's mom included a note that explained that her students had donated these things. *Take whatever you and your family need and share the rest with your friends and neighbors*, she wrote.

What a joyous task, I thought.

Caitlin also sent another two pairs of sneakers. The Filas fit me perfectly, so I gave Nation my beloved Nikes. Simba got the other pair, which meant now we all had proper shoes. Nation did a karate kick in his new shoes, and Simba copied him. I would have done one, too, but I was still unpacking: toothbrushes, shampoo, disposable razors, and a pair of cargo shorts that would impress my wealthiest friends at Nyanga. I couldn't wait to show them off when I returned to school. The most fascinating gift was a container of bright orange powder called Tang. The instructions said to mix it with water. My father got a cup and Nation went to fetch water from our jug beneath the bed. Following the directions, I spooned two scoops into the cup, added water, and stirred. Lois put her nose to the cup and said, "It smells like Starburst!"

I handed her the cup to have the first sip.

"Tastes like it, too!" she said.

I tried it next, and agreed. "Like Fanta without the fizz," I said, passing the cup to Simba. We each had a sip before giving it to our mother, who was still weak.

"Finish it, Mai," I said. "The jar says it has vitamin C, which will make you strong."

PART 5

A Changing World

Caitlin

I HAD NEVER HEARD OF malaria before Martin told me that his mother had it. I looked it up online and was startled. How could somebody die from a mosquito bite? It made no sense. Then I remembered a line from an early Martin letter where he wrote about Zimbabwean hospitals. He said that many people share one bed. And then he wrote *Fun.* That comment confused me back then, but now I know he was being sarcastic. There was nothing fun about any of it.

I read that quinine was used to combat the disease, which was potentially fatal if not treated. One website reported that Tylenol could help ease the symptoms. My urge to jump on a plane with two suitcases packed with pills was great. Instead, I went to Heather's house to talk to her dad. He worked in the pharmaceutical industry. I figured he could help me figure out what to send, and the best way to do it.

"Caitlin, you cannot send medication to Zimbabwe in the mail," he explained. "It is illegal."

Too bad, I thought as I walked back home. My mom bought aspirin in bulk, and I had already put aside two extra-large bottles for Martin and his family. Now I just needed to figure out how to get them to him without getting arrested. I asked my mom to talk with Solange, who confirmed what Heather's father had told me. Then one day I was talking to my nan, who is my mother's mother.

"Doesn't quinine help?" she asked.

"It does," I said. "Why?"

"I have a bottle you can have," she said.

"Nan, are you sure it's quinine?" I asked, slightly exasperated. How could she have malaria medicine? She'd never been to Africa.

"I'm sure," she said. "My doctor prescribed it for leg cramps, but it made me nauseated. The bottle is sitting in my medicine cabinet!"

I was flabbergasted. My grandmother had pills that could save Martin's mother's life.

"I will take them!" I said.

After we sent the last package to Zimbabwe, my mom set up a new box in the corner of our dining room—a place to put things for future deliveries. Richie was still living at home, going to community college. I hardly saw him, but I did notice one night that he'd thrown in a few T-shirts along with a pair of sneakers. I added Nan's quinine pills and two bottles of Tylenol.

By then, I had started my junior year at North Penn and enrolled in a woodworking class.

On my first day, before I even sat down, the teacher said, "You have to wear covered shoes in this class."

I was wearing my favorite wedge flip-flops and assumed he was joking.

"That's ridiculous," I said.

"Well, if you value your toes, and I can see you do, then you would want to protect them with proper shoes," he responded sternly. "I recommend steel-toed boots."

My mom and I went to the nail salon every Friday afternoon. That day, my toenails were painted a pale purple with silver swirls, which stood out against my black sandals. Stunned, I looked around the room and saw that I was the only girl in what was otherwise a sea of boys. They all wore sensible shoes. I grabbed my book bag and headed straight to the guidance counselor's office.

There, I sat down with a woman who reminded me of my mom. I told her my predicament.

"Don't you have closed-toe shoes?" she asked.

"I do," I explained. "But I don't want to have to wear them every day."

We discussed my dreams and goals beyond college, and when I told her I was considering mechanical drawing, she sighed.

"That means you would have to take other classes like woodworking, where there are uniform rules," she said.

"Well then, I need to think of a new career," I answered. I know it sounds silly, but I didn't want to be in a profession where I couldn't wear open-toe shoes. Period.

I explained the entire situation to my parents that night over dinner. My dad remained quiet.

"Well," my mother finally said, "you're the only one who knows what will make you happy. And it's better that you figure that out now than later!"

The only problem was that I had no idea what I wanted to be. I actually felt a bit jealous of Martin's focus. I knew I had the freedom of choice, but I was finding it difficult to settle on one.

A few days later, I woke up late, as usual. After hitting snooze for a third time, I dragged myself into the shower. Heather and I made it to school just in time for the first bell, which meant I got to class just as everyone was saying the Pledge of Allegiance. I was waiting to get called out by my teacher, but she seemed preoccupied. She asked everyone to take a seat and then stepped into the hallway.

During my first period, my home economics teacher asked us to open our textbooks and do an exercise, which was also unusual. I was on my way to third period when I saw a few teachers huddled in the hallway. One was crying.

Finally, in my fourth-period history class, our teacher made an announcement.

"This morning two planes hit the twin towers in New York," he said. There was a collective gasp as he switched on the television in the front of the room. The two skyscrapers looked like smokestacks, each spewing thick, billowy black clouds. A street view showed hundreds of people craning their necks, looking up in shock. Our teacher flipped through a few channels—every single one was talking about the twin towers. In another shot of one building, it looked as if Godzilla had taken a big bite out of its neck. Flames poured out of the gaping wound. It was like watching a horror movie, yet this was real.

All anyone talked about that morning was what was happening in New York City.

After lunch, I was in the auditorium waiting for English class to start when Richie came flying through the doors. He spotted me, and waved.

I waved back.

He yelled, "Caitlin, get your stuff. We have to go. Now."

I knew it must be serious, so I grabbed my book bag and started making my way down the aisle.

"What's up?" I said when I reached him.

He grabbed my elbow and started ushering me out of the auditorium.

"Mom told me to come get you," he said.

"Why?"

"Haven't you heard the news?"

"About the World Trade Center?" I asked.

"And the Pentagon?"

"No," I said, still unsure of what any of it had to do with me.

"Caitlin, another plane also crashed in Washington," Richie said. "The government is on lockdown—and we don't know if or when they may strike again."

"Who are they?" I was getting more and more anxious with each snippet of information.

Richie was five paces ahead of me, both physically and mentally.

"Where's Mom?" I asked. She'd make sense of all of this for me.

"She has to stay with her students at school," he said as we got into his car.

"Why do I have to go home now?" I asked. "We're not in any danger."

Richie must have sensed my panicked confusion, so he finally stopped to look me in the eye before he turned the ignition. "There was another attack in Pennsylvania," he said. "North Penn High is right between Washington and New York. Mom thinks it's an easy target and does not want to take any risks."

Those words sucked all the oxygen out of the car. I cracked open the window.

"And," he said, pulling out of the school's driveway, "Mom hasn't heard from Dad. He went to a military base this morning, Caitlin, and has not called since. She wants you and me to stay at home until we know he's okay."

I started connecting all the pieces: My dad worked for the government; he was at a military base; the Pentagon had been hit. I jumped to the impossible notion: My dad may be dead. I shook my head. That was preposterous. But then I remembered the fire I saw in the sky on the TV earlier that morning. That seemed impossible, too.

Once home, I clicked on the TV. The images were even more frantic, as the buildings had collapsed by then.

It looked as if it was snowing in downtown New York. I heard a reporter say, "The ashes are scattering as far as Brooklyn," and turned off the TV. It was too much to take in.

An hour later, I heard the dogs barking. Mom was home.

I ran downstairs.

"Have you heard from Dad?" I asked as soon as she walked in the door.

Her face was slick with tears so new I guessed that she must have just been sobbing in the car. When she shook her head, more tears sprang from her eyes. I ran over to give her a hug.

"He's going to be okay, Mom—he has to be," I said as I squeezed her. But I was not sure. All kinds of crazy thoughts went through my head, but rather than sit in front of the TV with my mom, I went up to my room and put Incubus on my CD player.

"I dig my toes into the sand," the song started slowly. When it hit the "I wish you were here" chorus, I turned the volume up.

Three hours later, the phone rang. My mom shouted, "Thank God it's you."

I ran down to hug her as she continued to talk to my dad. I'd never been happier hearing his deep voice booming through the receiver. He said that he had been stuck on the military base, which was on red alert. All cell service was blocked. He was finally on his way home.

I stayed home from school the next day—and the rest of the week. My parents were rattled by the experience, and so was I. Especially when we learned that the plane crashes were an act of terrorism. I'd learned that word the year before, after the embassy bombings. I never expected anything like this would ever happen on US soil. Damon thought it would lead to a full-fledged war. We talked on the phone every night for hours.

"If there's a draft, I'll have to go," he said somberly one night.

I kept quiet, but there was a maelstrom forming in my chest. The weekend before, Damon took me to Six Flags amusement park. We rode the Vertical Velocity and I had never been so scared in my life. That was just a ride. The thought of Damon leaving to go fight in some faraway war was terrifying in a different way.

"We can go to Canada," I responded. "My family has friends there."

"Baby, I will do what is right for my country," he said.

"I won't let you go!" I said. As those words left my mouth, I understood how everything I once knew to be true about my country had changed in an instant. My safe little world was quickly becoming unraveled.

I thought of Martin for the first time in days. Had he even heard about the attacks? I owed him a letter.

I eased in with a bit about my life in school before getting to the heart of what had been consuming me for the past six days since the attacks.

I guess by now you have heard of the terrible terrorist activities that have plagued our proud nation, I wrote. Those words released a torrent. I shared every single detail of that day, scene by scene. It was the first terrible thing that had happened to my country in my lifetime and I was still grappling with what it all meant. *This tragedy touches all who believe in freedom,* I continued. *Although the terrorists were nameless and faceless, we will recover. Our strength comes from knowing that we are a strong nation who believes in liberty and freedom for all. Our buildings may crumble, our hearts will bleed, we shed openly our tears at the loss of loved ones, but we will survive. These terrorists have not won anything.*

I did not even notice the tears that were streaming down my face until they splashed onto the keyboard as I typed. *Please pray that our leaders find the appropriate answer to all this violence and find inspiration and intelligence to provide the plan to hit this terrorism in its heart.*

There was so much more to say on this issue, one I thought Martin would somehow understand.

September 2001

Martin
—⁂—

BY THE END OF THE BREAK, my mother was back up on her feet, bossing everyone around. I'd never been so happy to wash dishes. On my last night home, Nation and I started laughing about it.

"What's so funny?" my mother shouted as she brought more plates to clean.

"You," I said. She swatted at me, and then went to finish tidying up.

Now that my mother was well, I could go back to school worry free. My bus left for Nyanga at nine the next morning. After breakfast, I said good-bye to my father and siblings. I hugged my mother for longer than usual. Her strength had returned. I could feel her squirm in my grip.

"No time for this," she said, pushing me away. "You will be late for your bus."

"Take care, Mai," I said. "Go easy."

"And you study hard," she responded.

"I will," I said.

On Monday, Mr. Muzawazi started his weekly assembly with a pep talk.

"We are entering the final semester," he started. "Half of you will be finishing your A-levels in December and heading to university to do great things. The rest have one more year to follow in their footsteps."

I had started to think about what I wanted to focus on at college. My grades were good enough to apply for scholarships in Harare, but I was more determined than ever to pursue university in America. Ever since the hospital experience with my mother, I was more determined to study medicine. Rabbit was going to start his medical degree at the University of Harare that January, and I had a few other friends who were planning to do the same. Zimbabwe certainly needed doctors, and I wanted to make a living where I could actually help people.

I was mid-reverie when Mr. Muzawazi began his inspection. For some reason, on that particular day, he was easy on all of us. He walked briskly up and down the aisles nodding and smiling. No one was called out. It was strange in a nice way.

Two days later, at breakfast, another assembly was called. This was unexpected. We all started chattering in the dining hall about what it could be.

"Someone must be in trouble," Rabbit said.

We filed into the assembly area quietly. Mr. Muzawazi was standing at the front with his hands clasped in front of him, his head nodded down, as if in deep prayer.

Once we all had taken our places, he spoke.

"Students, I have troubling news," he said. "There was a terrorist attack on the United States."

A ripple of sharp breaths and "How is that possible?" exclamations went through the rows of students.

"Two planes struck the twin towers in New York City," Mr. Muzawazi continued. "A third hit the Pentagon in Washington, DC. And according to news I read this morning, a fourth plane crashed in Pennsylvania."

I had never heard of the twin towers, though Mr. Muzawazi explained that they represented the financial capital of the United States. We had all heard of the Pentagon, and were shocked to learn that people had died as a result of this tragedy. But what alarmed me the most was the plane crash in Pennsylvania. That was where Caitlin and her family lived. What if the crash was near Hatfield? What if they had been hurt? With each new question, my throat constricted. I had to make sure Caitlin was okay. But how? A letter took two weeks to get to her. I shot my hand into the air.

Mr. Muzawazi stopped mid-sentence, surprised to be interrupted.

"Excuse me, sir," I said. "But do you know where in Pennsylvania?"

He shook his head. "I'm afraid not, Martin," he said. "All we know is that it was in the middle of a field, and everyone on the plane died."

As awful as the news was, it made me feel better. Caitlin

would have been in school and not on a plane. I could breathe again.

For the days that followed, everyone at school talked about the attacks. Not too long thereafter, we learned that the US and Britain were imposing sanctions on Zimbabwe, which was still involved in the Congo. While this was not directly related to September 11, the ripple effects of a changed world were being felt everywhere. The US was targeting any nation that abetted terrorists—that included my country. Still, I wasn't worried about the global consequences—I wondered, would these sanctions impact my relationship with Caitlin? I prayed every night that would not be so.

I also prayed for news from Caitlin, and was relieved to return home for the Christmas break to a letter that said she and her family were fine. As always, her words put all my fears to rest. I wanted to offer her comfort with mine. They were still all I had.

Dear Caitlin and family, I wrote. *I'm so sorry for the terrorist activities that rocked America and led to the loss of innocent lives. We Zimbabweans join you in this period of sorrow.*

I asked if she had heard of the sanctions, and then added, *I pray that all these potential problems and economic tensions between US and Zimbabwe will not affect our deep strong relationship.*

There were so many things I wanted to share with her: namely, that I was considering medical school seriously. Caitlin had already reached out to a few places for me, and then my headmaster even gave me a list of more top schools

285

to pursue. I included several in that same letter: *If you could please contact New York University School of Medicine, Stanford University School of Medicine, University of Washington School of Medicine, University of Michigan School of Medicine on my behalf.* I knew this was a lot, so I added, *I'm sorry for giving you such a huge task. I know it is time-consuming and may be boring. Maybe you don't have to do the whole task in one day, you may do it bit by bit. That is when you are free and feel like you want to do the tasks. So do not strain yourself! I thank you in advance for your help.*

I sent the letter right before Christmas and was amazed to receive one from her only a few days later. Our missives had crossed somewhere over the Atlantic Ocean, I thought as I ripped open the envelope.

Folded in between the pale pink stationery was a piece of silver. It looked like a very thin candy bar. I unwrapped it to find a twenty-dollar bill. I shook my head in disbelief. I'd forgotten to ask for money to secure a passport. I needed one now that I was planning to study abroad. Somehow my friend from so far away must have already known that. This was a sign.

Caitlin

EVERYTHING CHANGED AFTER SEPTEMBER 11. The attacks were proof that there were people who truly hated America. That was a new feeling. It was terrible, but it made me think hard about what it meant to be an American. I shared those thoughts with Martin in my next letter. *The terrorist attacks affected every American. But our country is so great, because we all stuck together in this time of need. We stand behind our government and trust that the terrorists will be brought to justice.*

The words just flowed out of me, as if the experience opened a new valve in my brain and heart. I hadn't heard about the sanctions Martin mentioned in his letter, but nothing could alter my feelings toward him. I made a point of that, writing, *Rest assured the political crisis between Zimbabwe and the US will not affect our friendship.*

If anything, I felt more indebted to Martin than ever. He had already changed the way I thought about the world.

And now he was having an impact on what I wanted to be in it. Ever since he wrote me about going to medical school, I started thinking about becoming a nurse. I told my parents over dinner one night. They were thrilled.

"You will always have a job," my dad said.

"And you have the right disposition," my mom added.

"Plus, if Martin does go to medical school, we can work together," I said.

We all laughed at this thought in a "wouldn't that be amazing" way.

Later that evening, my mom asked me to sit down with her in the kitchen.

"I've been thinking," she said. "Your father and I want to help Martin as best we can, but we cannot afford to send him to college here in the States."

"I know that, Mom," I said.

"But he won't be able to get here without our help," she continued. "You have so much on your plate, I don't want you to worry about helping Martin getting into college as well. Since I'm only going to be substitute teaching this year, I'd like to help Martin find a scholarship."

"That's the best news ever!" I said.

She smiled and then whipped out the letter she had drafted to Martin earlier that day in which she detailed the six universities she had already contacted about international scholarships.

"I didn't want to send this without your okay," she explained.

"You have my full support, Mom," I said. "But I still want to help."

She stuck out her hand and said, "Deal."

We shook on it.

I had already started to reach out to medical schools for Martin, and that process inspired me to make another appointment with my guidance counselor to talk about my own options. I told her I was thinking about nursing, and she asked if I had heard of the dual enrollment program. I had not.

"You only need to take homeroom and physical education next year in order to finish all your high school credits," she explained. "So why not start college at the same time? You can double up, and get a head start."

I was getting sick of high school and loved the thought of getting a head start on college.

"Where?" I asked.

"Montgomery County Community College offers all the prerequisite classes for a nursing degree," she said. "Your grades are good enough to go and you don't need any standardized tests to get in."

"You mean I don't have to take the SATs?" I said.

I went out with Damon the night before the PSATs and bombed them. I was dreading the SATs.

"You would still take them," she said. "But they won't matter."

"How can I sign up?" I said.

Martin

—◊◊◊—

I WAS SURPRISED TO RECEIVE a letter from Caitlin's mom. In it, she offered to help me navigate the complicated American college admission process. I was so happy to hear this. It was further proof that Caitlin was not the only angel in this family.

Anne asked me if I had ever heard of the SATs. I had, in fact, because my good friend Wallace had taken them earlier that year. He, too, was planning to go to school in the States that September.

Wallace lived in the dorm next to me but was always in my room because he was close friends with my roommates Bonaventure and Cornelius. We called Wallace "Lobe," short for Lobengula, the Ndebele warrior who fought the white colonialists when they invaded in the eighteen hundreds. Wallace was very buff. He worked out all the time, lifting weights. But he was also very calm, quiet, and reserved. He never said much unless you asked him direct questions, which was why I didn't learn sooner that he was going to the US to study. When I did find out, I started grilling him. That's how I found out his brother was already attending college in Canada, and that his parents owned a bed-and-breakfast in Victoria Falls, where he grew up. Despite his family's wealth, Wallace was humble, not showy like so many of our other classmates. I asked him one day why that was so, and he explained that his father was the first in his family to go to university, and that many of his relatives lived in the rural areas and were even worse off than my own parents. He understood poverty, even though he had not experienced it firsthand. He never judged me for mine. Instead, he inspired me to be the first to escape it in my family, like his father had.

When I received Anne's letter, I asked Wallace where I could take these SATs.

"You sign up for them through the Internet," he explained.

This was yet another reason I needed access to a computer. Anne had already mentioned that all of the information I needed for college was online, and she had recently asked if there was any way I could communicate with her via e-mail to save time, as it took a month for letters to get back and forth. There was an Internet cafe in Mutare, but I wouldn't be able to use that until I went home for break. I was getting frustrated, but then Wallace told me that Mr. Muzawazi had a computer—and online access—in his office.

I made an appointment to meet with Mr. Muzawazi, who was pleased to hear I was pursuing university in the States.

"Terrific news, Martin," he said.

"That is why I'm here," I explained. "I'm having trouble finding all the necessary information. I need access to the Internet."

"I see," he said.

"And so I was wondering if I could borrow your computer from time to time," I said. This was a lot to ask. I had to offer a compelling reason.

"I'd only use it after hours to correspond with my pen pal and her mother as they are helping me gather material," I explained.

"Other students have managed to get into universities abroad without a computer, Martin," Mr. Muzwazi responded. This was going to be a hard bargain.

"Yes, I understand, sir, but those students come from wealthy families," I said. "I will only be able to do it if I find an international scholarship."

Mr. Muzawazi remained silent.

"Caitlin's mother said she'd help me, but she needs to be able to get information quickly," I explained.

"Okay," Mr. Muzawazi said.

"Plus, I must register for SATs online," I explained. "Wallace told me this is the only way."

"I'll talk with my secretary," he said finally. "And we'll arrange to get you a key. You may use my office after hours."

"Fantastic," I said. I held back from hugging Mr. Muzawazi. He was not a touchy-feely guy, but after five years of waiting for letters to cross the Atlantic Ocean, this meant immediate access to Caitlin and her family.

"You can start this evening, after dinner," Mr. Muzawazi said. "But do not let word out. No one else is to use my office computer. This is our deal, okay?"

"Absolutely, sir," I said. "You have my word."

"And you have mine," Mr. Muzawazi said.

I left his office elated.

Later that evening, I returned to Mr. Muzawazi's office. The key was left for me with a note from his secretary explaining how to open the door, and how to turn on the computer.

I had only used a computer twice before in my lifetime, to type letters. Both times, the machine was already turned on. I walked up to the large beige box on Mr. Muzawazi's desk. Wires sprouted out its back side. That's where I found the power switch and watched in amazement as the screen buzzed to life. A row of numbers and letters appeared at the top corner, as if the machine was speaking its own language. Then a box appeared asking for a passcode. I typed in the secret word the secretary had supplied for me, written in neat capital letters on the school stationery. Next, I followed her specific instructions for getting online and accessing the school's only e-mail account.

Anne had sent me her e-mail address, and Caitlin's as well. I decided to send each one a message as an experiment. I had never sent an e-mail before, and the concept that they would receive it moments after I hit SEND was something I couldn't begin to grasp.

Hi Caitlin! I typed into the green screen. **It's me! Martin! My headmaster has allowed me to use his personal computer.**

Isn't that exciting? Please respond to this address so I know you received this. Your forever friend, Martin.

I hit the SEND button and the message disappeared with a whooshing sound. I worried that it may have done just that—disappeared. I sent Anne the same e-mail. And then I started to research SATs in Harare. I finally found the website and learned that I needed a credit card in order to register. I didn't have one nor know anyone who did. I made a note of it. Anne would know what to do. Then I started to look up other requirements for African students to go to the United States for school. Two hours later, I had two pages of notes and a heart brimming with hope.

August 2002

Caitlin

I HAD JUST LOGGED ON to the family computer when I saw a strange address pop up. The subject line said **CAITLIN!!!** I clicked it open and almost fell off my chair. I had been wishing for easier access to him, especially now that my mother was on a crusade to get Martin a full scholarship. Being able to e mail him made all the difference.

"Mom, look!" I shouted.

She needed some good news. Her quest was already off to a shaky start. She decided to start with Gwynedd Mercy, her alma mater. She thought Martin would be most comfortable at a Catholic school since Marist Brothers was one. And she also thought such a school would be open to supporting an impoverished African student.

"Plus, I was secretary for Kappa Delta Pi, an international honor society," she explained to me the week before. "They know me well there. This should be a breeze."

So she was particularly upset to learn earlier that week that Gwynedd Mercy rebuffed her request.

"Hypocrites!" she said.

"What happened?" I asked. I'd just finished the afternoon shift at Ray's and smelled like a pepperoni pizza. I kicked off my sneakers, and Kava started licking their soles. She figured out quickly that mozzarella cheese was often stuck in the treads.

"I called Sister Barbara today in the financial aid office and told her about Martin," she explained. "And she just cut me off and said, 'We don't offer financial aid to international students,' which I know isn't true because I had several friends who were there on scholarships from different countries."

"How weird!" I said.

"It gets even more weird," she continued. "I started to tell her Martin's story and was barely halfway through when she cut me off again and said, 'We're not giving this boy a scholarship.' "

My mother's jaw tightened and her nostrils flared as she continued her story.

"So I said, 'Sister Barbara, Martin is my daughter's best friend and through no fault of his own, he can't attend a US college on his own. So when our daughter said please help him, I immediately thought of Gwynedd Mercy's mission—to help those who cannot help themselves.' "

"What did she say to that?" I asked.

"She said, and I quote, 'We can't help him.' I think they wanted me to sponsor him myself. I think they thought I was wealthy because I had been so generous in the past in my giving. So I said, 'Okay, well then, you'll need to take my name off of the giving list. And the money I donate every year for the library? Not going to happen, because that's now all going to Martin Ganda.'"

"Wow," I said. "So what's next?"

"That's only one of ten Catholic schools in the area," she said. "Tomorrow I'll hit La Salle and Saint Joseph's in Philly, and then on Thursday I will drive over to Villanova."

"Aren't you glad you don't have to do this for me, too?" I asked. My community college program was just about to start, which meant no college applications, no tours, no essays. I was so relieved I didn't have to jump through all those judgmental hoops. And I was so thankful my mom was willing to do it for Martin.

By the end of the week, my mom seemed to have made up her mind.

"Villanova is the place," she said. "The campus is gorgeous and every student I met was friendly. One young man even asked me if Kava wanted water."

"You brought Kava?" I asked.

Our giant schnauzer was now snoring on the couch in the den.

"She's good company," Mom said. "Plus, she's a good test. When I walked her across the Saint Joseph's campus, all the kids ignored me."

"Maybe they were just shy?" I said. "Or busy?"

"Caitlin, they were all too cool for school, pseudo-city

sophisticates," she responded. "Nyanga is so rural, it does not even register on the map. And don't forget, Martin, no matter how intelligent, did not own shoes until six months ago. We have to pick carefully."

With that, she switched on our computer and sat down to start sending Martin her updates. Now that he was up on e-mail, she was sending him two to three messages a day. I still preferred writing him letters. I would write an occasional e-mail about college-related things, but those were always quick notes. I saved my thoughts and feelings for pen on paper. They felt more tangible and permanent, a real connection.

Martin
—ᗑ—

I SAID GOOD-BYE TO WALLACE right before our school break that August. Our school year doesn't end until December, but he'd been accepted to an American university and was leaving school early.

"You must reach out to my friend Caitlin," I said, handing him a slip of paper with her e-mail address, and her mother's as well. "They're good people. Do not hesitate to get in touch."

"I promise I will," Wallace said. He was packing his trunk up with all of his things. His uniform lay on top of his weekend clothes, books, and bed linens, likely never to be worn again.

"And don't forget to write me as well," I said. "I'll come looking for you next year."

"I know you will," Wallace said. "I will do anything to help."

First I had to get a scholarship. Wallace's parents were resourceful, so they had figured out a way to pay his tuition for him. I had to find another way.

I returned to Chisamba Singles for August break more determined than ever. People often asked if I was jealous that Wallace might meet Caitlin before I did. On the contrary, the idea filled me with joy. It was another step toward my finally meeting her.

As was collecting my passport. I had received a letter at Nyanga that said it was ready for pickup in Mutare. I went to get it my first day home. I had heard from friends at Nyanga that it was near impossible for most Zimbabweans to get passports. The international sanctions made the economic situation even worse; people who could afford to were fleeing the country. But Mr. Muzawazi said he'd make a call. The father of a Marist Brother student ran the passport office in Mutare, he told me.

That morning, I woke up early and went to the market with Nation. He was still selling clothes from Mozambique with three other friends. They traveled to the border, less than thirty minutes away, to buy bales of used clothing, which they then separated into piles: Nation sold shoes, his friend Cliff took the T-shirts, another guy would hawk jackets, and the fourth gathered up whatever was left. The used clothes market is huge in Zimbabwe. When Americans donate their old clothes to Africa, they often wind up being sold in markets. Nothing in Africa is free. It was not Nation's favorite job, but since things did not work out with his soccer career, it was better than nothing.

I helped him carry two big bags of shoes to the market. There, he laid down a tarp and placed the shoes side by side, like soldiers: worn-out pink Skechers, tattered blue Nikes, once-white tennis shoes, work boots missing laces. All of them had seen happier days, but for poor Zimbabweans, they were better than bare feet. As my brother began bargaining with an older man who wanted the boots, I scanned the market and was struck by how much bigger it seemed from the last time I had worked there a year earlier. More and more people were out, selling, hustling, bargaining, and trading. I saw so many familiar faces—neighbors as well as kids from my old school now scrapping with one another to carry luggage or pour tea. I spotted my friend Peter, still selling cold drinks.

"Martin!" he shouted as I waved to him. "Where have you been?"

I told him about Nyanga, and how I was hoping to go to university in the United States.

"I'm headed to the passport office right now, friend," I said.

"You're on your way to great places," he said.

"From your lips to God's ears," I said, offering him my fist, which he tapped with his.

The passport office opened at nine o'clock and I expected a long line, so I took an 8:05 AM bus. Shockingly, I was the only one there. I entered the squat cement building that looked more like a bunker than an official government office.

"I am here to collect my passport," I told the receptionist.

"Right this way," she said.

I followed her into another room, where a man in a navy

suit asked me for my birth certificate and the letter that stated my passport was ready for pickup. I produced both, and he handed me my passport within five minutes. I stood there, holding this small green book, waiting for more instructions.

"Is there anything else, sir?" I asked.

"No, that is all," he said.

Clearly, Mr. Muzawazi's assistance had worked.

My travel documents were in order, my family was doing okay—thanks to Caitlin and her family—and I even had a friend going to the US, leading the way for me. The only worry I had was that I had been doing quite a lot of thinking about pursuing medicine. The images of those people waiting on line at the hospital haunted me and often kept me awake at night. I wanted to help my fellow countrymen but had grown concerned that I did not have the stomach for it. I loved numbers, and was good at them. And so I decided to pursue actuarial science. I wanted Caitlin to know this immediately, as she was putting great effort into finding me scholarships at medical schools. I knew she'd understand. She had recently written me about changing her career focus to nursing. That gave me the courage to shift my own course.

As I walked toward the exit, I flipped through the many blank pages in this pocket-sized book waiting to be filled. I couldn't wait to get home and write to Caitlin.

Caitlin

MARTIN HAD ONLY EVER MENTIONED his family in letters before, so Wallace stood out. That he was actually coming to the United States was beyond thrilling. If Wallace could do it, Martin could, too.

The only problem was, Martin did not mention which school Wallace was going to. We'd have to wait for Wallace to get in touch. The thought made me giddy.

It was an exciting time for me. I'd just started my dual enrollment program. That semester, I had signed up for five college classes: English 101, General Psychology, history, liberal arts, and calculus, which I dropped quickly. I still hated math, but I liked being surrounded by older students who wanted to be there. It was so different from high school.

I'd always gravitated toward older kids. Damon was a year older than me, as was Heather, my neighbor. She had left for college, and I missed her. But Damon was still around. He wasn't interested in college, though, and couldn't understand why I was.

"Why don't you just work more shifts at the pizza joint?" he asked earlier that summer. He'd started working full-time at a factory in nearby Sellersville that made unfinished furniture. People could paint the chairs or dressers any color they wanted. He was happy doing that, but I wanted more out of my life than waitressing could afford me. I started to worry that he wanted me to be more like his mother. She married his father young and gave up any plans for college or a career to take care of her husband. Even though his father was disabled, he ruled the house. His mother jumped when his father said to. That was not the life I wanted for myself.

I worked every Wednesday and Saturday at the pizza parlor, and spent every spare moment in between doing homework. I never cared about it in the past, but I loved college and wanted to do well. It wasn't easy, and it left hardly any time to hang out with Damon. When I started studying with Jeremy, an older guy in my English class, Damon got jealous.

One night, he called me four times in a two-hour period. I was studying for my very first psych exam and didn't want to be bothered. By the fourth call, I thought it must be serious.

"Is everything okay?" I said, instead of hello.

"Why haven't you been answering my calls?" he said angrily.

"I told you I was studying," I said, wishing I had not picked up.

"You're always studying," he said. "It's bullshit."

"Actually, it's my future," I said, incensed. "You giving me a hard time about it is bullshit."

I stayed on the phone listening to his rants for fifteen minutes and then simply said, "I'm not going to argue with you about this. I have a test tomorrow. If you really loved me, you would want me to do well."

And then I hung up.

The next day, I aced my psychology test.

Martin
—∿—

BACK AT NYANGA, TWO E-MAILS were waiting for me.

One was from the SAT board telling me I was registered for the December 7 test date in Harare. It was happening.

My heart was racing as I opened the second e-mail. That was from Wallace. He hadn't been able to get in touch with Caitlin or Anne.

As for the e-mail addresses you gave me, he wrote, **it is a pity that none of them actually works. I tried them all but to no avail. Could you do me a favor by sending them to me one more time. I might have missed a spelling or phrasing.**

I e-mailed him back immediately to let him know my SAT exam date was set and to confirm Anne's e-mail address. I wanted to write a PS, that I would see him very soon. That I would one day be an African student studying in the United States, like him. But I decided to wait. I did not want to jinx it.

Caitlin

———— ⌾⌾⌾ ————

RICHIE WENT TO VISIT TEMPLE UNIVERSITY in Philadelphia that September and decided he wanted to transfer there in January.

"It seems like a super-fun school," he said.

"Fun does not necessarily mean good," my mom said.

"Or pay the bills," my father added.

"Jeez," Richie interjected. "I was also going to say that they have all the marketing courses I need to finish my degree."

"That sounds more like it," Mom said.

Ever since Richie got pulled out of college for choosing partying over studying, my parents had been giving him a hard time. The rule in our house was that you get one opportunity to screw up. Richie was still living at home because he had not figured out his best next step, and he knew he couldn't mess that one up.

I kept quiet. It irked my brother that I was taking freshman classes at the same community college where he had just finished his sophomore year. Earlier that week I teased him that if he didn't focus, I'd graduate before him.

"That will never happen," he said through clenched teeth. I knew better than to push any further.

A few days later, my mom finally got an e-mail from Wallace. Neither of us could believe where he was studying: Temple University.

"Richie was just there," my mom said excitedly. "He could have taken him out to lunch if we had known."

"He may have walked right by him," I said, getting goose bumps at the thought.

It felt like a sign, and we needed one. Mom was still gunning for Villanova for Martin but had also sent at least a dozen requests for scholarships to nearby schools. One had offered fourteen thousand dollars, half of what Martin needed. This was promising—colleges were at least interested in sponsoring Martin—but we needed a full ride.

"Maybe Wallace will have ideas," I said to my mom as she was going down her list.

"My thought exactly," she said.

She was planning to visit him the very next day. I was sad I couldn't join her. My schedule was so full, I barely had time to see her, let alone drive back and forth to Philly in the middle of a school week. We already agreed that this would be the first of many visits. My best friend lived ten thousand miles away from me, and his close friend just happened to get in to a school forty-five minutes away from our house.

The next night, I was up in my room studying when I heard

my mom's car pull into the driveway. I ran down the stairs. She had barely opened the door when I started pummeling her with questions.

"How was it?" I asked. "Did you take any photos? What's he like? Did he tell you about Martin?"

"Why do you want to know?" she teased.

"*Mom!*" I said. "I need to know everything!"

She told me that she arrived at his dorm room and was stunned to find his side practically empty.

"His roommate had a comforter and matching sheets, posters on the wall, and a computer set up on his side of the room," my mom said. "And Wallace had nothing—not even a pillow or sheets."

Her description reminded me of the photos Martin sent of his family. I wondered if Wallace's family was too poor to buy him things as well.

"I don't think he knew what he was getting himself into," my mom said. "So I made a list."

My mom spent a week gathering things on her list and by Friday morning had several shopping bags brimming with linens, clothes, and toiletries. We'd deliver them that night.

That day dragged on. My last class ended at 3:15. I watched the clock throughout the ninety-minute lecture, convinced it was broken. It took forever for the bell to ring.

Damon wanted to come as well. I wish I could say it was because he was sincerely interested in meeting Martin's dear friend. Honestly, I think he was just being protective and even a bit jealous.

Dad came home early from work and we all piled in Mom's Jeep Cherokee. My family rarely went to Philadelphia, so it always felt like an adventure. Temple was like a mini city itself. As we walked toward the dorm, we saw college-aged kids hanging out on building stoops smoking cigarettes, or playing Hacky Sack. It was Friday evening, so everyone was in a good mood. The security guard called up to Wallace's room to say he had visitors, and within minutes Wallace emerged through a door tentatively. He walked toward us with his shoulders hunched around his ears, his neck disappearing into his polo shirt like a turtle about to retreat.

"How do you do," he said, extending his hand toward me.

"I'm Caitlin!" I said, bursting inside, like I swallowed a firecracker.

"Yes, I know," he said. "Martin has shown me your photos."

I couldn't contain myself: I threw my arms around Wallace and said, "It's so amazing to meet you!"

I felt his body stiffen, so I pulled back to introduce him to Damon and my dad, each of whom were holding two huge shopping bags.

"We've already met!" my mom said, opening her arms to give Wallace another hug.

She must have felt his body tense up, too, because she said, "Wallace, one thing you'll learn about us quickly is that we're huggers."

His eyes grew wide and he let out a nervous laugh before saying, "That is fine. Would you like to see my room?"

"Lead the way," my dad said. "And Wallace, I'd like to clarify, the women are huggers in my family. When I set these bags down, I'll give you a proper handshake."

"Good," Wallace said, sounding relieved.

We entered his room to find his roommate lying on his bed listening to his Discman. He barely acknowledged us, or Wallace, as he rolled off the bed and walked out the door. I could tell from that short interaction that he was a total jerk.

Mom wasn't exaggerating: His side of the room was totally set up. He had tapestries on one wall, and photos of his grungy friends back in Seattle on his desk. His closet door was open, and stuffed with clothes. I opened Wallace's closet and saw that he had exactly two pairs of pants neatly folded on a shelf, and two hanging shirts.

My mom started unpacking bags.

"Damon, unwrap the comforter," she said. "Rich, the rug goes there. Wallace, this is an alarm clock. Do you know how to use one?"

I started hanging up the new clothes she bought for him, and was relieved to see that she had brought hangers as well.

Meanwhile, Wallace stood in the center of the room saying "Thank you, thank you" over and over again.

"You don't need to thank us!" my mom said. "Martin is like our son. And since you're his friend, that means you are part of our extended family as well."

Wallace bowed his head and said thank you again.

"How are things going at school?" I said, hoping to get him to open up.

"Fine," he said.

"Have you made any new friends?" I asked.

"Not yet," he said.

The entire conversation consisted of me asking questions and Wallace offering one- and two-word answers. At least I was trying. Damon stood in the corner of Wallace's room with his arms crossed. I wished he had just stayed home.

Within thirty minutes, Wallace's side of the room felt at least lived in, and my mom was making him try on the winter coat she found on sale at Ross.

"It snows here, you know," she said.

"Have you ever seen snow?" Damon finally asked a question.

"No," Wallace said. "But I'm very excited to do so."

An eight-word answer, I thought. He's opening up.

"I'm starving," my dad announced. "Let's go eat."

We had already chosen the Hard Rock Cafe in downtown Philly because it was typical American food, and only a short distance from the campus. I had never been, so I was excited. We walked to the car, where I squeezed in the middle between Wallace and Damon.

On our way to the restaurant, I interrogated Wallace about Martin.

"He's very smart," Wallace said. "And so funny."

"I knew it!" I exclaimed. "I can tell from his letters."

"Did you know Martin is from the bush?" Wallace said.

"I thought he was from Mutare," I said.

"He grew up there, but his people are from very rural areas," Wallace said. "Mine are, too."

Just then, my dad pulled into a parking lot by the historic Reading train station where the Hard Rock Cafe was located. As we got out of the car, I wondered how many other things I did not know about Martin.

Inside the restaurant, "Hot in Herre" was blaring on the speakers so loudly that the crystal chandeliers shook above us as we followed the hostess to the purple leather banquet reserved for our party. I slipped in first and told Wallace to sit next to me. Damon made a sour face, like he'd bit into a lemon. I didn't care. I could talk to him whenever I wanted. Wallace was the only person I was interested in that night.

Our waitress appeared with menus. She was wearing a short-sleeve shirt, which exposed the elaborate artwork that covered both of her arms.

I noticed Wallace's eyes widen as she passed him a menu. I leaned in and explained, "Those are tattoos." The space between his eyes crinkled. He then opened his menu and looked startled. I understood why. There were three columns of different dishes per page.

"Order whatever you want!" Damon said, finally trying to be nice.

"Do you like cheeseburgers?" my dad asked.

"I've never had one, sir," Wallace responded.

Everyone laughed at our table—except Wallace.

"Well, there's a first time for everyone!" my dad said.

I pointed at the list of cheeseburgers—there were more than twenty to choose from.

Wallace's eyes grew glassy.

"Do you want me to order for you?" I asked.

"Actually, I'm not very hungry," he said. "I had a late lunch."

"We'll order a bunch of different things, and you can try whatever you want."

"That sounds fine," he said, closing the menu.

After we placed our order, I continued grilling Wallace.

"How tall is Martin? What's his best subject? Does he have a girlfriend?" Wallace knew all of the answers.

"Quite short, math, and no, not to my knowledge," Wallace said. "Nyanga is an all-boys school."

Our food order covered the entire table. The cheeseburgers took up half the plate, and the French fries spilled over the sides. A slice of tomato was as large as the hamburger patty itself. Even I was shocked by the excess. Wallace had a bite of a cheeseburger, and tried a French fry and an onion ring. I think he liked all of it, but I could not tell if he was just being polite. My mom asked for all the leftovers to be boxed.

"You can take it back to your dorm room," my mom said.

"That's not necessary," Wallace said.

"I insist," my mom countered.

"I don't have anywhere to keep it," he responded.

"That's why we're going get you a mini fridge after dinner!" my mom said. That was news to all of us, including my dad. We got back into the car and drove to the nearest Sears, where we purchased a refrigerator the size of a large TV set.

Back on campus, we set up Wallace's new fridge and then filled it with food once it was plugged in and humming.

Just then his roommate walked in.

"Whoa," he said.

"Yeah, whoa," I responded. Then I turned to Wallace and said, "Anything you need, just call us."

My mom added, "In fact, we already set up the spare room in the basement and would love for you to come spend a weekend."

"I'll come pick you up," my dad said.

I gave Wallace a hug good-bye and then glared at his roommate as I walked out the door. I was so angry that he had not done more to make Wallace feel welcome. But then I heard my mom behind me, and my heart swelled.

"We'll see you soon, Wallace," she said. "Just think of us as your American family."

Martin

—✹—

WALLACE E-MAILED TO SAY HE had finally connected with Caitlin and her family. **Wow,** he wrote, **what nice people.**

I laughed out loud in the quiet dark of Mr. Muzawazi's office.

So very true, I thought.

I was gathering all of my teacher recommendation letters to send to Caitlin's mom. My physics teacher and guidance counselor each wrote a letter for me, as did the headmaster. The first one I'd received was from Mr. Makunura, my chemistry teacher, who had handed me his letter the day after my request. It looked so official, typed on Marist Brothers stationery. Class was just about to start, but my curiosity was strong: I quickly scanned the letter.

Academically, Martin is an outstanding student, the letter began. I looked around quickly to make sure no one saw what I was doing. It would be embarrassing to be caught reading about myself. I couldn't stop. He mentioned my O-level scores, and said that I was in the top 5 percent of my A-level class. He spoke about my academic achievements at Nyanga but then he wrote something that made me feel so proud. *Given his intellectual capability and motivation, I feel strongly that he will successfully go through the challenging course he has chosen. Martin is an exceptional student, one of the best I have come across.*

Mr. Makunura had started his lecture, so I quickly placed the letter in my folder and started to take notes, unable to contain the smile that was stretching clear across my face.

I'd always called Caitlin's parents Mr. and Mrs. Stoicsitz, but then Caitlin wrote me a letter in which she explained that her parents were informal and that most of her friends called them by their first names, Rich and Anne. She added, *You're not like most of my friends. You're more like family. So my parents would like you to consider them your parents from another country. I hope that is okay.*

I flipped through all the letters that Anne had sent me, and the dozens of e-mails I had printed. In one she sent in September, she listed the more than twenty universities she'd already contacted on my behalf. On October 1, she wrote, **Are you tired of me yet?** and then went on to detail her efforts at new schools, including Drexel, Villanova, and Franklin & Marshall. On October 2, she sent another note recommending I e-mail a woman at a college in Pennsylvania, as they offered full funding for superior students. And then the very next day, she sent another e-mail in which she wrote: **MARTIN!!!!! La Salle University!!!!** Her father had gone there, and they offered full scholarships. She signed off with **I have a good feeling about this one!!!!!** I had never seen so many exclamation points in one e-mail. Her enthusiasm was contagious.

Attached to that e-mail was information about the Christian Brothers Scholarship. It read: *These scholarships cover full tuition and fees. Only sixteen are awarded each year. The average SAT score is 1350.* I suddenly understood the importance of these SAT tests—and that Anne was doing for me what a mother does for her own child.

So on October 15, when I sent Anne and Rich my recommendation letters and my personal essay, I addressed the accompanying note, *Dear Mom and Dad.*

It didn't feel strange writing such intimate words to people I had not yet met. On the contrary, it felt right. I ended the letter with *I love you.* It looked spare on the page, not as robust as I wanted it to come across. So I drew a big heart around it. That looked much better.

Caitlin

WALLACE CAME TO VISIT THE last weekend in October, and then every weekend after that. I could tell he was really having a hard time adjusting to life at Temple.

"At Marist, we study on the weekends," Wallace told us that first stay. "But at Temple, everyone just wants to get drunk. I don't understand it."

Richie laughed. "Your way is better, Wallace," he said. "Trust me."

"I think so, too, but my roommate says it's why I am having difficulties finding friends," Wallace said.

My hatred of his roommate grew deeper that day.

"Do what you think is right," my mom chimed in. "You will meet people who feel the same way."

I wasn't so sure. Wallace seemed so lost. I realized that we had to carefully choose the right place for Martin. Wallace seemed more introverted than Martin, but I still wanted to make sure that Martin went to a school that would welcome him. No one at Temple seemed to care that Wallace had come all the way from Zimbabwe to study there. That really upset me. It also reminded me of all the times my high school friends teased me about Martin. I wanted to shake all those idiots by their shoulders and shout, "You are missing an amazing opportunity right now!" People are so scared of what they don't know. It's a terrible mistake.

Mom invited Wallace to spend Thanksgiving with our family, and we took lots of pictures to send to Martin. It was during that long weekend when we realized how badly Wallace was struggling. By then, Richie had been accepted to Temple to start in January. Since he was planning to commute to school and could drive Wallace back and forth, my parents invited Wallace to move in with us until we could find him better accommodations—and a nicer roommate.

I wrote Martin to tell him the news, and to wish him luck on the SAT exams. I knew he was scheduled to take them on December 7 in Harare. I bombed mine, but it didn't matter. For Martin, these tests were crucial.

Break a leg! I wrote as my PS. Just in case he didn't understand what that meant, I added, *That's American for "good luck"!*

Martin
—⁊⁊⁊—

WE SAT FOR FINAL EXAMS that November in Nyanga and had to wait until January for the results. We would all be back home by then. There was no graduation at Marist Brothers. Instead, Mr. Muzawazi hosted a final party in early December.

Most of my friends were headed to Harare for University that January. A few were going to England, and one guy was going to Canada. Two others had applied for early admission to American colleges, and had been accepted. I was the only one without a definite plan.

While my friends all had their places secured, they also had opinions for where I should go.

"Harvard is the place," Bonaventure said.

"I hear Princeton is even better," Cornelius countered.

They were both planning to study medicine at the University of Zimbabwe. At the party, they weighed all the pros and cons of my options—Brown, UPenn, Stanford, Villanova.

"Guys," I said, interrupting their fun, "I'd be happy at any of these places. I just need one to say yes to a full scholarship."

Both friends fell silent. They understood how high the stakes were. I had not applied anywhere else. If none of the US colleges worked out, I'd have to rethink everything.

Before I left Nyanga for good, I went to Harare to take the SATs. My American mother had arranged everything—she paid up front for the exam and then wired me money to the local bank in Nyanga so I had enough for the bus ticket and pocket money. I stayed with Alois and Sekai the night before the exam. I hadn't seen them since they helped me get in to Marist.

I arrived at the test site forty-five minutes early. I had been awake all night, whether it was from nerves or excitement, I didn't know. But I knew taking this important test on no sleep could be a problem. I watched nervously as two dozen or more students entered the room. All of them came from wealthy families—I could tell by their shoes.

The test was more difficult than I had anticipated. I had never taken an exam like that and worried I did not do well. The verbal section was very challenging. I struggled through it. But then I shook that thought from my head. There was no time to doubt.

I took the bus back to Nyanga to gather my things, and then continued on to Mutare the next day. Before I left that majestic campus, I popped in to see Mr. Muzawazi for the last time as a Marist Brothers student.

I was among the last students to leave, so the campus was

void of the usual hum of student life. I knocked on his door and heard the thumps echo through the great hall I had first walked two years earlier.

"Enter!" Mr. Muzawazi's voice boomed from the other side.

I opened the door and saw him sitting behind his desk. Finally, instead of having to convince him of anything, I simply wanted to thank him.

"Sir, if it weren't for you, I'd be stuck in Chisamba Singles," I explained.

"Martin," he interrupted me. "You don't get stuck."

"I try not to, sir," I said.

"But you do succeed," he replied. "I wish you continued success, wherever you land."

"Thank you, sir," I said, bowing as I backed out of his office.

"And don't forget to keep in touch!" his voice bellowed down the hallway after me.

Back home, I made daily trips to the only Internet cafe in Mutare to keep up my correspondence with Anne and Caitlin. Now with my A-levels and SATs behind me, I could concentrate on college admissions 100 percent.

PART 6

American Dream

January 2003

Caitlin

MARTIN'S SAT SCORES WERE SENT to my mother's e-mail address in mid-January. He did not do as well as we had hoped.

"In an ideal world, these tests don't matter," she said. "But our world isn't ideal, and this is bad news."

"They cannot be worse than mine," I said.

"That would be impossible," my mom deadpanned. "But seriously, yours did not matter. His mean everything. He got an eleven hundred, which is great for a kid from Chisamba Singles but not good enough to get him that full scholarship to La Salle."

"What are we going to do?" I asked.

"We need a new plan," she said.

We brainstormed ways to raise money for Martin.

"You write the US embassy in Harare, and I will get in touch with Mr. Muzawazi," mom said. "Two schools have already offered partial scholarships. Maybe we can get a Zimbabwean sponsor to do the rest?"

I had a contact at the US embassy already, from when we were trying to figure out where Martin could take the SATs in Zimbabwe. Her name was Rebecca Zeigler Mano. It was ten thirty PM in the US, but I wanted her to read this as soon as she got to work the next day. I reminded her who I was, and my relationship to Martin. And then I cut straight to the point: **We are searching desperately for scholarship money for Martin. My parents have two of us in college presently and are unable to take on the burden of a third tuition. They have paid all his application fees and arranged for him to take his SATs as well as forward those results to many different schools. They have currently spent over $1,000 and countless hours trying to help Martin receive a US education. But scholarships, both merit- and need-based, are rare.**

I asked her if she had any contacts or thoughts whatsoever as to who might be willing to help sponsor Martin. I signed off with **Any help would be appreciated** and then hit SEND.

I heard the whoosh sound that e-mails make when they are soaring off into cyberspace and imagined a letter folded into an airplane shape leaving Hatfield and landing on Rebecca's desk in Harare within minutes. Then I switched off the computer and bowed my head in prayer.

"Dear God, please help me find a way to bring Martin to the United States."

I made the sign of the cross and hoped God would not think badly of me for suddenly turning to him at this moment. We needed all the help we could muster.

Martin
—⟋⟍—

MY SAT SCORES ARRIVED FIRST, and they were not nearly as high as I'd hoped. This was bad news. I had one last chance. The SAT II was in mid-January, which was another version of the test, and so a second chance to do well. I took that and then I stayed on in Harare for another week to gather information about applying for an American visa. I was also awaiting my A-level results, which came around the same time. Finally, some good news: I received two As—one in math, one in chemistry—and one B for physics.

I took these results to the Ministry of Education to apply for a temporary teaching position, a popular thing to do for students who don't go straight to university. I wouldn't hear from American schools until April at the earliest, and even then I wouldn't have to leave until August. That meant I had eight months to start making money.

"We have an immediate opening for a science teacher," the minister told me the afternoon of my appointment.

"Great," I said. "Where?"

"Chigodora," he replied.

I'd never heard of such a place.

"It's four hours west of Mutare, and another four hours south of Marondera," he explained. "One school services a dozen or more villages. You'll be a great asset to your students."

I thought of Rabbit, who had come from the rural areas and was just starting his second year at medical school.

"I'll do it," I said.

The pay was nominal but enough to cover my basic expenses. I signed the paperwork that afternoon.

"Report as soon as possible," the minister said. "They've been waiting for a science teacher for two years now."

I shook his hand. It felt good knowing I might have some-thing useful to offer those less fortunate than I.

Before I left Harare, I popped into an Internet cafe to let Caitlin and Anne know I'd be teaching in an area where there was surely no Internet, let alone electricity. I promised to keep in touch through letters. I also sent Anne the list of things I needed for my visa. I knew this was premature, but I decided it was better to plan ahead. I added, **Well, this time I feel I did quite well on the SAT II. I think I made it this time. I love you all. I can't wait to be on US soil.** And then I signed off with my new favorite good-bye, a string of Xs and Os that Caitlin had recently taught me was American for hugs and kisses.

Caitlin

REBECCA ZEIGLER MANO RESPONDED THE very next day. She promised to keep her eyes open for opportunities, but made it clear that she did not expect any to present themselves.

The economic troubles in this country are dismal, she wrote.

I did not have the heart to share that news with Martin. Especially since his last e-mail to our family was so hopeful. The line **I can't wait to be on US soil** made me tense up. What if we couldn't pull this off?

My mom was still waiting to hear from Mr. Muzawazi. She had sent him a similar request for Zimbabwean sponsors, thinking perhaps the Delta Corporation that sponsored Martin for Marist would be willing to do the same for an American university.

He responded on January 30.

My mother showed me the e-mail and I understood why she looked so defeated. **I hope all will be well with Martin. He is** a committed and hardworking student with outstanding performance in mathematics. Unfortunately, our contacts from here are limited and there is no one that we can recommend to assist Martin. The economic situation is very difficult.

"Dismal" and "difficult" were the words swirling through my head that February as we waited for universities to respond to his application.

Meanwhile Damon continued to pester me about the amount of time I was spending on my college courses.

I finally lost it one night. He started picking on me again for not being able to go bowling with him and his friends on a Thursday night.

"It's a school night, Damon," I said. "I have homework."

"Just blow it off!" he responded. "It's no big deal."

"Dismal" and "desperate" started whipping around in my brain like empty plastic bags in a wind tunnel.

"It's a huge deal!" I shouted, stunned by how loud and angry my voice sounded. "I know I can blow it off, but I don't want to."

"What's your problem?" he said.

"Seriously?" I asked. "You know how hard my mom and I are working to find Martin a scholarship. You know how upset I am at the thought that he may not be able to come to the United States to study and fulfill his dreams."

"Oh Jesus, not Martin again," he said. "I'm so sick of your pen pal."

I saw red.

"Well, guess what, Damon, I'm so sick of *you*." I was

shouting again. "Leave Martin out of this. It's not about him. It's about me. I don't give you a hard time for not wanting more out of your life. So why are you constantly criticizing me?"

"You used to be more fun," he said quietly. "I miss that Caitlin."

"Well, that Caitlin has grown up," I said, retaining my composure. "And she cares more about college than bowling."

I held back from adding "and you."

I knew Damon was under a lot of pressure. His dad had taken a turn for the worse. There was talk that he would not live more than a few years.

I didn't judge Damon for deciding to stick close to home. But I was certainly not going to let him judge me, or hold me back.

April 2003

Martin
—·ɯ·—

CHIGODORA WAS EVEN MORE RURAL than Nyanga. The bus dropped me off at a small lean-to on the side of a dirt road. There was no town anywhere in sight. I saw smoke up in the distance and followed a path that led me to a small mud hut with a thatched roof. Two women were tending a fire, wearing only a scrap of material around their waists. Several children ran around nearly naked as well. Few had shirts on, none had shoes.

"Manheru," I said, "good evening" in Shona. The sun was about to set, and I was eager to get settled.

I introduced myself as the new science teacher and one of the elder boys ran to fetch someone who could lead me to the school.

He returned with an older man whose hair had gone completely white. He, too, was wearing just a pair of tattered shorts, nothing else. Poverty in the country was even more brutal than what I experienced growing up. At least in the cities, there were castoffs of wealthier people, whether used clothes or leftover food. But in Chigodora, there was nothing to cast off.

The older man asked me to follow him past a few more mud huts much like the first one I had encountered. Finally, we arrived at the school, which was at least made of concrete. It had one room, with several desks and chairs that were so rickety and old, I thought it might be better to teach outdoors.

There I met Frank, a teacher who was a few years older than me and had gotten his degree at Africa University, just outside of Mutare. He had arrived a few weeks earlier to teach history and invited me to stay with him.

We went back to his place, another mud hut not far from the school. When I finally lay down on the packed earth floor beneath a roof that smelled like damp hay, I understood why my mother moved to Chisamba Singles. It was an upgrade.

That night, I dreamed of my mother as a young girl. When I woke the next morning, I thought someone as smart as her could be in my classroom. That made me excited to meet my students.

Frank was already tending the fire when I emerged from the hut. He offered me tea and some of his mealie meal. I was very thankful, not only for the food but also for his company. I had so many questions for him, starting with, Where can I bathe? He pointed down a dirt path.

"There is a stream down that way," he said. "I prefer to bathe at the end of the day after the sun has warmed the water a bit."

He told me this was also the place to fetch drinking water, so I grabbed a bucket and went on an exploratory mission. If this was my home for the next eight months, I had better get used to it.

I reported to school an hour later and was excited to see a few students already there. Every school in Zimbabwe requires a uniform, and most of the kids in Chigodora had some semblance of one. One young boy, maybe fourteen, was wearing rags stitched together to resemble shorts. Another girl had a shirt that was several sizes too small. Clearly, she had been wearing it for years. My family was fortunate by comparison.

I introduced myself and told my students how I got there. I could tell by their faces that they were impressed. None of these kids had ever left Chigodora, let alone visited Mutare. That was the big city for them.

I went around the room and asked everyone to tell me his or her name, and where each lived, and what their parents did for a living.

Enough went first. She lived seven kilometers away.

"I wake every morning at four to help my father with the cows," she said. "I'm the eldest of five girls, so my mother needs me to prepare breakfast and clean the dishes before I can leave for school."

"How long does it take you to get here?" I asked.

"If I run, I can do it in forty minutes," she said.

Givemore went next.

"I stay with my grandmother," he said. "I had to take time

off from school when my mother fell ill, to care for her. I'm still catching up."

This explained why he looked my age or older. I didn't ask what I knew to be true: that his mother no longer was alive. The stories continued, each one as difficult as the next, though none of these kids thought so. To them, this was normal.

I started teaching that same day and saw how hungry they were for this knowledge. Givemore stayed after school that day, and every one thereafter, wanting to borrow my books, to take more notes.

"You remind me of myself," I said after several weeks. He was clever and hardworking. The biggest difference was that he had no support.

After two months, I learned I had no support, either. Frank and I would take the bus to Mutare together every Friday to spend the weekends with our families—and check our bank accounts.

We'd head back Sunday night, dejected.

"Nothing," I'd say as I boarded the bus to Chigodora.

"Me either," Frank said.

Our salaries were already meager—just enough to cover food and bus fare and not much else. But neither of us had been paid since we started, which meant we both had to pay out of pocket to teach. I wanted to stay for my students' sake. But I could not afford to. Frank felt the same way, but he didn't have any prospects to return to in Mutare. Plus, he was older than me, which meant all of the women in the village wanted him to marry their eligible daughters. While food was scarce, Frank and I never went hungry. The villagers, despite their poverty, took great care of us.

Leaving was a very difficult decision for me. I knew that college acceptances would start coming in and I needed to be accessible. I also had to focus on securing a scholarship. On one of my visits home, I learned that Temple University was one of the first places to offer me a place for September 2003—but they could only offer twelve thousand dollars, which was not even half the tuition. The same happened with three other colleges I had applied to. This was good news—at least I was getting accepted. I just needed proper funding.

My last day of school was in April, right before the first break. My announcement was met with an eerie silence. I was not the first to abandon these students.

Givemore stayed after school that day to speak with me one last time.

"I just wanted to thank you," he said.

"For what?" I asked.

"For coming," he said. "And for giving me hope."

April 2003

Caitlin

ALL OF MARTIN'S COLLEGE CORRESPONDENCE was being sent to me, so I started checking the mailbox every afternoon that spring. The anticipation I felt reminded me of being in seventh grade, desperately waiting for Martin's news.

My mom still had her heart set on Villanova. She felt like the two women on the International Admission staff were the most sympathetic to Martin's story. Her new strategy was to focus on one school versus dozens. She started calling Villanova every week.

"Hi, Candice! Any news?" My mom's chipper voice resonated through our house.

Or, "Valerie? It's Anne. I'm going to be on campus tomorrow and wondered if I could bring you lunch."

She was working every single angle.

The rejection letters came first. His SAT scores were likely the reason, though his personal essay was also a bit difficult to comprehend. He wrote about his dream of becoming an actuarial scientist, which I had never heard of until then. When I looked it up in our encyclopedia, I understood why: It was "a discipline that applies mathematical and statistical methods to assess risk in insurance and financial fields." The definition made my head hurt. I had just dropped a statistics class at college because the number problems looked like Mandarin.

The form rejection from an Ivy League college made me angry. I wanted to scream, "You are making a huge mistake!" It infuriated me that Martin's fate was being determined in this cold and impersonal way. If any one of these college presidents could meet him or correspond with him, they'd be begging for him to come to their school! They would feel lucky to get him.

Some schools saw this and offered him partial scholarships. Temple was one, but we already ruled that out after seeing Wallace's difficult transition. Yale was another flat-out no. I knew Martin would receive all this news via e-mail and just wished I could be there when he did, to say, "This means nothing. They don't know you. Don't give up."

The problem was, I was starting to.

Especially when I heard my mom talking to Candice one afternoon in late April.

"Are you certain?" she said, her voice cracking on the last word.

I walked into the kitchen.

"So there's nothing else we can do?" she added, her chin trembling. "Thank you, Candice. I know how hard you have been working on this."

After she hung up, my mother looked despondent.

"What is it?" I said.

"That was Villanova," she said. "They have a spot for him, but no money."

She could not hold the tears back any longer.

"I failed Martin," she said. "And you! I'm so sorry, honey."

It was difficult to see my mother defeated. I wanted to comfort her somehow. This was not the end of the road. It couldn't be.

"Mom, you have worked so hard make this happen," I said. "We cannot give up now! There has to be a way."

Mom just shook her head.

"Have you heard back from Oprah?" I asked. I knew she had written her earlier that spring, trying to get Martin's story on Oprah's show to raise awareness—and hopefully funds—about his story.

"No," my mom said, blowing her nose. "Or from Bill Gates or Bill Cosby."

My mom had a file for every wealthy celebrity she had contacted, every organization that offered international scholarships, and every institution that might sponsor a brilliant kid from Africa.

"We'll find another way," I said. "We can do a shoe drive, or a bake sale. I can get sponsors and do a bike ride across America!"

I was on a roll.

"Caitlin, you concentrate on your finals," my mother said, wiping tears from beneath both eyes. "I'll keep working on Martin."

Martin
—〰—

UPON MY RETURN HOME, I learned that Wallace was really struggling at school. His parents had written me a letter. They were so appreciative of my American family's help that they invited me to come stay with them in Victoria Falls while I waited for more news from the United States.

I was happy to accept. There was nothing to do in Mutare beyond hustling at the market for spare change. Wallace's parents offered me a place to stay and a job helping them at their bed-and-breakfast. This meant I would have access to phones and the Internet, which would help with securing a scholarship.

It was a two-day journey—the first stop was Harare, then Bulawayo, and finally Victoria Falls. The last leg of the trip was breathtaking as the train barreled up Zimbabwe's western corridor. It was nighttime when we passed through Hwange National Park, the largest game reserve in the country. I could see the silhouettes of the baobab trees rising above the grasslands in the moonlight and then a sea of red dots that suddenly stood still before disappearing into the night.

"Antelope," my seatmate said.

We had baboons and other monkeys in Mutare, but we didn't have antelope or elephants or lions hanging around. I didn't blame these majestic animals for staying so far away from the cities. I kept on the lookout all night, hoping to spot one. No luck. Perhaps the sound of the engine scared them off.

The sun had begun its rise as we pulled alongside the Zambezi River, which feeds the falls. Locally, we call them Mosi-oa-Tunya, which means "the smoke that thunders." I saw the spray rising in the distance, a shimmering fog, and truly understood.

I recognized Wallace's parents, Tecla and Phanuel, immediately. I saw Wallace in each of them. They were waiting for me at the station, and their accents were familiar, as they come from the Eastern Highlands, like my family. I felt immediately at ease. We drove back to their house, which reminded me of the picture Caitlin sent me of hers. I was astonished by how humble Wallace's parents were, as it was clear they had great wealth.

Tecla showed me my room and the bathroom.

"I'll make sure to bathe early so as not to disturb you," I said.

"That's not necessary," Tecla said. "We have our own bathroom—this is for your use."

She then invited me downstairs for breakfast. I took my seat and was stunned when a maid entered the room with a platter of scrambled eggs.

I said hello, and she bowed her head at me as she served me.

I'd never been served by someone in this manner. It made me think of my own mother, who had started doing this work in Mutare. I wanted to say, "I'm happy to serve myself," but I didn't want to cause a scene, so I kept quiet.

She disappeared back into the kitchen and returned with cereal, tea, and orange juice, which I had never tasted before. It remains my favorite drink to this day.

Tecla and Phanuel filled me in on Wallace's news. I did not know that he had moved in with Caitlin's family for a while, or that Anne and Rich had helped him find a new apartment with a much nicer roommate to finish his freshman year with.

"Anne treats Wallace like her own son," Tecla said. "We'll never know how to repay her kindness."

"I feel the same," I said. "This family is the reason I'm sitting here with you."

Phanuel asked about my own college news, and I told them I was still waiting for a scholarship.

"Anne and I speak often," Tecla said. "She's determined to find one."

"And from what she tells us, so are you," Phanuel said.

I was determined—and I really had to be, as I had not made any other alternative plans. Optimism was key. If I doubted now, even for a moment, I would never get to the United States.

We finished eating and I went to unpack. I had only brought a few things: the three shirts Caitlin had sent me over the years, my dungarees, cargo shorts, and Fila sneakers. As I hung things up in my closet, I saw that every item of clothing I owned came from Caitlin. Somehow, they gave me hope. I showered, and then changed into fresh clothes. Tecla was waiting for me downstairs to take me to the falls.

As we approached the national park, I heard a dull roar—it sounded like an army of angels clapping. We pulled into the parking lot, which was thronged with mostly white tourists. From there, we walked down a dirt path to the first viewpoint. The ground beneath my feet trembled so much, I could feel the vibration in my teeth. Soon, a damp spray was enveloping me. It moistened my skin and turned trapped sunlight into soft rainbows. The vegetation became more lush and vibrant green as we neared the first gorge. The sound was deafening by the time we reached the cliff's edge and I finally saw why: The cascade of water was so vast and mighty, I thought, the angels were not only clapping—they were giving a standing and stomping ovation for a spectacle only God could have created.

From there, Tecla took me to the bed-and-breakfast a kilometer away and introduced me to the staff as the new receptionist. My job was to greet and check guests in, and then help with any travel requests.

My first day, I met two Americans, four Australians, and a group of people from the United Kingdom who had arrived on a tour bus. Victoria Falls is a must-see stop on any Zimbabwe package tour. Tourists would stay for two days before heading down to Hwange. I'd never seen so many white people in my life—I told everyone I met about Caitlin.

At the bed-and-breakfast there was a computer connected to the Internet, so I was able to communicate with Caitlin and Anne frequently, though there wasn't much news. Waiting was quite painful.

In the meantime, I read an ad in the newspaper about a pre-departure orientation for Zimbabwean students who were planning to study in America. It was taking place at the US embassy in early June.

I called the number listed and spoke to a woman called Rebecca Mano. I told her I was very interested in the orientation but wasn't sure if I'd be going to college that September, as I was still awaiting a scholarship.

"Tell me your name again?" she said.

"Martin Ganda," I said.

"I know you!" she responded. "Your pen pal e-mailed me a few months ago!"

"Caitlin?" I asked.

"Yes," Rebecca said. "She got in touch to see if I could help find Zimbabwean sponsors. I wish we could."

Caitlin had never told me this, but I didn't let on.

"Oh yes, of course," I said. "We're not giving up."

"Nor should you," she added. "I was recently on the phone with Villanova's office. The recruiter was raving about you. Come to the orientation. This way you'll be prepared when they do find the money."

Those words instilled such hope—as if the angels were clapping for me, too.

I asked Tecla if it was okay for me to go to Harare that weekend, to attend the course.

"You must!" she said.

Alois and Sekai once again greeted me warmly.

"When you do go to America, don't forget everyone here," Alois said.

"That would be impossible," I replied.

I'd never been to the American embassy before, but it was like they planted what I'd imagined was a building from New York City or Washington, DC, in the middle of Harare. I walked through the wrought-iron gates and felt like I was suddenly transported to the States. Even the doorknobs were different—big, heavy, and polished. Proud.

I entered the building and walked up to the security guards, who asked me for identification. My name was on a list, and the guard pointed down a long hallway to a room where the orientation was taking place.

I saw a white woman with long blond hair holding a clipboard and asked her where I could find Rebecca Mano.

"Mai Mano," she said.

I was shocked—I was certain Rebecca was black. When we spoke on the phone, her Shona was impeccable. As I was still reeling, she asked if I got my majeksen—Shona for "vaccination injection." She spoke my native tongue fluently.

I had just started wandering around the room when Rebecca called everyone to take seats and explained that the orientation was to prepare us for some of the bigger cultural differences between Zimbabwe and America.

"Money is quite different, for starters," she said. "US bills are all the same size, so make sure you look at the number in the corners," she explained.

I knew this already. This was going to be a breeze.

But then she handed around coins. They were totally confusing. She said the ten-cent coin was smaller than the five-cent one, but was worth more, and was also called a dime.

I started taking notes.

There were about twenty other students there, all going to the US for the first time. Most were black kids from Harare whose parents were paying for everything, but a few came from far away like me. I was the only one awaiting a scholarship.

Next, Rebecca introduced Freedom, who was already studying in the US.

"Americans are funny about food," he began. "To start, there's so much, you won't believe your eyes. A hamburger is the size of your plate."

Everyone laughed. This was something we all wanted to see.

"If you have a roommate, you don't have to offer them any of your food," he continued. "And if your roommate leaves food in the fridge, you have to ask permission before you eat it."

We all started laughing again. In Zimbabwe, everyone shares. I wouldn't eat if you weren't eating, too. That would be rude.

"I learned this the hard way," Freedom continued. "My roommate reported me for eating his leftovers."

One girl raised her hand. "Why?" she asked. "Leftovers means you are full."

Everyone agreed, including Freedom.

"That's how we feel here," he said. "But America is different."

This was important information. Freedom next talked about clothes. Same deal: Americans don't share their clothes. For us, there is no mine or yours. I could wake up and my mom would be wearing the T-shirt Caitlin gave me, or my brother would have on the shoes I often wore—it wasn't a big deal. In Shona, we say the little we have, we share.

Even at Marist everyone shared. Some people would bring cans of fish from home because we didn't get fish at school. Or they would bring peanut butter. If my peanut butter runs out, I'd say, "I'm getting peanut butter from your jar." No one cared.

Rebecca introduced another student, who told us about parties and how everyone drinks beer. That was shocking. We didn't do that at Marist. Our parties were alcohol free— at that point I saw myself as someone who would never drink in my life—I'd had one sip of beer and thought it tasted nasty. Many students at the orientation were already over twenty-one, so this guy said, "Be careful. Buying alcohol for under-age US students can get you in serious trouble."

"What kind?" someone asked.

"You can be arrested and deported," he said.

I jotted that down, too.

American greetings were another topic.

"If someone asks, 'How's it going?' The answer to that question is, 'Fine.'" Freedom explained. "No one has time for anything else."

This was fascinating. We have six different ways of saying hello in Shona, each appropriate for a specific time of the day. "Mangwanani" means "good morning," and is usually the start of a five-minute conversation, like, "How did you sleep? What are you going to do today?" In the States, Freedom said, people just say "Hi" and keep going.

I'd taken four pages of notes by the time the American ambassador arrived. He told us that he went to Harvard with Edson Zvobgo, the first black Zimbabwean to go to that famous university. "He eventually became a professor in the United States," the ambassador said. "People often talk about the American dream—Edson had one. And now you do, too."

By July, I hadn't heard anything from Caitlin or Anne, and I was starting to get nervous. I sent them a quick note, using all caps, to stay positive. Somehow these large letters helped. I told them I was waiting patiently—which I was truly trying to do—and to please keep me updated on any news. I signed it with a string of Xs and Os, and then *MARTIN (2003 UNDERGRADUATE AMERICAN UNIVERSITY STUDENT)*.

Caitlin

⎯⎯⎯∞∞∞⎯⎯⎯

BY THE END OF APRIL, we had heard from all of the colleges Martin applied to: Five accepted him; three offered him partial scholarships, and two offered him a place but no money. The last letter came in from NYU—another rejection. That was it. We had reached the end of the road. I crumpled it up in the driveway and burst into tears. I'd failed my friend. I promised him we would find a way for him to study in the United States, but it felt impossible. The only thing I could do was work even harder and start saving money to bring him here myself.

"More bad news," I shouted as I entered the house.

"What now?" my mom asked.

I threw the paper ball onto the kitchen counter.

"That's it," I said. "It's over, Mom."

"Not yet," she said. I knew she was working on other avenues—she had reached out to local politicians and the papers. She was even organizing a bake sale to raise money.

"I sent Rebecca Mano an e-mail this morning," she continued. "I'm going to see if we can get him here on a visitor's visa."

"How does that help?" I asked.

"He can accept the spot at Villanova, and then we'll keep working once he's here to raise money to cover the fees," she said.

I knew this was a last resort for my parents. They were paying for Richie to go to Temple, and I was planning to continue at the community college in the fall.

In the meantime, my high school graduation was coming up, and my mom wanted to take me dress shopping. I didn't have the heart to tell her I didn't care about a new dress—or graduation, for that matter. I couldn't wait to be done with high school.

The day my mother and I planned to go shopping, she surprised me.

"I wrote a letter to Father Dobbin this morning," she said, sliding a piece of paper in front of me. I knew he was the president of Villanova because my mother had been talking about him lately. He was her last shot at a miracle.

"I wanted to make sure he realized what a big mistake Villanova was making by not giving Martin a scholarship," she said as I began to read:

Dear Father Dobbin:

We are contacting you as our last resort for helping a young man from Zimbabwe. Martin Ganda is a twenty-year-old from Mutare,

Zimbabwe, and has been our daughter's pen
pal since 1997. Our daughter initially paid for
Martin's schooling fees with her babysitting money
until his family became destitute from declining
economic conditions. At that point, we took over
the support and tuition for Martin and his family.

Martin has been accepted at Villanova
University for fall 2003. Unfortunately, our
daughter and son are both college students, which
means we are unable to finance Martin's college
education as well. Your colleagues at VU have
been very supportive of our plight, yet we still do
not have any funds.

Martin graduated from Nyanga High
School with honors last fall. He secured a
part-time teaching position and is currently
working in a tourists' cottage to earn money for his
family.

Father, we know you have a very heavy load of
responsibilities and we would never ask for our own
children, but this young man has nothing.
We are his only hope. Do you have any connections
or programs seeking students like Martin to
sponsor? Would you know of any other avenues for
us to pursue? Please explore any resources you may
have to help our dear young friend. His information

should be available in Admissions and I have copies
of the e-mails, including a story of Martin's sad life
and how he touched our hearts.

Thank you in advance for your help.

Sincerely,

Richard and Anne

Neville Stoicsitz

Tears were streaming down my face as I read my mom's last-ditch effort.

"Send it," I said.

"Let's bless it first," she said.

She placed it in the stamped envelope and held one end as I took the other. We both closed our eyes and said a silent prayer.

I leaned down and kissed it—for good luck.

In July we had our bake sale; we raised $350. I was working full-time at the pizza parlor and picking up any baby-sitting jobs I could, and had only saved another $900. I had another $28,750 to go.

Then I got an e-mail from Martin saying he was waiting patiently—but I could tell that even Martin's optimism was wavering.

"How am I going to tell him that it might not happen?" I asked my mom, once again fighting back tears.

She stayed quiet as she considered my question. Usually, she'd snap right back and chastise me for a bad attitude. She'd say, "Don't give up! That's not going to solve this problem.

Save all your energy for figuring out how we can do it, not how we can't."

Today was different.

"We'd better start thinking about how to break it to him," she said, her voice barely a whisper.

July 2003

Martin
—ᴍ—

I WAS SURPRISED THAT CAITLIN and Anne hadn't responded to my e-mail right away. I assumed they were very busy. I was, too. It was peak tourist season and the bed-and-breakfast was booked solid every single day. It was hard to take time off, but I had to go fill out a few more forms at the embassy, so I'd be ready to go when we found the scholarship money. Rebecca was helping me figure out a visa without a benefactor. It was very difficult.

There was an Internet cafe not far from Alois and Sekai's house. I checked in my first morning there on my way to the US embassy to see if there was any news. There was an e-mail from Villanova dated July 15, 2003.

I was trembling as I clicked it open.

Caitlin

⊶∞∞⊷

I WOKE UP STARTLED. MY mother was screaming so loud, I thought something terrible must have happened. It was a rare day off, and I had been out with Damon until one AM playing pool. After our big fight that spring, Damon really backed off and gave me space. I appreciated it. But he was really happy when school was over, as I had more time for him. I was happy, too.

I heard another shriek and looked at my clock—it was 9:15 AM. I stumbled downstairs to make sure everything was okay.

That's when I heard her say, "That's fantastic news!"

I had to tap her on the shoulder to let her know I was there, waiting to hear what on earth was so exciting on a Thursday morning.

"Caitlin, they did it!" she cried. She then told me the story at breakneck speed:

"Father Dobbin marched my letter down to Candice,

placed it on her desk, and said, 'Martin Ganda.' Candice said, 'Yes, Father Dobbin. He's an extraordinary young man, but we don't have the money for a full scholarship.' And then Father Dobbin tapped his finger on her desk, and said, 'Find the money.' That was in June, and this is Candice on the phone right now saying they found the money! Martin is going to Villanova!"

The rush of emotions was so intense, I thought it might swallow me whole.

Martin

—◊◊◊—

THE FIRST LINE OF THE e-mail was like rocket fuel:

We are pleased to offer you a full scholarship beginning with the 2003–2004 academic year.

It propelled me from my seat. The breath I'd been holding for the past few months came barreling out of my mouth as I shouted, "Yesssssss!"

The cafe was already filled with people. Several turned to look at me like I was crazy. I did not care.

"I am going to America!" I shouted. "AMER-I-CA!!!"

I managed to sit back down to read the rest of the message. It said a package was sent to Rebecca Mano on my behalf with all the paperwork necessary to secure my visa.

I was so excited that I ran out without paying for the computer use. When I saw the shop owner come after me, I grabbed money from my pocket and shoved it into his hand and then started sprinting.

The bus to the embassy took forever that day. There were plenty of seats, but I was too excited to keep still. I paced up and down the aisle, my heart pounding, my mind racing. As soon as I saw the white gleaming building in the distance, I pulled the cord to stop the bus and then ran down the street and through the wrought-iron gates.

"Congratulations, Martin!" Rebecca said as I burst through her door.

She handed me a FedEx package that was as heavy as a textbook. I pulled the cardboard strip and the contents fell onto my lap.

VILLANOVA UNIVERSITY was written in navy blue across a thick cream-colored cardboard folder. I opened it and saw a version of the e-mail I had just received. This was the official acceptance letter. This was real.

I looked up at Rebecca, who was beaming.

"A lot of people believe in you, Martin," she said. "Including me."

I thought of every single person who helped me get to this very place, sitting in the American embassy across from a blond-haired and blue-eyed woman who spoke fluent Shona. The list was long, but it started with Caitlin. I had to share the news.

"Shall we call them?" Rebecca asked.

"Can we?" I said.

She picked up the phone and started to dial.

Caitlin

⎯⎯⎯∞⎯⎯⎯

THE NEWS WAS STILL SINKING in two hours later when the phone rang. I picked it up and said hello, but there was a funny echo, like the person on the other end was calling from the moon.

"Caitlin?" I heard a few seconds later. "It's Martin."

I started to shake.

"You got the scholarship!" I shouted.

My mother came running, so I put him on speakerphone and kept shouting, not because I thought he couldn't hear me, but because I was too excited to speak otherwise.

"You need to be here by August twenty-fourth!" My mom was now shouting, too. "I just spoke to Candice. We know everything."

"Mom?" Martin said. "Is that you?"

"Yes, it is me," my mom said. "We are finally going to meet you!"

"My brother from another mother!" I chimed in. That's what we had started calling Martin in my household.

"I look forward to that day," Martin said.

"Where are you?" I asked.

"Here in your embassy, with Rebecca," he said.

"Well, tell her that I will arrange for the airline tickets immediately," Mom said. "In fact, may I speak with her?"

My mom got out her notepad and started making a list of things we needed to do as Martin's sponsors once he was here in the United States.

"You did it, Mom!" I said after we hung up.

"Honey, none of this would have happened without you," she said. "Don't ever forget that."

We called my dad and Richie to tell them the good news. Wallace was in Colorado working for a friend his parents had met in Victoria Falls. I called Damon last.

"That is amazing news, Caitlin," he said. "I'm so proud of you."

"You're finally going to meet him," I said.

"It will be like meeting a celebrity at this point," Damon said. "I can't wait."

"I can't, either," I said.

The very same day my mom booked a one-way ticket for Martin. He would leave Zimbabwe on August 15 and arrive in Philadelphia the next day. After waiting nearly six years for this moment, a month felt like forever.

Martin
—⚬⚬⚬—

I DIDN'T HAVE MUCH TIME to get ready, so I returned to Victoria Falls to tell Tecla and Phanuel the great news and get all my vaccinations.

From there I went to Mutare to say good-bye to my family. I wanted to tell them about the scholarship in person. I also had to say good-bye. I had a feeling it would be a long time before I saw them again.

I waited until my father and Nation came home that evening. We were all sitting around the fire, eating together. George was now seven, no longer a baby but a grown boy. Lois was twelve, the same age Caitlin was when she started writing me. She had maintained the number one position in her class since grade one without once slipping. Anne still sent my mother money to keep everyone in school, which meant Lois, too, would go to college if she wanted to.

I was thinking of her when I stood up to make the announcement.

"Mai, Baba, I have news," I started. "I will be leaving in a few weeks to study in America."

I saw a smile grow across my mother's face—but it quickly turned to a frown when my father leaped from his seat and started to run around shouting, "Martin is going to the United States! He did it!"

My mother started hissing, "Keep quiet! This is no time to brag."

Some things would never change.

My father was so happy for me, and this news, but my mother was superstitious. "You don't brag about things ever," she scolded my father when he finally calmed down again. "We cannot jinx this."

Then she turned to me and said quietly and composed, "We're very happy for you, Martin. You have made your poor parents so proud."

Her eyes shone in the firelight, happy tears.

I was scheduled to take the train back the very next day. Before I left, I took my mother aside. Anne had sent one hundred US dollars to the Victoria Falls Western Union with a note that said *for travel expenses*. I priced the least-expensive round trip train ticket to Mutare and kept a small amount of money for food during the two-day journey, and gave the rest to my mother.

"This is for you, Mother, from my American mother," I said, placing ninety-six US dollars in her hands.

"You keep this, son," she said.

"No, Mai," I said, wrapping her hand around the cash.

"Once I get to America, I will send more. But until I get there, I need to know you're going to be okay."

My mother looked me in the eyes and said, "Martin, we are fine—because of you. Now go!"

I hugged her, and then my father placed both of his hands on my shoulders and said, "I am so proud of you, son. So, so proud."

I said good-bye to Nation and Simba, both grown men by then. It was hardest to say good-bye to Lois this time.

"I will miss you, brother," Lois said as she hugged me good-bye.

"Keep your grades up and you will soon come after me," I said.

I returned to Vic Falls the first week in August, to wait for the plane tickets to arrive. Each day felt an eternity. By August 11, the tickets had still not arrived.

I knew Caitlin and her mom had sent them, but that didn't help. The waiting kept me awake at night, and fed the wildest dreams whenever I did drift off. In one, I was lying on a dirt floor in a hut similar to the one I shared with Frank in Chigodora. It was pouring rain—the water sounded like pounding hooves on the thatched roof, which I was convinced would collapse at any moment. Suddenly, water started seeping in from the sides and rising up from the floor. When it reached my face, I startled awake, drenched with sweat.

I looked around and was relieved that I was not in Chigodora, or even Chisamba Singles, but still in the guest room at Wallace's house. Still, I couldn't shake the feeling that the lost ticket was a sign that this was not meant to be.

That morning, at breakfast, Tecla informed me a prophet was coming to see me.

In Zimbabwe, prophets are like witch doctors. They can foretell the future. My mother made my father see one many years ago, before I was born, when he was misbehaving. That meeting, she claimed, cured him of his womanizing. I didn't entirely believe in their powers, but they are hugely popular in my country. People turned to witch doctors more often than regular doctors, and many friends and family members claimed that it worked. I was so desperate at this point, I was willing to put aside my skepticism and try anything.

The prophet arrived dressed in a robe. His silver hair was clumped into dreadlocks, steel wool snakes slithering down his back.

We sat in the living room, and I told him my troubles. He grabbed my hands and started to chant with his eyes closed. When he started speaking gibberish, I was so terrified that I closed my eyes as well.

His entire body started shaking violently as he kept chanting. I cracked open my eyes and saw that his were open, too, but rolling in the back of his head. He started moaning, and sounded like an animal in heat. The shaking grew more intense until finally he let go of my hands with such ferocity that I fell backward. When I regained my composure, the prophet was sitting quietly, with his hands folded in his lap.

"Your aunt doesn't want you to go," he said. "She has a bone to chew with your mother, so she's placed a hex on you."

I had never met my aunt, but I know she stayed behind in the rural area and was worse off than my mother was. I thought of the topless women I saw in Chigodora, and of Enough, the young girl who walked seven kilometers to get to school. I thought of all the people in Zimbabwe who were struggling, who deserved the chance I was being given.

"What can I do?" I asked.

"Let us pray," the prophet said.

I grabbed his hands and closed my eyes and I made a litany of silent promises. If those tickets came, if I was allowed on that plane, if I actually made it to the United States to study, I'd never forget those who couldn't go with me. I would always remember Enough. And my mother. When I opened my eyes, I saw the prophet staring at me.

"That's all you can do," he said.

Afterward, I was so exhausted that I went upstairs and fell asleep. It was the middle of the day, but I was so tired that I slept straight through dinner and until the following morning. It was a sound, restful sleep, the first in a very long time.

August 12, 2003

Caitlin

FEDEX CLAIMED THAT ITS forty-eight-hour guarantee did not apply to Africa. My mother was livid. When I left for the pizza parlor at noon on August 12, she was on the phone screaming at them. And when I got back later at night, she was pleading with the consolidator whom she'd bought the ticket from.

"We already paid for it," she said. "Can't they reissue one at the airport?"

I couldn't hear the response, but I knew it wasn't good when my mother shouted, "Thank you for nothing!" and slammed down the phone.

My father arrived moments later.

"How is it going?" he asked.

"Horribly!" she said. Her voice was scratchy. "I'm at my wits' end. I already called Villanova to say he might not get here in time."

"What did they say?" I asked, alarmed that it had come to this.

"That they would hold his spot until January," my mother said. "But Martin can't wait that long. He needs to come now."

"Let me make a few calls," my dad said.

We ate dinner first, and then my father took over the phone, starting with the consolidator and then working the airlines and FedEx.

At one AM, he was still on the phone. It was seven AM in Vic Falls. My mom thought we should call Martin to tell him the news.

"What news?" I said, exasperated. "There is no news!"

"Tell him to go to the airport," my father said. "He's getting on that plane."

Martin

—⟡—

MY FLIGHT WAS SCHEDULED TO leave in three hours when the phone rang. Tecla jumped to get it. She then handed the receiver to me. It was Anne.

"Mom," I said, relieved. "Am I coming?"

"We're still working on it," she said.

I could tell she had been crying, and that started my own tears.

I was so stupid to believe that these voodoo rituals might work—and angry that I allowed myself to think they would.

The tears were now stinging the backs of my eyes. I handed the phone to Tecla and ran up to my room. I couldn't cry in front of Wallace's parents. It was too undignified. As soon as I was able to shut the bedroom door, I fell onto my bed and buried my head beneath my pillow. The sounds that came from my belly were as primal and terrifying as the prophet's. They hurt my throat as they clawed their way up and out.

Ten minutes later, there was a knock at the door. I wiped my face dry before opening it.

Phanuel and Tecla were there.

"Get your things, we're taking you to the airport," they said.

"How come?" I asked, confused.

"We're not sure how, but you're getting on that plane," Phanuel said.

I grabbed the few things I was taking: my money belt with all my paperwork, a toothbrush, and one of the very first photos of Caitlin, in which she is wearing her mother's sun hat. I placed that picture with my passport in the money belt and followed Tecla and Phanuel downstairs and into the car. They had already packed a suitcase of African art for me to bring to Anne, who would send it to another friend in the US to sell to raise funds for Wallace.

Wallace's father drove so fast, I thought we might actually crash. We now had less than an hour before my flight left. We pulled into the airport and went to the British Airways desk to explain the situation. The attendant pointed us toward the manager's office, down the corridor.

The manager was on the phone when we arrived. Phanuel knocked on her window—we knew this was rude, but the flight was boarding. There wasn't time for manners.

She looked up from her desk and waved us in.

"Martin Ganda?" she said.

"Yes," I answered, stunned.

"I'm talking to a man who claims he's your American father," she said.

The hex had been lifted.

Five minutes later I walked outside onto the tarmac with a ticket in my hand.

I was the last person to board the small jet to Johannesburg. I took my seat, by the window, and waved at Tecla and Phanuel, who waited to make sure I got on the plane.

"Welcome to British Airways Flight 429," the stewardess announced as the propellers outside started to whir. "Please prepare for takeoff."

I had never been on a plane before and had no idea what that meant, so I looked around at the other passengers. There were only thirty or so people on board, most of them white men in business suits. A few were likely tourists, I guessed, based on their khaki pants and matching shirts. There was one other black guy a few years older than me.

Copying the others, I snapped my seat belt on and tugged it extra tight. As the plane began to move, I held on to the arm rest with both hands, my knuckles straining through my skin. When the nose of the plane tilted upward, I thought I might throw up the meal I had eaten at Tecla and Phanuel's house earlier that morning. I closed my eyes and prayed.

I opened them when the stewardess announced that it was fine to walk around. All these people snapped off their seat belts and got up to get books or stretch or use the restroom. I looked out the window and saw clouds and blue skies forever.

I closed my eyes again and did not open them until we had landed safely in Johannesburg.

The airport was the busiest place I'd ever seen. All these

people, many talking with funny accents, or in languages I had never heard before. There were signs with lists of flight numbers followed by the names of exotic places they were heading to. Tecla had given me ten US dollars to get snacks. I saw a McDonald's and got very excited. Some of the wealthier kids from Marist Brothers had bragged about it. So I walked up to the counter and bought my very first hamburger. It cost eight dollars, but I did not care. It was delicious.

I went in search of my next flight, but did not know how to find it. My ticket had so many numbers on it, but I was not sure which ones corresponded with the flipping and flashing board. So when I saw the one black guy from my Victoria Falls flight walk by, I asked him for help. As it turned out, he was heading to Paris, as well, where his father was a diplomat. We walked to the gate together and then waited for the flight to board. When he had to use the bathroom, I followed him. I didn't want to get lost.

That was a huge plane. I watched movies, ate food served on very fancy trays, and wished I could keep the cozy blanket and pillow they offered all the passengers.

We arrived in Paris, and once again, I didn't want to take any chances. This time, I asked the attendant to bring me to the next gate. My flight was not for a few hours, but it did not matter. I wasn't going to risk it. I just stayed there, not moving. Once the flight began to board, I was the first person in line. The next stop was Philadelphia.

August 15, 2003

Caitlin

⸏∞⸎

I DIDN'T WAKE UP THAT morning because I never went to sleep. I stayed awake all night tracking each of Martin's flights online.

The day before, we made a poster that said, *WELCOME TO AMERICA MARTIN* with bubble letters, which I colored in with red Magic Markers. I laid that in the trunk of my mom's car that morning, and then climbed into the backseat. My grandparents Nan and Pop drove their own car, so I had the entire seat to myself. I didn't invite Damon to come along. I had been waiting for this moment for six years, which was three times as long as I had known Damon. This meant too much to me to share with anyone but my family. Damon was pissed and I didn't care.

We arrived an hour early and camped out as close to the international flight exit as possible, right next to the swinging doors that led down the long hallway to customs.

Every time a new wave of people arrived, I would pick up my poster.

"Who's Martin?" an elderly man asked my mom.

"Our African son," my mom answered, beaming.

He looked utterly confused, but we didn't care. We had already told everyone on our street that Martin was coming. We were hosting a welcome to the neighborhood barbecue the following day. That evening, our closest relatives were coming to finally meet Martin. Everyone was excited, but no one more than I.

We'd been there for an hour when Paris flight passengers started coming through. We knew because I kept asking, "What flight were you on?"

I started counting people. When I hit one hundred twenty, I got nervous.

"What if he got stuck in France?" I asked my mom.

"He's here," she said. "I can feel it."

We kept peering down the hallway until it was just a trickle. And then no one. My stomach did a somersault. Something must be wrong. I was just about to go find an airline representative to make sure he had gotten on the flight when I saw a young black man emerge.

As he got closer, his face erupted into the biggest smile ever.

"That's him!" I cried.

I was standing on one side of the plastic barrier that corralled the arriving passengers in one direction. He didn't even get to walk around it—I just reached over and grabbed him. We stood there hugging right over the fence.

"You made it!" I said.

"I did," Martin answered.

The crowd of people around us waiting for their loved ones burst into applause as my mother rushed up and started snapping photos.

Martin pulled back and said, "Hi, Mom!"

My mother burst into tears. "We're so glad you are here!"

My dad was crying, too, as he held out his hand to shake Martin's. "Welcome home, son."

Martin grabbed his hand and pulled him close. My grandfather was videotaping the whole thing, but that did not stop Martin from saying, "Hi, Nan. Hi, Pop."

He knew who everybody was.

"Is that your only bag?" PopPop asked, pointing to the suitcase full of African art.

"This is for Wallace," Martin explained.

"I told him to just come with the clothes on his back and we'd take care of the rest," my mom said.

"I have this," Martin said, pulling a toothbrush out of his back pocket. We all laughed.

On our way home, we took a slight detour to drive by Villanova. The stone buildings looked majestic against the green carpet-like lawn.

"That's where you're heading, Martin," Mom said.

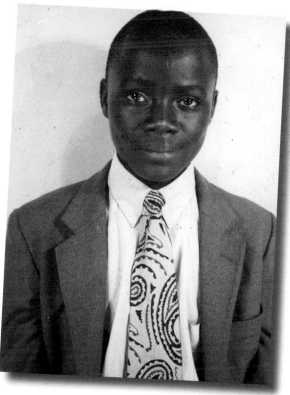

These were among the first pictures we sent each other.

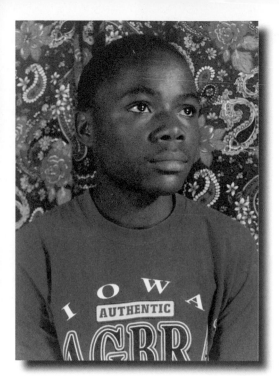

This photo was taken in Harare,
where I worked as a tea boy.
I am wearing a shirt Caitlin sent me.

Around the same time,
I attended my school's Winter Ball.

Nation, my mother, and me. (The tins under the bed were used to fetch water for drinking and cooking.)

My family saying thank you to Caitlin and her family for all the wonderful gifts (like the rain boots!). Seated (left to right): my mother, my father, Simba; standing (left to right): Lois, George Jr.

At Marist Brothers Nyanga High School, 2001.

In June 2001, I was a camp counselor.
Here I am with Louis the rabbit.

Relieving some exam stress and anxiety with classmates
outside the classrooms at Marist Brothers Nyanga High School.

Relaxing with friends. Left to right: Bonaventure, Cornelius, me, Kennedy.

Waiting for Martin at the airport in Philadelphia, 2003.

We greet each other for the first time in person with a big hug
(over the barrier wall!).

I risk introducing Martin to Louis the rabbit,
even though he once mentioned eating rabbit for dinner.

Happy Holidays
2003
RICH, ANNE,
RICH, CAITLIN,
MARTIN, WALLACE,
KAVA,
ROMEY, and
MICK

The 2003 Stoicsitz family Christmas card, including Martin and Wallace.

Together at Caitlin's wedding (that's her husband, Dzmitry, on the left), 2008.

Another wedding photo, this one with Rich (left) and Wallace and Richie (right).

Martin
—⁓—

HEARING CAITLIN SAY "YOU MADE IT!" when we first embraced made me realize this was real. For so many years, I thought I had conjured her. But here she was, as beautiful as I imagined, but much taller. She towered over me. No longer the twelve-year-old girl with jewelry on her teeth that I first met six years ago. I wouldn't wake up in Chigodora, or Chisamba Singles, or Victoria Falls in a sweat. I had made it.

As I was telling her about all my adventures, I saw that the girl who became my best friend in her letters was the woman sitting right next to me in the car. I still couldn't believe it. But I felt immediately at ease with her. Anne and Rich were asking questions from the front seat, smiling, so loving as well. She got this demeanor from both parents, I thought.

They drove me by Villanova's campus and it took my breath away. It was difficult to imagine I would be walking across that campus as an American student in less than two weeks. I could barely believe I was sitting there, in the back of a four-by-four Jeep, next to Caitlin.

We pulled into their driveway, which I immediately recognized from the photos Caitlin had sent me. Richie came out to embrace me.

"My African brother!" Richie said. "Very cool to meet you."

Caitlin took me inside and showed me around. They had set up a room for me in the basement, where my dear friend Wallace had spent many nights. We called him after I showered. He was still in Colorado finishing his summer there. I would see him in a week or so. Then Caitlin said, "Let's go."

She wanted to take me shopping at the legendary mall to get some things for my new American life.

Walking into the glimmering palace with its magic sliding glass doors and gusts of cool air was everything I had imagined and more. The smells of sweet cinnamon and fried food overwhelmed me as we walked through what Caitlin called "the food court." We shared something called a Cinnabon, and to this day, I have never eaten anything that delicious. Then she took me shopping. That I found overwhelming.

To start, her father gave her his credit card. This was a new concept, that a small piece of plastic could purchase so many things. Caitlin bought me pants and shorts, T-shirts and long-sleeved shirts, flip-flops, sunglasses, and more. I kept saying it was unnecessary, but soon just gave up. When she picked out not one but three belts, I had to say something.

"I only have one waist," I said.

I had never witnessed such excess, not even at Marist Brothers. Eventually I just went along with it, like I was in a dream. Or an American movie, like the ones I'd watch sitting on my brother's shoulders and peering through a window all those years before in Chisamba Singles.

Back home, Caitlin insisted I put on a new outfit for dinner, my first with my American family. When I came downstairs in my chinos and button-down shirt, everyone erupted in applause. The feeling reminded me of my first day slipping into my uniform at Marist Brothers: But this was even bigger. I was dressed now as an American student. My dream had been realized.

I sat down at the table, which my American mother had covered in food: a meat dish she called pot roast with potatoes and carrots that made my mouth water with its rich smell. The bowl of salad was so large I could wrap both my arms around it, and there was a small spinning device next to it with an assortment of bottles that Caitlin called dressing. I had never heard of that word, nor was I the slightest bit hungry. I was still full from the Cinnabon—and too ecstatic to eat. But I helped myself to a bit of everything. I wanted to taste it all; each bite was further proof that this was real. I was in Hatfield with my American family wearing my new clothes and about to go to university.

The next day, Anne and Rich hosted a party for me and invited all of Caitlin's relatives and neighbors. I met aunts and uncles and cousins who greeted me as if I were a long-lost relative who had finally come home.

After we ate, Anne stood up to make a speech. She introduced me to the family formally, and as she did, her voice grew wobbly, shaking with emotion. This stirred something in me. It brought me back from the high-in-the-sky feeling I had had ever since I boarded the plane in Paris. It reconnected me to the ground, and to the fact that I was standing next to my best friend in her backyard, in Hatfield, Pennsylvania. Anne paused mid-sentence to collect herself and I began to speak. It was not rehearsed, or even intended. These words came from deep inside me, waiting to emerge.

"I just want to thank you. You really don't understand what part you have played in my life, and in the lives of people who are dependent on me. This is going to bring a great change to my family. It has always been my dream to go to college. It will give me a platform to exploit my potential and get some help to my family and friends in Zimbabwe. I just want to hope that God will give you maximum blessings."

I felt Caitlin squeeze my hand, and I squeezed back. After six years of imagining what it would be like to see her, to hug her, to hear her laugh, to hold her hand, here she was, my best friend from afar, now standing right next to me.

EPILOGUE

Martin

—⚏—

I CLINKED A CHAMPAGNE GLASS to get everyone's attention.

"I would like to say a few words," I said, rising from the table to face Caitlin, who looked more radiant than ever before. "I'm so happy that you have met Dima. Not only do you have a wonderful new husband, but I now have another brother."

Her face, already set in a smile, went a slight pinkish color as she raised her glass toward me and then turned to kiss the man she had just married.

"Here, here!" Wallace shouted. He was sitting across the table from me, next to Richie, our other brother from another mother. This is what we call each other still to this day.

A few weeks earlier, Caitlin had phoned me in Manhattan, where I was living and working, to say she was going to marry Dzmitry, a guy she had met on a cruise with her parents the year before. It was a quick engagement, but I knew this was a relationship that would last. Dima was different from Caitlin's previous boyfriends. He and I shared a similar worldview, perhaps because he came from a faraway place, like me; he was from Belarus, a country in Eastern Europe. We both saw that Caitlin's beauty was way more than skin deep. He saw her generosity and kindness and was not threatened by it. He is a good man.

Watching him exchange vows with Caitlin earlier that day, I got a bit choked up. Caitlin and I had already shared so many milestones—and still have many ahead. I did not know then that I would go on to do my MBA at Duke, or that Caitlin would finish her nursing degree, as she had planned since she was sixteen, or give birth to a beautiful baby girl. All I knew was that we both had witnessed so many of each other's dreams come true.

This day was another in a long list of special moments I got to share with her, starting with the very first letter she had sent eleven years earlier.

I sat back down and looked around the table. Anne had happy tears streaming down her face, and Rich was so proud I thought his head would pop off. Nan and Pop were beaming, as was Grandpa Stoicsitz. Richie was there with his wife, Jenilee, as was Wallace with his, Doreen. There was so much happiness at that one table.

I only wished that my family back in Zimbabwe could be there as well.

I kept in touch with everyone back home through letters and phone calls. In fact, as soon as I was settled at Villanova, I got a job in the admissions office and told Anne that I wanted to take over sending money to my parents. She had done enough. But she insisted on sending money to them the first year so that I could focus on my studies. I began saving, and got a second part-time job at Taco Bell to earn more. That summer, I got a full-time job working for an insurance company, then continued to work and study during the following school year as well.

It took some time, but finally I was able to save enough to buy my parents a new house in Mutare. They moved out of Chisamba Singles the same year I graduated from Villanova. Knowing that my mother has a water faucet in her own home, and a bathroom with a toilet, and her very own bed brings me peace. It makes the richness of my new American life all that more enjoyable. To this day, I continue to send money home to my parents, and I made sure that my siblings stayed in school, no matter what. I kept my promise to my mother, the one I made right before I left for Victoria Falls and Villanova, that even though I was leaving her, it was only to be a better son to her and my father, and the best brother to my siblings. My dream to come to America was never for me alone.

Lois remained number one in her class and is planning to come to college in the United States. I promised her she would, just as Caitlin had promised me that I would. Soon my sisters will meet for the first time.

My family and Caitlin's stopped being two separate families a long time ago. It started with a letter—and then all of our lives were changed forever.

October 2015

Caitlin
⎯⎯⎯⎯⎯⎯

WHEN I SAT DOWN TO write that pen-pal letter eighteen years ago, I had no idea that it would lead to me finding a best friend, or helping him come to the United States for college, or that we would write a book together about that life-changing experience. I just wanted to make a connection with someone whom I had never met before. I wanted to reach out beyond my small, insular world of Hatfield to see what life was like for other kids in faraway places. I was curious.

And while my life is so much richer for having connected with Martin, I still live in Pennsylvania, only thirty minutes from my childhood home where I now take my two daughters to visit with "Money" and "Pop Pop," Mila's nicknames for my mom and dad. Dasha was born on December 21, 2014, making Mila a big sister and, in between my pregnancies and writing this book, I switched jobs and became a registered nurse at a local emergency room.

I stayed in Pennsylvania for the entire writing process, while Martin was either Skyping from South Africa or texting me from an airport tarmac en route to Texas or WhatsApping me from Manhattan where he'd found a job as an Africa analyst for a midtown investment banking firm *while* finishing his MBA at Duke. Everything has seemed to change for Martin since the rumbling-stomach and dirt-floor days of his youth, and yet he remains the same energetic, always-on-the-move person he has been since he wrote me that very first "Hallo!" His optimism and enthusiasm has never once wavered. Neither has his love for surprises.

I turned thirty on March 28, 2015, three weeks before our book was published. My mom and dad threw a small birthday party for me, inviting Nan and Pop, my Aunt Kim and Aunt Joanne, and Wallace and his wife, Doreen, and their one-year-old son, Aiden. I invited Martin, too, but didn't hear back from him, nor did I expect him to come. I assumed he was somewhere far more exotic—like Uganda or Zambia. So when I heard my mother shout, "You made it!" over the din of music and people chatting, my heart quickened.

I was sitting in the living room nursing Dasha when Martin appeared. He flashed his electric smile and said, "Happy birthday, sis!" and I burst into tears.

I was emotional for so many reasons—it was Martin's first time meeting Dasha and the last time we would see each other before our book was out in the world. It was beginning to dawn on me that our story was no longer just ours.

I let everyone at the party swarm Martin first. They had the same questions I did: How is everything? What are you doing? Where have you been?

We learned that he had moved his parents into yet another new house, in an even safer neighborhood, and that Martin was traveling so much for work that he was no longer sure what time zone he was in.

As the party started to break up, I pulled Martin aside to talk about the months ahead. Our story was going to be excerpted in *Seventeen*, my favorite magazine growing up. That was the first of many "I cannot believe this is happening" moments for me. We had other requests for interviews—on radio and TV as well as a book party in Manhattan to look forward to. It was all so exciting—and daunting, too.

"Only good things can come from this," Martin assured me.

"It's why we decided to do it," I concurred. "If we can inspire just one person to do something kind, we will have done enough."

The next time I saw Martin was at our book party at his company's headquarters in midtown Manhattan. He was dressed in a suit and tie, and he walked me through the crowd of similarly well-dressed city sophisticates—women in high heels with matching handbags, men with slicked-back hair and shiny loafers. Cocktails were served on the terrace that overlooked the city, which was particularly sparkly that evening.

I felt a bit self-conscious. This was a different world than I was used to—suits, not scrubs—and yet one Martin fit into effortlessly. So when he clinked his wine glass and asked me to stand next to him to address the glamorous crowd, my stomach did a double backflip. I started to sweat. I hate public speaking, and I got panicky, thinking, What can I possibly say to impress this crowd? Martin is the star—he's the smooth talker!

And he was just that. I stood next to him and watched in awe as he wowed the crowd, hoping no one would notice that I was trembling beside him. When he said, "With her babysitting money, Caitlin helped me finish school," I felt everyone's eyes fix on me. "I would not be here without her."

It was my turn to speak. I introduced myself and explained that I was an emergency-room nurse. As I spoke those words, I realized the connection: "I see people at the worst times in their lives—that's when I want to help. Martin inspired me to do that."

Everyone applauded and I noticed a few people even dabbing their eyes. If our story could move people to tears, could it move them to act? I wondered. To be kinder to one another? To take a chance and do good things for deserving people?

On the drive home that night, my heart swelled as I started to think that the answer to all those questions was yes. That was just the beginning of this realization.

Martin and I created a Facebook page and a Twitter account, and the messages arrived almost daily. Lila, a seventh grader from Brooklyn, wrote that our book "changed her world view" and that she was working at a soup kitchen for her school project because of our story. Ellen and Caroline, two ninth graders from Denmark, wrote to thank us for creating such an inspiring story, and Becca, a student from Kenya, sent us a photo of herself with our book. Lauren sent me a photo on Twitter of a poster she had made based on our book, which she'd chosen for her school project. She wrote a whole paragraph on my quote, "People are so scared of what they don't know." That blew my mind. When I posted an old photo of me and Martin visiting Mrs. Miller, my seventh grade English teacher, another teacher commented, "Teachers change lives!" I agree.

So when I was contacted by a parent whose daughter goes to West Chester East High School, an hour away from me in Pennsylvania, about Martin and me coming to talk to the entire school, I wrote back an enthusiastic "YES!"

The school had chosen our book for their school-wide summer read and wanted Martin and me to come talk about our experience as pen pals, friends, and now authors. Martin and I had done this once before, years earlier, right after he arrived in the States. The local paper wrote a story about us, and we were invited to speak at Pennfield Middle School, where I wrote that first letter. (That's when we took that photo with Mrs. Miller that I posted.) I had let Martin do most of the talking then. I thought that he was the one everyone was interested in. He had the incredible story; I just helped him realize it. I figured this would be the same— he'd charm everyone, and I'd add a few anecdotes, like I did at the book party. When Martin told me he could not make it because he'd be traveling, I was so disappointed. I wrote Brian Dakin, the father organizing the event, to say it was not going to work out after all.

"Would you consider coming on your own?" he responded.

Without thinking, I typed back, "Sure!"

But as soon as I hit SEND, I realized I had made a terrible mistake. How on earth would I entertain an entire school?

I spent days working on a PowerPoint presentation, mostly photographs of everything that had happened after Martin's arrival in the US. All the Christmas cards my mom sent out that showed him as part of our family; photos of his graduation from Villanova, and from Duke, too. Pictures of him meeting our dogs—he looks so petrified! And one of him holding Mila for the first time. In that photo, he's elated. Then I worked on my talking points—how my life had become so much better because of this relationship. How I would never have met and married my husband, or become a nurse, if it had not been for Martin. And then, for fun, I decided to play the Spice Girls at the beginning of the program to set the mood. I was ready, even a little excited.

I had to be at the high school by 7:30 AM for a 7:45 AM assembly, and it was an hour-and-six-minute drive from my house according to my GPS, which I'd checked four times the night before.

I showered, ate a quick breakfast even though I felt a bit nauseous from nerves, and then kissed Dzmitry, Dasha, and Mila good-bye before grabbing my purse. On my way out the door, I felt a snag—the zipper on my bag had grazed my upper thigh and got stuck on my stockings. I tugged at it and felt the sudden release—as well as a faint tickle across my leg, as if a mouse had run across it. I looked down to see a spiderweb pattern spread the width of my leg. I was already late, so there was no time to change. Instead, I ran to the car thinking, At least my dress is knee length.

In the car, I glanced down to see the webbed design now creeping toward my knee. Thankfully, I had some clear nail polish in my bag, which I quickly used to stop the spread and then drove toward West Chester, trying to focus on what lay ahead. As I felt the lacquer adhere to my skin, I could not help but think that the rip was an omen.

I was literally shaking by the time I pulled into the school driveway. There was still time to turn around. I could feign food poisoning, anything to get out of the embarrassment of what I was about to face. But then I saw the big school billboard, which read, WELCOME CAITLIN ALIFIRENKA!

Instead of calming me down, the sign made me queasier. I started second guessing everything in my presentation, especially the decision to start off with the Spice Girls. As I parked the car, I thought, They won't even know who the Spice Girls are! And they certainly won't care about a thirty-year-old lady talking to them about kindness!

I entered the school feeling an overwhelming sense of dread. Then a student spotted me and asked, "Are you coming to speak to us today?"

I was surprised and said, "I am!"

She smiled and said, "I'm getting out of my class so I can come see you! I am really excited!"

My dread started to fade.

I met Kim, the head of the English department, in the

lobby and followed her through the locker-lined hallways to the auditorium, with its row upon row of chairs, all lined in semicircles facing the stage where I was about to stand, in ripped stockings, in front of several hundred teenagers.

"We couldn't fit the whole school in here so we're live streaming it into classrooms as well," she explained.

Butterflies had started to swarm in my stomach just as the head of library services introduced herself. "We are so happy to have you here!" she said, hugging me. "Your book speaks to these kids. You're a local girl. Our students see themselves in you. If you could change someone's life, they can, too."

Her words gave me the courage to climb up onto the stage.

Kim introduced me, and as I looked out across the crowd—the mix of football jerseys and flannel shirts, the too-much makeup or none at all, the quiet kids and the class clowns—I realized that high school had not changed that much since I had been there. It was still a vast mix of kids—each one capable of changing someone else's life. And they were all looking at me.

"Eighteen years ago, I wrote a letter." I started to speak and a silence fell over the crowd. I talked for the next forty-five minutes, clicking through photos, telling stories—of how a Hatfield girl like me could write a letter that turned into a book that I hoped would move others to do the same.

"One small act of kindness," I said in closing. "You have no idea how powerful that can be, whose lives it can change, including your own."

The applause was so loud I could feel it through the

floorboards, humming up my legs. I had forgotten about the rip in my stockings, and my early-morning jitters. As I walked off the stage, a line started to form of teenagers holding my book, wanting *me* to sign it. Both girls and boys wanted to take selfies with me, and one young man even asked me to sign his cell phone case. One girl had tears in her eyes when she told me that my book meant "everything" to her.

I have no idea what any of these young people will do with the emotions our story stirred in each of them—but I am excited by the possibilities. It's why I wanted to write this book.

Kindness is contagious. It changes lives. It changed mine. What will it do for you?

Acknowledgments

Martin Ganda would like to thank:

Caitlin for changing my life.

My Zimbabwean family: Nation, Simba, Lois, George, and my parents, George and Chioniso; Alois and Sekai Munyaradazi; Peter Muzawazi; Brother Brito; and Phanuel and Tecla Mugomba. In memory of Grandma Majokwiro.

My American family: Anne Neville, Richard Stoicsitz, Dzmitry Alifirenka, Richie and Jenilee Stoicsitz, Bill and Joanne Neville, Jim and Kim Neville, and both of their families. Nan and Pop Neville, Grandpa Stoicsitz, and in memory of Grandma Stoicsitz.

My Villanova family: Michael Gaynor, the admissions director; Candice Keith; Valerie Furman; and Father Edmund Dobbin—I never would have made it to the US without your help. And Derik Rosa, Chris Hill, Jack Zawora, and Joseph Pantini, my first friends at Villanova who introduced me to America!

Mentors: Amy and Jeff Towers for believing in me. Tom Wilcok and Ken Farhman for friendship and unwavering career support and mentoring. Ali Naqvi and Linda Holliday for molding me into who I am today. Thanks to the following mentors for hand-holding and guiding me in my business career: Alex Dibelius, Keith Ferrazzi, Dr. Mthuli Ncube, Noah and Florence Ziumbe, Advocate Brenda Madumise, James Makamba, Mutumwa Mawere, Gerald Rem, Luke Ngwerume, Phil Heilberg, and Maureen Erasmus. Ben and Claire Spillard for their friendship and continued guidance. Thanks to Mark, Lesley, and Dirk Goldwasser, Jonathan Plutzik, Kenneth Allen, Michael Civitella, Bret and Marissa Rosen, Ashley Bendell, Cass Almendral, and Clive Ginsberg, for their friendship. And to the very many others who have played a pivotal role in my journey from Sakubva Mutare to where I am today!

Friends: Elias Mutambikwa, Karen Nyawera, Simba Mhungu, Simba Marekera, Edwin Mushambi, Kevin Portmann, Sam Njanike, Stephen Mutsongodza, Ronnie Rukambe, Tinashe Machaka, and Tapiwa Gurupira for their friendship. Shikshya Khatiwada for being an amazing sister from another mother.

I thank Peter Godwin, Sarah Burnes, Judy Clain, and Farrin Jacobs for their encouragement and guidance with the book. And lastly, Liz Welch for helping Caitlin and me tell our story.

Caitlin Alifirenka would like to thank:

Thank you to my parents, Anne Neville and Rich Stoicsitz, for their unyielding guidance, love, and constant belief in me. Without your assistance, dreams would remain unfulfilled and this story may have never unfolded. Special thanks to my grandparents, Bill and Marie Neville and Joseph Stoicsitz, for loving me when you were unsure of the paths I was taking! And to my brother, Richie, for allowing me to grow and supporting my passions, and to Heather Witta, for being such a constant and supportive friend. Also to my uncles, aunts, and cousins for readily accepting Martin into our family as a new nephew and cousin. To my mother-in-law, Irina Olifirenko, and my sister-in-law Diana Olifirenko for loving and supporting me and making Martin your family as well. And most important, to my beloved husband, Dzmitry, who supported me and was always my rock. And finally, to our dearest daughter, Mila, who listened to hours of me retelling this story. You are the future, and I want you to see the world as your playground.

And special thanks to my brother, Martin Ganda. We believed in each other. It's impossible to imagine my life without you. You truly opened my eyes to a bigger, better world.

To Liz Welch, without whose thoughtful planning and execution our story would have remained in file folders. We lived the story, but you brought it to life!

Liz Welch would like to thank:

Martin Ganda and Caitlin Alifirenka for entrusting their inspiring story to me; to their agent, Sarah Burnes, for making the introductions; and to my agent, Brettne Bloom, for her always smart and thoughtful support. To Anne Neville, for her fastidious fact-checking and enormous heart—this book could not have happened without you. To Farrin Jacobs for her expert edits, to Judy Clain for her spot-on instinct that this story must be told, and to everyone in Karen Braziller's workshop who read early pages and fell in love, as I did, with Martin and Caitlin's story.

Discussion Guide

1. Why does Caitlin choose someone from Zimbabwe as her pen pal, rather than someone from somewhere more relatable, like Germany or England?

2. Describe Martin's day-to-day life. In what ways is it similar to and different from Caitlin's?

3. Explain what Caitlin learns from Martin's second letter.

4. Why is Martin's father impressed with Martin's correspondence with Caitlin?

5. Does Caitlin understand Martin's life? How is her idea of his life different from reality?

6. How does Martin feel about the dollar Caitlin sent him? Why does he feel this way? Does this make you think differently about the money you have right now?

7. Describe some of the struggles Martin faces just to send his letters.

8. Why does Caitlin keep disregarding some of the things Martin says, like how one shirt "greatly increased [his] wardrobe"? Why do you think she misses these details?

9. Why does Caitlin feel bad about telling Martin about her teen drama? Should she feel bad? How do you keep your everyday problems in perspective?

10. How has Martin's life changed by January 1999? Why does he tell Caitlin the truth about his situation?

11. Cite evidence that reveals Martin's feelings toward Caitlin and her privileged life.

12. Paraphrase some of the problems Caitlin faces in trying to get Martin the first care package. What are some of the things Martin receives from it? Classify the items from most to least important and be prepared to defend your answers.

13. Compare and contrast Stephie and Caitlin.

14. What aspects of Martin's photos accurately represent his life and what aspects are embellished, if any?

15. Describe the boys from Marist Brothers School and compare them to Martin.

16. Describe Caitlin's attraction to Damon. How is he different from her previous love interests? How have Caitlin's ideas about the future changed?

17. Compare and contrast the health clinic in Zimbabwe to one found in America. What can be done about the inequity?

18. How does 9/11 change Caitlin's perspective on the world? Does it have an impact on Martin's as well?

19. Describe some of the ways the Internet helps Martin. Can you imagine your life now without the Internet?

20. Explain why Caitlin disregards Damon's concerns about her studying too much and wanting to go to college. Compare and contrast Damon's and Caitlin's attitudes toward learning and college.

21. In what ways is Wallace similar to Martin? In what ways is he different?

22. List the struggles Martin faces in trying to get to America.

23. How does Martin's attitude toward Caitlin and her family change throughout the years?

24. Describe the village of Chigodora and the people who inhabit it.

25. Is Caitlin's mother optimistic about Martin's future? Explain.

26. List some cultural differences between the US and Zimbabwe. Which ones do you think are the most notable, if any? Why?

27. Explain how Martin manages to get into Villanova with a full scholarship. How does this change more than just the trajectory of his own life?

28. Describe Martin's feelings toward his trip to America and the lost airplane ticket.

29. Describe some of the culture shock Martin faces in America.

30. Summarize Martin's and Caitlin's lives as described in the epilogue chapters.

Anne Neville

Caitlin Alifirenka and **Martin Ganda** met as pen pals in 1997 and are still best friends today. Caitlin, an ER nurse, lives outside Philadelphia with her husband and young daughters. Martin currently lives in New York. He has dual degrees in mathematics and economics from Villanova University and an MBA in finance from Duke University.

Liz Welch is an award-winning journalist and memoirist whose critically acclaimed first book, *The Kids Are All Right*, coauthored with her sister Diana Welch, won an ALA Alex Award. Her stories have appeared in the *New York Times*, *Parade*, *Life*, *Cosmopolitan*, *Vogue*, *Glamour*, *Real Simple*, *Self*, *Marie Claire*, and other publications.